TEILHARDISM

AND

THE NEW RELIGION

TEILHARDISM

AND

THE NEW RELIGION

A Thorough Analysis of
The Teachings of Pierre Teilhard de Chardin

by

Wolfgang Smith

*"That henceforth we be no more children tossed
to and fro, and carried about with every wind of
doctrine..."*

—Ephesians 4:14

TAN BOOKS AND PUBLISHERS, INC.
Rockford, Illinois 61105

TAN BOOKS AND PUBLISHERS, INC.
P.O. Box 424
Rockford, Illinois 61105

1988

To the Blessed Virgin Mary,
Mother of God,
and Unfailing Help of Christians

"My people have been a lost flock, their shepherds have caused them to go astray, and have made them wander in the mountains: they have gone from mountain to hill, they have forgotten their resting place."

—Jeremias 50:6

Contents

About Teilhard de Chardin

Pierre Teilhard de Chardin was born on May 1, 1881, at Sarcenat, near Orcines, Puy-de-Dôme, in south-central France. His father was a gentleman farmer with an interest in geology, and his mother a descendant of Voltaire. Teilhard was educated at the Jesuit College at Mongré, and joined the Society of Jesus in 1899. He studied philosophy and continued his seminary education from 1901 to 1905 at the Jesuit house on the Isle of Jersey. This was followed by a three-year sojourn in Cairo, Egypt, where he taught physics and chemistry at a Jesuit school and developed his paleontological interests. Teilhard returned to England in 1908, studied theology at Hastings, and was ordained in 1911. He subsequently returned to Paris and devoted himself to the study of paleontology at the Museum of Paris under the direction of Marcellin Boule, a noted authority of the time. These studies were interrupted by the outbreak of World War I. Refusing to serve as an army chaplain, Teilhard joined the French forces as a stretcher bearer. In recognition of his bravery he was subsequently decorated and received into the Legion of Honor.

Teilhard continued his paleontological studies after the war, and took a doctorate in 1922 from the Sorbonne. For a brief period he taught geology at the Catholic Institute in Paris. His less-than-orthodox theological opinions, however, especially with reference to Original Sin, led to the termination of this employment and his *de facto* exile to China. Thus, in 1923, Teilhard came to Tientsin, where he took up research as an assistant to the Jesuit paleontologist Émile Licent. He subsequently collaborated in the excavations at Choukoutien which led to the discovery of the so-called *Sinanthropus* ("Peking Man"), supposedly a "missing link" in the evolution of man from subhuman ancestors. And although this presumed discovery was later challenged (if not indeed disproved), it caused Teilhard to become widely looked upon as a paleontologist of note. His reputation was further enhanced in 1931 when, together with the well-known Abbé Henri Breuil, he supposedly established that *Sinanthropus* had known the use of fire and primitive tools.

During World War II Teilhard continued his activities in Peking, where on account of the Japanese occupation he lived in virtual captivity. He returned to France in 1946 and tried unsuccessfully to gain permission from the Church for the publication of his philosophical writings and to secure a teaching post at the Collège de France. Unpublished copies of his numerous writings were widely circulated, however, and commenced to arouse great admiration and enthusiasm in Catholic circles, beginning with high-placed members of the Jesuit order. In 1952 Teilhard accepted a position with the Wenner Gren Foundation for Anthropological Research in New York. He died in that city on Easter Sunday, 1955.

Preface

Charles Darwin would have been greatly surprised to see his atheistically slanted doctrine turned into a religious creed, a self-styled ultra-Christianity, no less, hailed and embraced by men of the cloth. Yet as we know, this unlikely turn of events did come to pass in our day, thanks to Pierre Teilhard de Chardin, the once-exiled Jesuit of posthumous fame who introduced the world to Point Omega, the "God of Evolution," and forged what purports to be a kind of scientific theology.

For many years, it will be recalled, the prophet of theistic Darwinism was silenced under orders from Rome. Yet all the while he wrote prodigiously, and communicated his thought to an ever-widening circle of admiring and influential friends. And when at last he emerged from the underground, the moment was opportune. The stage had been set, and it appears that a goodly portion of the believing and unbelieving world was ready and most willing to receive his message. And the doctrine did spread like wildfire, especially within the Roman Catholic Church. It struck on the eve of the Second Vatican Council, with an impact that could be felt around the world. Translated before long into twenty-seven languages, the posthumous treatises of the controversial Jesuit have exerted an inestimable influence.

Today, of course, the rage has abated. The picture has changed: by now Teilhard's ideas (which in the sixties had appeared so revolutionary) have become almost commonplace, and in their essentials seem to be accepted in many quarters as an unquestionable truth. And it is plain that the fashionable theologies of our day are in fact rooted in the Teilhardian Weltanschauung, and that the New Christianity, in its multiple forms, owes a lasting debt to the priestly scientist, who in the eyes of many was its martyr and prophet.

Our concern, however, is not with the person of Teilhard de Chardin, nor with the history of his influence, but purely and simply with the fundamental ideas of his doctrine, and particularly with the question of their validity. And herein lies the weakness of those numerous writings, not a few of which were penned by intimates and sympathizers of the French savant: the fact is that despite the extensive literature on Teilhard produced in the sixties, and notwithstanding recent studies (more than ten have been published in the U.S. since 1980), there exists as yet no definitive critique, no cogent and comprehensive treatise, which dispels rather than perpetuates Teilhardian fictions.

We wish to emphasize, however, that the present work is intended, not just as a critique of a particular thinker, but primarily as a contemporary exposition of perennial truth. It views questions in the light of the metaphysical traditions, and seeks to promote a deeper understanding of orthodox Christian doctrine. The problematic of the Teilhardian system serves mainly as a point of departure for the application of universal principles to a number of basic and vital issues, such as the status of Darwinism, the so-called mind-body problem, and the meaning of history. In a way, the present book follows along the lines of the ancient "adversus" treatises, wherein polemic and didactic are intertwined. From start to finish we have been motivated and spurred in our endeavor by one paramount concern: to safeguard and render intelligible a living legacy which is incomparably more than a mere philosophical system or formal doctrine.

Acknowledgments

The author and publisher gratefully acknowledge permission to reprint excerpts from the following material:

Activation of Energy by Pierre Teilhard de Chardin, copyright © 1963 by Editions du Seuil; English translation copyright © 1970 by William Collins Sons & Co. Ltd., London. Reprinted by permission of Harcourt Brace Jovanovich, Inc.

Christianity and Evolution by Pierre Teilhard de Chardin, copyright © 1969 by Editions du Seuil; English translation copyright © 1971 by William Collins Sons & Co. Ltd., and Harcourt Brace Jovanovich, Inc. Reprinted by permission of Harcourt Brace Jovanovich, Inc.

Human Energy by Pierre Teilhard de Chardin, copyright © 1962 by Editions du Seuil; English translation copyright © 1969 by William Collins Sons & Co. Ltd., London. Reprinted by permission of Harcourt Brace Jovanovich, Inc.

The Heart of Matter by Pierre Teilhard de Chardin, copyright © 1976 by Editions du Seuil; English translation copyright © 1978 by William Collins Sons & Co. Ltd., and Harcourt Brace Jovanovich, Inc. Reprinted by permission of Harcourt Brace Jovanovich, Inc.

The Future of Man by Pierre Teilhard de Chardin. Translated by Norman Denny. Copyright © 1964 in English translation by William Collins Sons & Co. Ltd., and Harper & Row, Publishers, Inc. Reprinted by permission of Harper & Row, Publishers, Inc.

The Phenomenon of Man by Pierre Teilhard de Chardin. Copyright © 1959 in the English translation by William Collins Sons & Co. Ltd., and Harper & Row, Publishers, Inc. Reprinted by permission of Harper & Row, Publishers, Inc.

Science and Christ by Pierre Teilhard de Chardin, copyright © 1965 by Editions du Seuil, Paris. Reprinted by permission of Editions du Seuil.

List of Abbreviations
For the Writings of Teilhard de Chardin

AE   *Activation of Energy*
     (New York: Harcourt Brace Jovanovich, 1970)
CE   *Christianity and Evolution*
     (New York: Harcourt Brace Jovanovich, 1971)
DM   *The Divine Milieu*
     (New York: Harper & Row, 1968)
FM   *The Future of Mankind*
     (New York: Harper & Row, 1964)
HE   *Human Energy*
     (New York: Harcourt Brace Jovanovich, 1969)
HM   *The Heart of Matter*
     (New York: Harcourt Brace Jovanovich, 1979)
MN   *Man's Place in Nature*
     (New York: Harper & Row, 1966)
PM   *The Phenomenon of Man*
     (New York: Harper & Row, 1965)
SC   *Science and Christ*
     (London: Collins, 1968)

TEILHARDISM

AND

THE NEW RELIGION

Chapter I

Evolution: A Closer Look

Today, a hundred and twenty-eight years after it was first promulgated, the Darwinian theory of evolution stands under attack as never before. There was a time, not too long ago, when it seemed to the world at large that the theory had triumphed once and for all, and that the issue was henceforth closed. And yet, within the last two or three decades the debate about evolution has not only revived but is showing signs of heating up. Indeed, the question whether the evolutionist claims are justified is currently being discussed and argued, not just in fundamentalist circles, but also on occasion in research institutes, and in the prestigious halls of academe. The fact is that in recent times there has been increasing dissent on the issue within academic and professional ranks, and that a growing number of respectable scientists are defecting from the evolutionist camp. It is interesting, moreover, that for the most part these "experts" have abandoned Darwinism, not on the basis of religious faith or biblical persuasions, but on strictly scientific grounds, and in some instances regretfully, as one could say. We will presently examine some of the major reasons which account for this shift; but first let us assay how the status of evolution was perceived by the celebrated Jesuit whose doctrine constitutes the subject of this book.

For Teilhard de Chardin, evolution is not simply a scientific theory, but an established and henceforth irrefutable truth. It is in fact the rock upon which he would found his entire doctrine.

1

"Is evolution a theory, a system or a hypothesis?" he writes. "It is much more: it is a general condition to which all theories, all hypotheses, all systems must bow and which they must satisfy henceforward if they are to be thinkable and true. Evolution is a light illuminating all facts, a curve that all lines must follow."[1] What is quite amazing, however, is that nowhere does this prolific author explain with even a modicum of precision on what basis he is putting forth these sweeping claims. We are told dogmatically that evolution is an established fact; but we are never told who has established it, and by what means. We are told, often enough, that the doctrine is founded upon evidence, and that indeed this evidence "is henceforward above all verification, as well as being immune from any subsequent contradiction by experience"[2]; but we are left entirely in the dark on the crucial question wherein, precisely, this evidence consists.

In *The Phenomenon of Man,* it is true, Teilhard leads us to believe at one point that the doctrine of organic evolution has been confirmed by paleontological findings. When in 1859 Darwin first promulgated his discovery, Teilhard admits, the theory had not yet been adequately verified. "But things are now changing. Since the days of Darwin and Lamarck, numerous discoveries have established the existence of the transitional forms postulated by the theory of evolution."[3] But it happens that this statement is misleading, to say the least. For as George Simpson (an ardent evolutionist, and one of the foremost authorities) points out, "It remains true, as every paleontologist knows, that most new species, genera, and families, and that nearly all categories above the level of families, appear in the [paleontological] record suddenly, and are not led up to by gradual, completely continuous transitional sequences."[4] One also knows, moreover, that this circumstance has been from the start one of the major stumbling blocks for the proponents of evolution: the fossil record is definitely unfriendly to their cause. So much so that evolutionists have all along been obliged to postulate *ad hoc* hypotheses of even the most farfetched kind in order to explain away the persistent and ever-recurring difficulty of "missing links." To be sure, the Jesuit paleontologist knows this very well, and is in fact himself the originator of one of these ingenious postulates (the so-called "automatic suppression of origins"[5]). But then, if the expected transitional forms have not been discovered, and if, according to an hypothesis which he himself has introduced, they cannot be found at all, why does he inform his readers that "numerous discoveries have established the existence of the transitional forms postulated by the theory of evolution"? In the sense, at least, in which this statement is sure to be read, it is not only misleading, but undeniably false.

It has sometimes been pointed out by philosophers of science that the theory of evolution is not in fact empirically based. Even Haeckel, the celebrated Continental evolutionist (reputed to have been "more Darwinian than Darwin himself") must have been aware of this when he wrote to a scientific friend that "One can imagine nothing more absurd, nothing which indicates more clearly a total lack of comprehension of our theory, than to demand that it be founded upon empirical evidence."[6]

Now it may come as something of a surprise that Teilhard himself implies as much sixty pages later in *The Phenomenon of Man*. "In view of the impossibility of empirically perceiving any entity, animate or inanimate, otherwise than as engaged in the time-space series," he writes in a footnote, "evolutionary theory has long since ceased to be a hypothesis, to become a (dimensional) condition which all hypotheses of physics or biology must henceforth satisfy."[7] In other words, we are now led to believe that the truth of evolution can be established, not by direct empirical evidence, but somehow, Kantian style, on *a priori* grounds, by analyzing the conditions to which all observation must submit. And this, too, must be the reason why the truth of evolution is said to be "above all verification," and why it is "immune from any subsequent contradiction by experience." It is "above all verification" because it cannot be empirically verified at all.

Everything, then, appears to hinge upon Teilhard's "Kantian argument," or rather, upon the question whether that argument is correct. If it is, then the issue has indeed been settled once and for all, as Teilhard insists. It is quite surprising, therefore, that this crucial discovery has been relegated to a footnote and mentioned only in passing, as it were. And it is surprising, too, that it should have been left to the reader to ascertain why the impossibility of perceiving physical entities "otherwise than as engaged in the time-space series" leads ineluctably to the conclusion that "organic evolution exists, applicable equally to life as a whole or to any given living creature in particular."[8]

Nonetheless, let us try to understand what Teilhard is suggesting, however obscurely. The point seems to be that inasmuch as the emergence of living forms can be "empirically perceived," this genesis can be conceived or imagined in none other than transformist terms. Now this could well be true. But the crucial difficulty lies precisely in the initial premise: in the postulate, namely, that the emergence of living forms *can* be "empirically perceived." First of all, one knows that such a perception has never taken place. As Jean Rostand points out, "We have never been present even in a small way at *one* authentic phenomenon of evolution"[9]; which is to say that no one has ever observed a *bona fide* transformation of species, be it by direct or indirect means. Furthermore, there is absolutely no reason to suppose that everything within Nature can in fact be "empirically perceived," and that all happenings without exception can be neatly parcelled out in what Teilhard is pleased to call "the time-space series." This is not an *a priori* condition at all, but simply an unwarranted assumption. What it amounts to, basically, is that one limits the possibilities of the real by postulating that in principle it must fall entirely within the scope of human observation. But we know for a fact that this is not true: if it were, there could be no such thing as an electron (seeing that an electron is both a particle and a wave, or better said, is neither of the two, and is therefore definitely *not* "empirically perceivable"). The point is that neither the perceivable, nor the much larger category of the imaginable, can cover the entire ground of even physical reality.

It thus turns out that Teilhard's Kantian argument in support of evolution is spurious: its central premise proves to be "human, all too human." At bottom his reasoning reduces to a confession of incapacity: like Jean Rostand, he firmly believes in evolution "because I see no means of doing otherwise."[10]

★   ★   ★

Let us recall a few vital facts regarding the Darwinist doctrine. In the first place we need to underscore a distinction which is crucial, and which has all too often been overlooked: the distinction, namely, between what is currently termed micro-

and macroevolution. Now microevolution (which is an undeniable fact) involves relatively minor changes in the structure and function of plant or animal forms: a microevolutionary transformation is thus one which pertains to the fine-structure of the taxonomic scale. Macroevolutionary transformations, on the other hand—if such exist!—would entail, so to speak, a change in the underlying form, the very prototype of the organism. Such a transformation would constitute a leap from one of the major taxonomic groups to another. Now it requires no doubt a certain familiarity with the realities of the biological world to appreciate the full magnitude of this distinction, which might not unreasonably be compared with the difference between inches and light-years: the point being that the concepts of micro- and macroevolution belong actually to entirely different domains. The first domain, to be sure, is empirical: microevolutionary transformations can indeed be observed—which is precisely what Darwin has very convincingly detailed in *The Origin of Species*. Macroevolutionary changes, on the other hand, have not in fact been observed—which is what Jean Rostand must have meant when he said that "We have never been present even in a small way at *one* authentic phenomenon of evolution."

One might add that more, perhaps, than anything else, it was the failure to distinguish clearly between these two conceptions—or these two domains—that has obfuscated the early evolutionist debate. We should also remember, in this connection, that the physics of Darwin's day had not yet penetrated to the discovery that Nature harbors discontinuities: it was, as we now can see, a naive and uncorrected physics of continuity, a physics according to which the extrapolation from inches to light-years was indeed perfectly feasible. It is small wonder, therefore, that in an age dominated by Newtonian physics naturalists, too, tended to be a bit overconfident, to say the least.

In any case, it is only after the distinction in question has been carefully noted that it becomes possible to make cogent and indeed apodictic pronouncements on the subject of evolution. And the salient fact is this: *if by evolution we mean macroevolution* (as we henceforth shall), *then it can be said with the utmost rigor that the doctrine is totally bereft of scientific sanction.* Now, to be sure, given the multitude of extravagant claims about evolution promulgated by evolutionists with an air of scientific infallibility, this may indeed sound strange. And yet the fact remains that there exists to this day not a shred of *bona fide* scientific evidence in support of the thesis that macroevolutionary transformations have ever occurred. One is reminded in this connection of Colin Patterson, senior paleontologist at the British Museum of Natural History, who in recent times has shocked the public—and the experts—by challenging anyone to come up with even a single piece of authentic knowledge about evolution. Despite a voluminous amount of mail response, most of it irate, it seems that no one was able to supply information of the desired kind. When a reporter questioned Patterson on this point, he was told that one person had written in to say that the polar bear is descendent from the brown bear. "Do we really know this?" the reporter asked. "No" replied the paleontologist.

It has often been said, of course, that there does exist evidence for evolution (macroevolution, to be sure!); only it happens that this purported evidence never quite seems to pass the test of scrutiny. We have already encountered an instance of this kind in Teilhard's statement to the effect that "numerous discoveries have established the existence of the transitional forms postulated by the theory of evolution": an optimistic assessment, it seems, when a contemporary authority can say that "the known fossil record fails to document a single example of phyletic (gradual) evolution accomplishing a major morphological transition"![11] For the most part, however, the purported evidence is based, not so much on vagaries of fantasy, but on *ad hoc* hypotheses or hidden premises which need to be assumed before the facts in question can be perceived as evidence that evolution has occurred. One should add, moreover, that this kind of "evidence" tends to be short-lived: ere long the *ad hoc* hypothesis falls or erodes under the impact of new knowledge, with the result that the old showpieces lose their evidential status.

To give an example: in Darwin's day, much was made of so-called vestigial organs. Just about any anatomical structure, in fact, whose origin or function was insufficiently understood—the pineal gland, for instance—could be viewed as a degenerate and no longer functional vestige of an ancestral form, and paraded as evidence that evolution has taken place. The requisite *ad hoc* assumption, in this case, was the thesis that the structure in question serves no useful function in the living organism, and can furthermore be explained only on evolutionist grounds. This problematic premise, moreover, was supposed to have been guaranteed in numerous instances by what Darwin referred to as "the plain stamp of inutility." However, one has since found that apparently useless structures have an uncanny way of turning out to be quite essential, so much so that few reputable authorities, if any, would nowadays be willing to commit themselves on issues of that kind.

It is also worth noting, in this connection, that what the theory of evolution actually calls for are not vestigial, but nascent organs: rudimentary structures, that is, which will become useful only in a later and more highly developed state. In fact, if Darwin were right, it would stand to reason that the fossil record should be filled with the imprint of nascent formations; but it appears that no such fossils exist. As Douglas Dewar has pointed out, "The earliest known fins are fully developed, so are the earliest legs and wings, whether of insect, bird, bat or pterodactyl."[12] What is perhaps still more damaging to the evolutionist, however, is that under Darwinist auspices there is no reason to suppose that the phenomenon of organic evolution has now come to a halt, which means that even in our age there should exist transitional forms, living species, therefore, which exhibit structures of a nascent kind. As Dewar goes on to point out, "If these species be really evolving, the majority of them ought to exhibit nascent structures in all states of completion, from unrecognizable excrescences to structures almost ready for use. Not a single one seems to exist!" It is quite ironic, finally, and perhaps revealing, that whereas the so-called vestigial organs have been extensively discussed and publicized (so long, at least, as this notion could yet be plausibly maintained), the subject of nascent organs—which by right is of far greater importance!—has rarely been brought up, and has in any case not been touched upon in the popular evolutionist literature.

There is more to be said, however. Not only have the standard categories of presumed evidence eroded to the point of disappearance,[13] but in the meantime new and hitherto unsuspected facts have emerged which are turning out to be exceedingly hostile to Darwinism, and are forcing Darwinist loyalists to fabricate *ad hoc* hypotheses of the most fantastic kind just to keep their theory alive. Let one example (the most striking, we believe) suffice: everyone knows that with the discovery (in 1953) of the double-helix structure of DNA by Watson and Crick the youthful discipline of microbiology has entered upon a new era of breathtaking discovery. It has often been claimed, moreover, that these new and momentous findings have at last unearthed the true mechanism of evolution, and that we are presently on the brink of discovering precisely how macroevolution has come about. However, the truth of the matter is very much the opposite: now that the actual physical structure of what might be termed the biochemical mainstays of life has come into view, scientists are finding—frequently to their dismay—that the evolutionist thesis has become more stringently unthinkable than ever before. For the first time one is now in a position to speak of the distance or separation between living species in a rigorous quantitative sense (for example, in terms of so-called percentile sequence differences of certain proteins, such as cytochrome C), and this has led, first of all, to a rediscovery of a fundamental fact which in a way goes back to Aristotle and has always been recognized, in any case, by taxonomists as holding on the phenomenal plane: the fact, namely, that the biosphere breaks up into well-defined and widely separated classes, organized according to a hierarchic— and not sequential—principle. Only it happens that, on the molecular level, these separations, and this hierarchic order stand out with a mathematical precision which once and for all silences dissent. On this fundamental level it becomes a rigorously demonstrable fact that there *are* no transitional types, and that the so-called missing links are indeed non-existent. And this is not only embarrassing to the evolutionist, but virtually fatal to his theory.

Consider, for instance, the circumstance that a carp is 13 percentile sequence differences (based upon cytochrome C) removed from a horse, 13 from a turtle, and 13 from a bullfrog. Now, the fact that a fish is thus "equidistant" from a mammal, a reptile and an amphibian is hardly compatible with the evolutionist postulate that mammals have descended from reptiles, reptiles from amphibians, and amphibians from fish. Indeed, as Michael Denton has pointed out, "The only way to save evolution in the face of these discoveries is to make the *ad hoc* assumption that the degree of biochemical isolation of the major groups was far less in the past...There is, however, absolutely no objective evidence that this assumption is correct."[14]

Once again the partisans of evolution are driven to postulate a totally ungrounded and indeed most unlikely tenet simply to save their theory in the face of incompatible facts. Now this is of course something at which evolutionists have been adept from the start; yet, even so, it seems that these are trying times for the Darwinists, and that their apparently boundless faith in the miracles of molecular accidents is being tested close to the breaking point. It may be that Arthur Koestler has overstated the case when he referred to Darwinism as "a crumbling fortress"; however, one cannot but agree with Ludwig von Bertalanffy (a distinguished biologist, let us add) when he writes: "The fact that a theory so vague, so insufficiently verifiable, and so far from the criteria otherwise applied in 'hard' science has become a dogma can only be explained on sociological grounds."[15]

★   ★   ★

Yet Teilhard, to be sure, perceives the matter otherwise. "Using the word 'evolution' in its most generally accepted meaning, and in a purely experiential context," he writes, "I would say that man's origin by way of evolution is now an indubitable fact of science."[16] Indeed, the point is made in the most emphatic terms: "There can be no two ways about it: the question is settled—so finally that to continue to debate it in the schools is as much a waste of time as it would be to go on arguing whether or not the revolution of the earth is an impossibility."

We seem here to be in the presence of a strange phenomenon: what should one say? How can an informed and seemingly rational person make such misleading claims? We will get back to this question later; but first there are several points that need to be considered.

To begin with, it is to be noted that the concept of organic evolution, as it is generally understood, not only postulates the occurrence of macroevolutionary transformations, but also entails certain assumptions regarding the *modus operandi* by which the conjectured transformations have been accomplished. For indeed, even though evolutionists may disagree about many things, and although they may no longer be Darwinists in the full sense, it remains true nonetheless that their fundamental outlook is still conditioned by a certain residual Darwinism. What is agreed upon, basically, is the idea that speciation comes about, not by design, or by the operation of final causes, but simply by means of a random process. Life emerges and unfolds its myriad forms by accident, or as we say, by chance: that is the fundamental idea.

But what does this mean? What is chance, after all? The notion turns out to be inherently negative: to say "chance" is no more than to deny that the event in question has a sufficient reason, that it fulfills a purpose or a design. With reference to the origin of life and to speciation, moreover, this is tantamount to the denial of any efficacious creative act. So long as it is admitted that the origin of species conforms to the will or the plan of God, one can no more speak of natural selection (or of any other statistical mechanism) than one could speak of probabilities with reference to a card game in which the deck has been stacked. At bottom, therefore, Darwinism amounts to no more and no less than a denial of God's creative efficacy in the sphere of biogenesis and speciation.

It may not be without interest to point out that Darwin's own road to discovery confirms the atheistic underpinning of his doctrine. One knows from his early notebooks that he was a thoroughgoing materialist who had ruled out from the very start the possibility of any divine creative act; and clearly, as Stanley Jaki has observed, "Darwin could not proceed along lines of inductive reasoning in the *Descent* if he had reached its main conclusions more than thirty years earlier."[17] Where God is denied, the origin of species must indeed be viewed, not only in transformist, but more specifically in statistical terms. Under such auspices Darwinism of some kind becomes the only thinkable option. One has then no choice but to accept the Darwinist postulate of organic evolution, despite the scientific unlikelihood of its claims. As James Gray (himself an eminent evolutionist) has said: "No amount of argument, or clever epigram, can disguise the inherent improbability of orthodox evolutionary theory; but most biologists feel it is better to think in terms of improbable events than not to think at all."[18]

But let us get back to Teilhard de Chardin. Unlike Darwin, the French Jesuit was certainly not an outright materialist: it appears that he wanted to have God and evolution too. Or better said, perhaps, he would have evolution, and as much of God as that concept will permit. And let there be no mistake about it: for Teilhard evolution was far more than simple transformism in the minimal sense. There can be no doubt that when it comes to what he takes to be the earlier stages of evolution (right up to the first appearance of man) his vision of the evolutive process is Darwinist to a high degree. Thus, not only does Teilhard speak repeatedly of such things as "happy accidents" and "means of survival," which are then "promptly transformed and used as an instrument of progress or conquest,"[19] but he goes so far as to propound a theory of "groping" as "the specific and invincible weapon of all expanding multitudes."[20] At one point he seems to differentiate his own theory from the classical Darwinist conception by telling us that it would be a mistake to interpret "groping" as mere chance. "Groping is *directed chance*. It means pervading everything so as to try everything, and trying everything so as to find everything."[21] But the difference turns out to be slight. For as Teilhard himself explains later on, "It is only really through strokes of chance that life proceeds, but strokes of chance which are recognized and grasped—that is to say, psychically selected."[22] What this amounts to is that in addition to "natural selection" Teilhard postulates "psychic selection" as yet another evolutionary mechanism. Meanwhile it remains true, in the new doctrine no less than in the old, that life proceeds "only through strokes of chance."

*   *   *

Whether or not Teilhard regarded this additional article of evolutionist belief as having been validated by what we have called his Kantian argument, it is clear in any case that he presents what might be termed the stochastic postulate as nothing less than an irrefutable truth of science. That evolution proceeds "only through strokes of chance" has become for him a fundamental dogma. It will therefore be of interest to show that some of the latest discoveries of science (in its most exact branches, no less) are not in fact propitious to this claim. We are referring in particular to the so-called anthropic principle, which could well be described as one of the most startling and philosophically significant discoveries of contemporary physics. It is based upon a remarkable recognition: it happens that the physical evolution of the universe is controlled by a number of fundamental constants, the values of which turn out to be *precisely* what they need to be to admit the appearance of man. In the words of Paul Davies:

> All this prompts the question of why, from the infinite range of possible values that Nature could have selected for the fundamental constants, and from the infinite variety of initial conditions that could have characterized the primeval universe, the actual values and conditions conspire to produce the particular range of special features that we observe. For clearly the universe is a very special place: exceedingly uniform on a large scale, yet not so precisely uniform that galaxies could not form; extremely low entropy per proton, and hence cool enough for chemistry to happen; almost zero cosmic repulsion and an expansion rate tuned to that energy content to unbelievable accuracy; values for the strengths of its forces that permit nuclei to exist, yet do not burn up all the cosmic hydrogen, and many more apparent accidents of fortune.[23]

And let us point out immediately that what distinguishes these "apparent accidents of fortune" from the "happy accidents" of the Darwinists is the fact that the former have nothing whatever to do with "endless ages of groping," or with any conceivable stochastic mechanism. It is not possible, therefore, to pretend that these apparent accidents can be somehow explained on a statistical basis.

Yet "all this prompts the question why." Now the anthropic principle is not so much an explanation of the facts as it is a formal recognition of what these facts seem to imply. Formulated in its so-called strong form, it affirms that "the universe must be such as to admit the creation of observers within it at some state." In other words, the universe has from the start been designed, so to speak, to serve as the future habitat of man. One cannot but agree with Paul Davies when he observes that "in this respect the strong anthropic principle is akin to the traditional religious explanation of the world: that God made the world for mankind to inhabit."[24] Or as another physicist has remarked in even more poignant terms: "God made the fine structure constant to be 1/137 so that we could arise and worship Him."[25]

It is no doubt remarkable that many leading physicists have argued in support of this principle, and that they have done so on ostensibly rational and scientific grounds. The fact is that the anthropic principle marks a complete reversal from the position of nineteenth-century materialism, for it implicitly recognizes the existence of an intelligent, creative agent as the Architect or Lawgiver of the universe. And so it recognizes (again *implicitly*) an agent that can only be conceived of as *transcendent* in the authentic metaphysical sense: for it would make no sense whatsoever to suppose that the cosmos is able to determine or to select its own fundamental constants. But this means that in this regard, at least, modern physics has moved as close as it possibly can to the traditional belief in God.

But if it happens that the determination of the universal constants and of the so-called initial conditions of cosmogenesis can only be understood as an intelligent creative act which includes in its intention the emergence of man, by what right can it be supposed that in the sphere of biogenesis and speciation everything proceeds "only through strokes of chance"? If God is able to determine the fine structure constant with unerring accuracy "so that we could arise and worship Him," why then should He leave the remainder of the process to chance, or to "endless ages of groping"? By what right can we restrict the efficacy of God's creative act to some hypothetical first moment of cosmic history? The Darwinist thesis (which as we have noted before is tantamount to a denial of God's creative efficacy in the sphere of biogenesis and speciation) was no doubt very much in harmony with the prevailing world-view of nineteenth-century physics; but it is scarcely compatible with the anthropic principle. Step by step the new physics has retreated from its former materialistic stance, right up to the point of admitting the perennial conception of an intelligent Creator who has fashioned the world as a habitation for man. The scientist has thus been released from the imperative (or the spell) of the stochastic postulate, the gratuitous assumption that biogen-

esis proceeds "only through strokes of chance."[26] No longer
need he think in terms of astronomical improbabilities if he
is to think at all. And this, quite clearly, pulls the rug out from
under the Darwinists.

*   *   *

Yet, for Teilhard, not only is evolution a fact: it is the all-
important fact. "What makes the world in which we live specifically modern is our discovery in it and around it of evolution."[27] And in this modern world, dominated by the discovery
of evolution, all basic beliefs are to be rethought and reformu-
lated: that is what Teilhard maintains. Evolution is for him the
touchstone by which all human truth is henceforth to be tested.
And not only human truth, but all that earlier generations had
held to be a sacred and more-than-human truth. "What we
have to do without delay," Teilhard tells us, "is to modify the
position occupied by the central core of Christianity. . ."[28]
    The first conception that needs to be thus reworked is the
Judeo-Christian idea of creation. It is no longer possible (Teilhard claims) to accept what biblical revelation, as interpreted
by two thousand years of Christian tradition, has to say concerning the creation of the world and the origins of life. It
appears that Bible and Tradition must henceforth bow before
Darwin's *Origin of Species* and *The Descent of Man*. Not that
we need to deny God or reject the idea that He has created
the world: Teilhard's doctrine is a good deal more subtle than
that. Certainly he does not align himself in this regard with
Darwin and the atheistic materialists. The problem, then, is to
recast the idea of God, and the conception of His creative act,
so as to conform this Christian teaching to the magisterial truth
of evolution. According to Teilhard de Chardin, Christianity
has hitherto been too generous in its estimate of what God
can do; it has grossly overrated His creative efficacy. God does
create, Teilhard assures us—but not in the absolute sense of
traditional theology. God creates, we are told, but *only by way
of evolution*: that is the new dogma. "God cannot create except
evolutively"[29]: that is what we must henceforward believe.
    But why? To begin with, of course, the question remains
whether the Darwinist theory is correct; which is to say that

there is absolutely no reason to assume that the "evolution" to which God is supposed to be committed exists in the first place. But even if evolution could indeed be substantiated as a scientific theory, this still would not provide a sufficient basis upon which to challenge the traditional Christian doctrine of creation, let alone found a new theology. And the reason for this insufficiency, clearly, lies in the fact that *as a scientific theory* the doctrine is strictly confined to the realm of phenomena: it then speaks only of things that can in some sense be empirically observed, and only insofar as they *can* be observed. But this obviously excludes from consideration not only God, but His creative act. Even Teilhard admits elsewhere that "where God is operating it is always possible for us (by remaining at a certain level) to see only *the work of Nature*," and that "we shall never escape *scientifically* from the circle of natural explanations."[30]

But then, if that be the case, by what right does he maintain that the traditional Christian doctrine, which is in the first place theological and metaphysical in its content, has in fact been invalidated by the discovery of evolution? If science is unable to penetrate beyond the level of phenomena to behold the secret working of God, how can it enlighten us on the subject? At best it can say that the phenomena do not suffice, that the pieces do not fit together into a coherent whole, and that consequently (on the strength of a certain categorical imperative) there *must* be something beyond the total phenomenon: a factor X, which by virtue of its transcendence remains forever unknown and unknowable. This, quite clearly, is as far as science can ever go in the direction of theology; and one might add that today the physical sciences, at least, are already approaching that limit. Is not the anthropic principle a case in point? And what about the amazing discovery that the cosmos is bounded in its temporal duration? In the domain of biology, moreover, do not the "missing links" point in exactly the same direction, no matter what the Darwinists might say?

Our point, in any case, is that science can at best intimate that God exists, but cannot enlighten us further on theological issues. It can indeed suggest that God created the world (as a habitation for man, no less!); but it can tell us absolutely nothing about the manner in which God's work of creation

has been accomplished. Nothing, therefore, obliges us to conclude that "God cannot create except evolutively." Howsoever
Teilhard may have arrived at this remarkable notion, it is clear
that the dogma has absolutely no foundation in scientific fact.

★   ★   ★

But there is another (and far more serious) difficulty with
the idea that God creates by way of evolution. For as St. Augustine observes, "Beyond all doubt the world was not made
in time, but *with* time."[31] The point is that time belongs to
the created order and does not extend beyond the world. And
so the primary creative act cannot take place in time. Evolution, on the other hand, does of course take place in time (if
indeed it takes place at all). It therefore cannot be the primary
creative act. In the words of St. Augustine: "Let them see that
without the creature there cannot be time, and leave off talking
nonsense."[32]

Let us try to understand this more clearly. There is first of
all the question, "How did the world begin?"; and the answer,
quite obviously, could *not* be that it began by evolution. Now
it appears that Teilhard is intent upon obviating this question
by insisting that the world did not begin at all. "The universe
is no longer endless in space alone," he tells us. "In all its strands,
it now unfolds interminably into the past, governed by a constantly active cosmogenesis."[33] His idea, apparently, is that the
cosmos is constantly generating itself, and that this process of
autogenesis extends "interminably into the past." But one knows
today (with a high degree of assurance) that *it does not*. According to the latest findings of astrophysics, the cosmos (and thus
time itself) came into existence some twenty billion years ago.
And if it be admitted that the world was created by God, then
the fact of finite duration is alone sufficient to rule out Teilhard's contention that "God cannot create except evolutively."

On this question, therefore, it seems that contemporary physics
stands squarely on the side of traditional Christian doctrine,
the very teaching which Teilhard regards as being scientifically
untenable. But let us go on. Perhaps, when it comes to the
later stages of creation, the idea of "creation by evolution" may
yet be vindicated.

But here another difficulty presents itself: there *are* in reality no "later stages of creation." To quote St. Augustine once more: "God, therefore, in His unchangeable eternity created simultaneously all things whence times were to flow. . ."[34] The point is that the creative act, by virtue of being atemporal, does not break up into earlier and later phases. The ideas of "before" and "after" do of course apply to the *effects* of this act, but not to the act itself. Multiple in its effects, and absolutely simple in its own right: that is the point.

The act of creation may thus be viewed from two directions, as it were: from the side of the cosmos, and *sub specie aeternitatis,* as the Scholastics would say. According to the first point of view, things are created in temporal sequence: first one thing, then another, and so forth. Let us observe, moreover, that this corresponds to the perspective of the first chapter of *Genesis,* the perspective of the *hexaemeron* or the "six days." But let us not fail to observe, too, that in the second chapter one encounters an entirely different outlook: "These are the generations of the heaven and the earth, when they were created, in the day that the Lord God made the heaven and the earth, and every plant of the field before it sprung up in the earth, and every herb of the ground before it grew." (*Gen.* 2:4-5).[35] Now this corresponds to the second point of view. From "the standpoint of eternity" there are no longer six days, but only *one.* On its own ground, so to speak, the work of creation is accomplished in one absolutely simple and indivisible act. As we read in *Ecclesiasticus* (*Ecclus.* 18:1): *Qui vivit in aeternum creavit omnia simul* ("He that liveth in eternity created all things at once").

It is worth pointing out that this perennial teaching comes to us from a double source: it derives on the one hand from the Judeo-Christian revelation, and also from the metaphysical traditions of mankind.[36] For as St. Augustine has observed, the metaphysical recognition that "the world was not made in time, but with time" entails the scriptural *omnia simul* as a logical consequence: "God, therefore, in His unchangeable eternity created simultaneously all things whence times flow. . ." They were not made in temporal succession, because they were not made in time.

Yet, to be sure, created beings come to birth in time: they enter the world, as it were, at some particular moment. Each creature, in its cosmic manifestation, is thus associated with its own spatio-temporal locus: it fits somewhere into the universal network of secondary causes. But yet it is not created by these causes, nor is its being confined to that spatio-temporal locus: for its roots extend beyond the cosmos into the timeless instant of the creative act. That is the veritable "beginning" to which *Genesis* alludes when it declares: *In principio creavit Deus caelum et terram.* It is "the day that the Lord God made the heaven and the earth, and every plant of the field before[37] it sprung up in the earth, and every herb in the ground before it grew." Let there be no doubt about it: the creature is more—incomparably more!—than its visible manifestation. It does *not* coincide with the phenomenon. Even the tiniest plant that blooms for a fortnight and then is seen no more is vaster in its metaphysical roots than the entire cosmos in its visible form: for these roots extend into eternity. And how much more does this apply to man! "Before I formed thee in the womb, I knew thee." (*Jer.* 1:5).

Here then, in the scriptural and metaphysical teaching of the *omnia simul,* we have the definitive answer to evolutionism. With the adoption of an authentically metaphysical standpoint the seemingly interminable debate between the evolutionists and the so-called creationists has at last been put into perspective: it now becomes clear that both sides are in fact looking at only half the picture: the outer or phenomenal half, one could say, forgetting that things have also an inner dimension, an essential core which transcends the plane of the phenomenon. From this truncated point of view, moreover, the riddle of origins becomes truly insoluble—for the simple reason that things ultimately derive, not from the phenomenal plane, but from the side of transcendence. Likewise, they grow and unfold their potential from inside out: the essential, in other words, has primacy over the phenomenal, whatever the empiricists might think. Metaphysics, therefore, is neither a luxury nor an idle speculation; it is there to complete the picture, and is needed if ever we are to make sense out of first origins or final ends. One might add that its neglect in modern times is both a symptom and cause of our contemporary intellectual predicament.

Getting back to the subject of evolution, no one doubts that living forms have emerged successively as evolutionists insist:

this is an empirical fact, after all. Indeed, it is precisely what the fossil record does permit us to conclude. What is objectionable in the evolutionist position, on the other hand, is that it oversteps what we actually know, first through the transformist hypothesis (for which there is no evidence at all), and secondly by maintaining that the process of speciation can be accounted for in terms of molecular accidents (an assumption which is not only unfounded but astronomically improbable to the point of absurdity). The fact that these unpromising postulates have nonetheless commended themselves to countless individuals derives no doubt from the circumstance that in conjunction they seem to offer a rational means of approach to the mystery of life for minds closed to the metaphysical outlook. As one evolutionist has said: "It is better to think in terms of improbable events than not to think at all."

The creationists too, of course, maintain the successive origin of living forms, oftentimes basing themselves on the *hexaemeron* doctrine of *Genesis* 1. Our only criticism of these biblicists would be that for the most part they do not avail themselves of the biblical teaching in its integrality, and that in particular they generally ignore the *omnia simul* doctrine which proves to be the key to the entire problem.[38] Getting back to *Genesis* 2:5 it needs to be pointed out in this connection that the terms "every plant" and "every herb" admit of a symbolic interpretation which is metaphysically illuminating.[39] For in marked contrast to animals, a plant exists, as it were, in two domains: above ground, namely, and beneath the earth. Now the former is evidently suggestive of the phenomenal sphere, the domain of visible manifestation; whereas the latter can then be taken to refer to a transcendent realm of causes, an invisible domain wherein the seeds of living beings are to be found, and where also they incubate and begin to sprout. One thus obtains what might indeed be termed an "icon" of the perennial ontology: through the figure of a natural symbolism, *Genesis* 2:5 is actually speaking of profound metaphysical truths.

One should add that under this interpretation the "seeds" correspond precisely to the *rationes seminales* of patristic doctrine: they constitute the essential reality of the creature, one could say, as it emerges directly from the primordial creative act. To be sure, these are not physical seeds, not physical entities, in fact: they are situated "below ground," after all, which is to say that they belong to a prior ontological plane. One must remember, moreover, that whereas the physical or corporeal domain is subject to the spatio-temporal condition, "below ground" one can speak neither of spatial separation nor of temporal sequence in a literal sense. Here we encounter the truly primordial realm—the corona of God's Act—where everything is still concentrated at a single point, or "fused without confusion," as Meister Eckhart says.

Such, in brief, is the metaphysical panorama revealed to us—as in a flash—by *Genesis* 2:5. And it happens that this picture is not propitious to the evolutionist. Indeed, the doctrine of evolution may henceforth be likened to a botany which supposes that plants originate abruptly at the level of the ground—as if they had neither seeds nor roots! And let us add, with reference to Teilhard de Chardin, that this misbegotten doctrine remains such even if one brings God into the picture via the dictum, "God creates evolutively": this bit of rhetoric hardly compensates for the fact that now as before "seed and roots" are missing. With or without God—if one may put it thus—what has been excluded from the evolutionist purview is nothing less than the essential thing, the "core of reality," of which the visible phenomenon is merely the outward manifestation. Furthermore, inasmuch as this essential core—the *ratio seminale*—is not subject to terrestrial time (being situated "below ground," as we have said), there can be no question of evolution in this domain: the *ratio seminale* of a simian, for instance, can by no means be "hominized." And finally, how can temporality be predicated of the creative act itself (as demanded by the phrase "God creates evolutively")? As St. Augustine has admirably put it, "Let them see that without the creature there cannot be time, and leave off talking nonsense."

*   *   *

This brings us at last to a question regarding Teilhard de Chardin which may prove to be enlightening: what is it in the idea of evolution which so greatly fascinates and inspires this man? Is it simply the notion that lizards have descended from fish, mammals from lizards, and man from primate stock?

As Teilhard himself informs us in a most interesting piece entitled "Note on the Essence of Transformism," that is not really the point at all. Transformism, in its true and essential sense, he tells us, is far less specific than that. What it really means is that the origin of life and of species can be adequately understood in terms of physical causes, or in terms of a "physical connection." Surprisingly enough, however, that "connection" need not necessarily be understood in terms of filiation or lines of descent. "Without as yet pre-judging in any way the particular physical nature of this connection," he explains, "and without even asserting that there is a line of descent, properly so called, linking organic beings, we hold firmly to the belief that the various terms of life appear as a physical response to one another."[40] At the same time Teilhard is careful to point out that the idea of transformism (thus understood) does not exclude the notion of a divine creative act: "For the transformist retains the right, as much as anyone else, to believe that a creative act is necessary to set the world in motion. What he postulates is quite simply that this perennial and indispensable act on the part of the first cause comes to us in the order of history and experience in the form of an organically established movement."[41]

Now this, of course, can hardly be denied. What we encounter "in the order of history and experience" is indeed an organically established movement: what else could it be? Is this all, then, that the transformist postulates? Obviously, there must be more to the transformist hypothesis; and this more, quite clearly, must lie in the idea that the network of physical causes is in itself sufficient to explain the phenomena of biogenesis and speciation. Or to put it another way: the point of transformism, as Teilhard presently informs us, is to rule out "the intervention of an extra-cosmic intelligence"[42] in the operations of Nature.

One might remark that there is something distinctly Newtonian (or Cartesian, even) in this notion of all-sufficient causality. One has the impression that Teilhard still stands under the spell of the Newtonian world-picture, with its rather unsophisticated and materialistic conceptions. His idea of an unbroken network of physical causes in terms of which everything can be somehow explained seems to belong to an era in which the notion of "complementarity" in the sense of Niels Bohr had not yet come to light, and the sobering recognition that our scientific knowledge of Nature is perforce fragmentary had not yet dawned upon mankind. It is in the spirit of this unrefined and unchastened Weltanschauung of a bygone age that Teilhard envisages Nature as a seamless garment of organic inter-relationships, in which every living form can be regarded as the resultant of other forms that have preceded it. Thus conceived, transformism is in essence the biological counterpart of Newtonian physics, and the biosphere an analog of that "clockwork universe" which had been the dream of the classical physicist.

There must be a rigorous physical connection, a "physical agent," Teilhard maintains, in terms of which biogenesis and speciation can be explained; but what exactly this connection, or this agent, might be is another question. What alone is essential to the transformist cause, he believes, is that there be such a connection, such a physical determinism. This is what every "natural scientist worthy of the name" presupposes: "He may hesitate about the precise nature of the physical agent shared by the successive forms of life; but the belief that such an agent exists, whether it be confused with the generative function or not, the dream that one day we shall be able to put a name to it and define its behavior, it is there we find his most precious conviction and his grandest hope."[43]

It is worth pointing out that this passage flatly contradicts what Teilhard has so often and so vehemently affirmed elsewhere: for if it has not yet been established that the postulated "agent" resides in the generative function, how can it be said that evolution (in its "most generally accepted sense") must henceforward be regarded as an "indubitable fact of science"? If more than half a century after *The Origin of Species* scientists are still dreaming that someday they will know whether or not there exist actual lines of descent connecting higher to lower forms of life, how then can one say that the matter has been settled ("so finally" that it would be a "waste of time" to discuss it further)?

One wonders, too, what it is about the transformist hypothesis that inspires such strong convictions and powerful sentiments in its votaries. Why does the transformist believe (or dream) with such vehemence? From whence does he derive "his most precious conviction and his grandest hope"? It appears to be an act of faith, as Teilhard himself suggests: "It is 'faith' in one organic physical interaction of living beings, it is that and *nothing else,* which constitutes the necessary and sufficient disposition for an evolutionist mind."[44]

But the question remains: what is the basis of that faith? And why does the issue loom quite so large? Why this almost religious intensity? The reason, as we would like now to point out, is that the issue *is* in fact religious at the core. Teilhard himself, moreover, has made this clear: "We have to make a choice: there is either evolution or intrusion," he declares. And what might be the nature of this "intrusion"? It is precisely "the intervention of an extra-cosmic intelligence." This, then, must be the crux of the matter: the essence of transformism reduces ultimately to a denial of God's role or efficacy in the generation of living forms. In the final analysis, this is what Teilhard perceives as the quintessential faith of the evolutionist, "his most cherished conviction and his grandest hope"!

At first glance this conclusion may strike us as rather strange: was it not in fact the express intention of the Jesuit paleontologist to reintroduce the Christian God into the scientific worldview? Was it not the great ambition of his life to demonstrate that the idea of evolution, in its full-blown format, demands actually a Christic Omega Point as a universal center of attraction and confluence? Now this assessment is almost correct: it is right except for one crucial point: the God to be installed upon the evolutionist horizon is no longer the traditional Christian God, the supposedly "extrinsicist" and "immobilist" God of a pre-scientific humanity. It had never been Teilhard's intention to defend and reinstate the traditional Christian teaching; instead, his objective from the start has been to *reshape* the doctrine. "What we have to do without delay is to modify the position occupied by the core of Christianity. . ." In a word, Teilhard's objective is to found a new Christianity. And that must be the reason why he is willing to join forces with the materialists, the atheistic Darwinists, in their well-camouflaged campaign against "interventions by an extra-cosmic intelligence." The thrust is aimed, not at the new, but at the old religion: at traditional Christianity, with its time-honored belief in an eternal, transcendent, and absolutely omnipotent God. It is this

"God of the Above" who needs to be overthrown to make way for the new deity. "This is still, of course, Christianity and always will be," Teilhard assures the reader; "but a Christianity re-incarnated for a second time in the spiritual energies of Matter. It is precisely the 'ultra-Christianity' we need here and now to meet the ever more urgent demands of the 'ultra-human.'"[45]

To be sure, whether "this is still, of course, Christianity" is another question, with which we shall have to deal later. For the moment what concerns us is the recognition that a new (or "re-incarnated") religion has appeared upon the scene, and that Teilhard is its prophet. And this seems to be the decisive fact, the key, we would say, to the phenomenon of Teilhard de Chardin.

NOTES

1. PM, p. 219.
2. PM, p. 140.
3. PM, p. 82.
4. G. G. Simpson, *The Major Features of Evolution* (New York: Columbia University Press, 1953), p. 360.
5. According to this doctrine (presented by Teilhard de Chardin before the Congress on Philosophy of Science, Paris, 1949), the birth of a new phylum is accomplished in a short period of time through a small number of individuals, all of slight stature and fragile composition, which consequently disappear without leaving any trace in the fossil record.
6. Quoted by Louis Bounoure in *Déterminisme et Finalité* (Paris: Flammarion, 1957), p. 48.
7. PM, p. 140.
8. *Ibid.*
9. *Le Figaro Litteraire*, April 20, 1957. Quoted by Titus Burckhardt in *The Sword of Gnosis*, ed. J. Needleman (Baltimore: Penguin, 1974), p. 143.
10. *Ibid.*
11. S. Stanley, *Macroevolution* (San Francisco: Freeman, 1979), p. 39.
12. *The Transformist Illusion* (Murfreesboro, TN: Dehoff, 1957), p. 166.
13. See W. Smith, *Cosmos and Transcendence* (La Salle: Sugden, 1984), chapter 4, for further details and references to the literature.
14. *Evolution: A Theory in Crisis* (Bethesda, MD: Adler & Adler, 1986), p. 291.
15. Quoted by Huston Smith in *Beyond the Post-Modern Mind* (New York: Crossroad, 1982), p. 173.
16. SC, p. 139.
17. *Angels, Apes, and Men* (La Salle: Sugden, 1983), p. 53.

18. Quoted by Stanley Jaki in *op. cit.*, p. 65.
19. PM, p. 104.
20. PM, p. 110.
21. *Ibid.*
22. PM, p. 149.
23. *The Accidental Universe* (Cambridge: Cambridge University Press, 1982), p. 111.
24. *Ibid.*, p. 121.
25. Quoted by S. Jaki in *op. cit.*, p. 120.
26. It will be recalled that Teilhard qualifies this principle by postulating some form of "psychic selection." Let us add that in rejecting the notion that biogenesis proceeds "only through strokes of chance" we do not deny that psychic selection may play a role in the unfoldment of life. We see clearly that it does have its use. Our point is only that this role is restricted, that it cannot be primary. It is obvious, for example, that psychic selection may help us to utilize our senses to best advantage; but it cannot account for the formation of the eye.
27. PM, p. 229.
28. CE, p. 77.
29. CE, p. 179.
30. SC, pp. 27 & 28.
31. *De Civ. Dei.*, 11:6.
32. Conf., 11:40.
33. CE, p. 78.
34. *De Gen. ad Litt.*, 8:39. As St. Thomas Aquinas has put it: "Succession is proper to movement. But creation is not movement. Therefore there is in it no succession" (*Summa Contra Gent.*, II. 19).
35. *Genesis* 2:5 can also be interpreted as follows: in place of the phrase "and every plant of the field before it sprang up in the earth" some have read "and no plant of the field had yet sprung up in the earth." The ambiguity stems from the Hebrew word *terem*, which can mean either "before" or "not yet." The fact that Christian tradition has opted for the former sense (*"et omne virgultum agri antequam oreretur in terra"* reads the Vulgate) does not of course rule out the second option; it only legitimizes the first.
36. See especially A. Coomaraswamy, *Time and Eternity* (Ascona: Artibus Asiae, 1947).
37. To be sure, this "before" is not to be understood in the sense of temporal precedence: that would be to miss the entire point! The precedence in question is ontological, or causal, as one could also say.
38. It has sometimes been charged by Christians of a fundamentalist persuasion that the Catholic Church has bestowed sanction upon evolutionism; now this is not correct. To be sure, ever since Canon Dorlodot was commissioned to represent the Catholic University of Louvain at the celebration of Darwin's birth centenary (held at Cambridge in 1909), one has repeatedly witnessed the spectacle of prominent Catholic thinkers, not infrequently theologians, flirting quite openly with Darwinism; so much so that the term "Catholic evolutionism" has come to enjoy a certain vogue. Yet the fact remains that evolutionism has been censured in a number of Magisterial documents which have never been retracted. More could and should perhaps have been done; but that is another question.
39. It would seem that the double reference to plants and herbs should in itself dissuade the exegete from a literalist interpretation.

40. HM, p. 110.
41. HM, p. 112.
42. HM, p. 113.
43. HM, p. 112.
44. HM, p. 111.
45. HM, p. 96.

Chapter II
The Cartesian Connection

According to Teilhard's usage of the word, "spirit" is more or less synonymous with "consciousness" and "thought." And it is scarcely surprising that he thinks of spirit in evolutive terms: "From a purely scientific and empirical standpoint, the true name for 'spirit' is 'spiritualization.' "[1] It is a process, then, "a gradual and systematic passage from the unconscious to the conscious, and from the conscious to the self-conscious."[2] Now this second mode of consciousness appertains to the human sphere: it is a characteristic of man. We humans not only know, but know that we know; and let us add that this reflective mode of awareness is evidently connected with the specifically human phenomenon of language. Once symbols have taken the place of things, one is able to manipulate these symbols, move them about at will; and by virtue of this inner freedom one finds oneself, as it were, in a new space: the space of concepts, the inner world of thought.

Consciousness and thought: this is what Teilhard is referring to when he speaks of "spirit." There is a birth or genesis of spirit, moreover, because there is an emergence of consciousness and thought. Spirit has become in effect a phenomenon—an "internal" phenomenon, perhaps, one that, strictly speaking, can be "observed" only in ourselves; but still a phenomenon. And as such it is related to other phenomena: to biological complexities, and to brain function. At Teilhard's hands spirit becomes a variable correlated to other variables, other parameters.

27

Spirit, then, is growing; it is evolving via a more or less continuous trajectory, along which it is possible to distinguish various stages, ranging from the most dim and rudimentary consciousness in the lowest forms of life right up to the peaks of human thought. And beyond this, what for us unimaginable heights of thought, or hyper-thought, may yet be attainable in the far distant future if our individual powers become more and more amplified through ever-greater strides of socialization? What if Teilhard is right in conjecturing the formation of a super-organism, a Gargantuan creature endowed with a brain within which each of our brains is but a single neuron as it were?

But let us take spirit at its present high-water mark: it is, then, thought. This is Teilhard's position; and it is not without interest to note that this thesis has a distinctly Cartesian ring. It was Descartes, as we know, who implicitly identified the inner man, the spiritual man, with thought: *"cogito ergo sum."* It was Descartes who reduced the spirit to a *res cogitans,* a "thinking entity." Until then, spirit (in the form of intellect) had generally been distinguished from "mind," or the discursive level of psychic function. And this fundamental distinction had been clearly marked in the ancient metaphysical vocabularies: it is the difference between *nous* and *dianoia* in Greek, *intellectus* and *mens* in Latin, or *buddhi* and *manas* in Sanskrit, to mention the most important examples. But with the advent of the modern age, the two levels of cognition came to be *de facto* identified; or, what amounts to the same, the higher of the two came to be dropped. Men forgot all about "intellect" in the high and time-honored sense of that term. And today the word has acquired an altogether different connotation: in fact, its use is commonly associated with an attitude which could almost be characterized as a denial of *intellectus* in the ancient sense. It is one of the signs of our time that the "intelligentsia" has become hostile to intellect.

But these are matters with which we shall have to deal later. For the moment it suffices to say that Teilhard, for his part, conforms to this modern trend, and seems to accept its implicit presuppositions without the slightest qualms. In fact, he goes considerably further than the Cartesians: whereas Descartes still believed in "mind" as a spiritual substance, a *res cogitans,* whose activity is thought, Teilhard veers towards the position that mind or spirit *is* thought. His outlook represents thus a decisive step beyond the *cogito ergo sum*: not only is thought an indication that I exist as a spiritual entity, but it *is* that entity. According to this view the "I" is nothing but the epicenter of the thought; what else could it be from a radically evolutionist standpoint? The traditional picture, of course, is quite different. In the light of what some have called the "perennial philosophy," one would have to say that thought is an activity arising from the interplay of spirit (or soul) with the body, or more precisely, with the brain. It could thus be compared to the music which results when a pianist plays upon his instrument. There is, of course, an observable correlation between the sounds and the movement of the keys and hammers; and in a certain sense it is true that the sound is produced by the piano. And yet the fact remains that the piano as such does not account for the music. It could not be said that the music is an "epiphenomenon" of the instrument, or that the two constitute complementary aspects of one and the same underlying reality or process (a view which would correspond roughly to the position of Teilhard de Chardin). The point is that in either case we have left out of account a vital factor, in the absence of which there can be no music at all: the pianist, namely. And so, too, it needs to be realized that the brain, though necessary to the phenomenon of thought, is not in itself sufficient to produce that phenomenon. As Wilder Penfield, a noted neurologist and brain surgeon, has put it:

> Because it seems to be certain that it will always be quite impossible to explain the mind on the basis of neuronal action within the brain, and because it seems to me that the mind develops and matures independently throughout an individual's life as though it were a continuing element, and because a computer (which the brain is) must be operated by an agency capable of independent understanding, I am forced to choose the proposition that our being is to be explained on the basis of two fundamental elements.[3]

It is clear, moreover, that the second of these two fundamental factors could not be *thought*, which is, after all, an effect:

the result of the postulated interaction. It must therefore be something else: an unknown, a factor X, which we may call "mind," "soul," or "spirit," as we wish. In the words of Sir Charles Sherrington, it "goes in our spatial world more ghostly than a ghost. Invisible, intangible, it is a thing not even of outline, it is not a thing."[4] No wonder the renowned neurophysiologist was forced to concede that science "stands powerless to deal with or to describe" that elusive element.

Yet it exists and is no doubt the crucial factor: the active principle, the determinant of our thought. And by the same token, is this not, too, the decisive factor which spells the difference between one man and another? Are we to suppose that the difference between a Mozart and an average man is simply a matter of neurons? Are not their respective brains presumably very much alike? And if there be some differences, could *this* be the cause on account of which one is a musical genius and the other is not? To say so, clearly, would be to fall once again into the old materialist position which Wilder Penfield has rejected: it would be to assume that the workings of the mind can be explained on the basis of neuronal action within the brain. Let us admit it once and for all: the mind cannot be thus explained. It cannot be "explained away," in other words; there is an inner man, a spiritual man, as religion has always proclaimed. And science "stands powerless" in the face of that being.

What, then, can we say about that inner man? We say that he is not the body, but an "indwelling spirit"; he is not the thought, but the author of the thought, the thinker. We do not know this man directly: he is invisible to our senses; but yet we *do* know him. And this is perhaps the greatest miracle of all: he is no stranger to us. We know him by his words, we know him by his actions, we know him by his countenance, by the expression on his face and the look in his eyes. After all, the body is *his* body, *his* instrument— his *icon,* one is tempted to say.

Now this is the simple and eminently natural doctrine in which mankind had always believed—until just yesterday, when it was replaced amongst the modern intelligentsia by a scientistic teaching which explains nothing, and for which there is not a shred of evidence.

★   ★   ★

What Teilhard has failed to grasp is that spirit and matter are situated on different levels of reality. They are not simply two faces of a single cosmic substance or principle, but two tiers of the cosmic edifice: the two poles, one could say, between which the entire drama of cosmic existence is played out.

There is in reality no single cosmic substance, no "stuff of the universe" in Teilhard's sense. It is a pure fiction, a carry-over from the old Newtonian materialism which science itself has since been forced to disavow. Now it is true, certainly, that we cannot stop at the idea of multiplicity, or of duality: our intellect craves unity, it would know "the One." But as all the traditional schools of metaphysics have recognized, that One is not a part of the cosmos, nor is it the cosmic whole (what our contemporaries would call "the holistic universe"): instead, it is the Absolute, the Infinite: it is none other than God.

The great fact is that the world begins with a primordial duality: *In principio creavit Deus caelum et terram*. Theologians do not always agree in their interpretation of this "heaven and earth"; and no doubt the expression can be legitimately understood in more than one sense. What is beyond dispute, however, is the fact of duality: after the One comes—not three or four— but precisely *two*.

We have said that the biblical "heaven and earth" can be understood in a number of senses: as the active and passive principles of cosmogenesis, as *form* and *matter* in the Scholastic sense, as the angelic and the corporeal orders of existence, as soul and body, as the male and female principles, and so forth. But it will also be noted that all these senses are somehow related; they are so many exemplifications, as it were, of a single underlying idea. Spirit and matter, let us say; the terms are well suited, on account of their deep and manifold associations, to convey some slight intuition, at least, of what is actually at stake.

There are, then, these two poles, between which the entire gamut of cosmic existence is spread out—but not, of course, in a spatial, but in an ontological sense. And yet we can hardly avoid the temptation to spatialize even the purest of relations: we are never at peace until we have discovered an icon, a visual representation of the ideal or metaphysical. Now this, of course, is exactly what the ancient cosmologies—such as the much-maligned Ptolemaic world-picture—were attempting to do: their deeper function, quite clearly, was to provide a symbolic representation of the cosmos in its ontological entirety. And as we have pointed out elsewhere,[5] it could hardly have been an accident that Europe began to lose its metaphysical sense at precisely the time of the so-called Copernican revolution. Most assuredly, there is more—incomparably more!—to the Ptolemaic *Weltanschauung* than meets the modern eye. Let us not forget that the very terms "heaven" and "earth" in which the biblical revelation apprises us of the primordial duality are spoken from a distinctly Ptolemaic point of view. Their direct reference is to a natural icon, an icon which we behold, not with telescopes or Geiger counters, but with our God-given eyes. And how wonderful, how infinitely expressive that icon is!

But there is yet another image, another icon, which is equally biblical; for it has also been said that Heaven lies "within." Here the standpoint has changed; from an authentically metaphysical perspective, the two "worlds" are no longer separated; they interpenetrate, one could say. But here, too, we need to go behind the image, behind the figure of speech. Spirit and matter interpenetrate, no doubt; but they do so without mixture or confusion: they interpenetrate in a most marvelous way.

What we actually perceive, moreover, and what alone we know in our earthbound existence is neither matter nor spirit as such, but the effect or offspring, rather, of their enigmatic union. The corporeal world does not in fact exist in isolation from the spiritual, nor is it intelligible in its own right: to think of it thus is to fall prey to an illusion. And of course, one does often enough think of it in these terms; the fallacy is implicit in the very conception of the physical universe (which goes back to Descartes). One knows today, after centuries of philosophical debate, that the Cartesian notion of a physical universe (made up of self-existent *res extensa* or "particles") is thoroughly untenable; and is this not, too, the reason why the physicist's "matter" has proved to be chimerical? For today one also knows, from a purely scientific direction, that there exists no such thing as a "particle" in the classical sense. For those who believe in the so-called physical universe, this means that the cosmos itself is void, not only of qualities, but of substances as well. Yet in reality the cosmos is far from void. What has happened is that we have lost our grip on reality; we have systematically filtered out the real.[6]

The universe is not in fact an empty space-time, whose curvatures and singularities conjure up an appearance of solidity. The material (or corporeal) world does have a *bona fide* content, but that content turns out to be immaterial and non-corporeal in its own right; it derives from that enigmatic interpenetration, from that "conjugal embrace of the spirit" through which the cosmos receives its fecundity. Furthermore, it is precisely this "spiritual content" that renders the universe intelligible. Let us understand it well: the content of the cosmos coincides with its intelligibility. What we know in all things is spirit—or spirit reflected in matter, to be more precise. That is what matter does: it reflects the spiritual light. And that light is again perceived, not by matter, but by a spiritual faculty: the mirror reflects, and the eye perceives.

The cosmos is not empty, as we have said. What appears as a void when viewed through telescopes and Geiger counters, turns out to be a plenum, a perfect fullness, when viewed with a spiritual eye. For as St. Maximus has said, "The whole of the spiritual world appears mystically represented in symbolic forms in every part of the sensible world for those who are able to see."[7] But we must not think that this perception, to which the Saint alludes, is reserved only for mystics of high rank. In its purest form, yes; but let us also remark that all of us, whether we realize it or not, have yet some share in that vision: for it is this, and this alone, that makes us human.

*   *   *

These are the rudiments of traditional cosmology. The secret of Nature, the alchemical secret of its innermost operation is perceived to hinge upon a primordial duality: the ontological pairing of spirit and matter. This entails, moreover, that the cosmos may be conceived as a hierarchic order of ontological planes held together and dominated, as it were, by a vertical axis: the so-called *axis mundi* by which Heaven is joined to Earth. This is the veritable Jacob's Ladder on which "the angels of God" are said to ascend and descend perpetually. And in this hierarchic and vertically ordered cosmos the material world—the world that is normally visible to us—corresponds to a single rung, a single horizontal plane: the lowest, no less.

For Teilhard, on the other hand, that world, that single rung, has become the cosmos in its ontological entirety. "All that exists is matter becoming spirit"[8]: these words express the quintessence of his thought. And this means that in Teilhard's eyes matter and spirit are situated on one and the same plane: they constitute two faces of a single cosmic reality. As Teilhard himself observes, "There is neither spirit nor matter in the world; the 'stuff of the universe' is spirit-matter."[9]

The cosmos has thus become flattened out. We must understand that the idea of the primordial duality and the notion of metaphysical verticality go hand in hand: they are inseparable. Whosoever, therefore, denies the primordial duality has in the same breath denied the concept of an *axis mundi*. There is then no more Jacob's Ladder, and presumably no more "angels of God" to ascend and descend thereon. We then find ourselves in this familiar universe, this narrow world, which remains such in spite of what Teilhard has euphemistically termed "the discovery of Space and Time."

Now it may well be true that our ancestors were less well informed about physical and quantitative matters than we are today. But they cannot be accused of "thinking small"; it is we, rather, who tend to be guilty of that charge.[10] Far better to think that the world was created six thousand years ago, while realizing that there exists a spiritual realm which is incomparably more lofty than this Earth, than to know that the physical universe began some twenty billion years ago and imagine that this one domain is everything.

But let us get back to Teilhard's vision: having abolished verticality, he immediately proceeds to find an analog, an Ersatz, if you will, within the remaining plane. This is in fact the salient characteristic of his system: he has replaced the *axis mundi* by the "arrow of time," or more precisely, by the trajectory of evolution. In the language of geometry, he has rotated the axis through ninety degrees. And the result of that transformation, quite clearly, is that "the above" has been replaced by "the ahead." According to Teilhard's theory, Heaven is neither "above" nor "within," but ahead of us in time: it is situated in the indefinite future.

★   ★   ★

This is the artful shift which in a way characterizes Teilhard's entire Weltanschauung and bestows upon it the stamp of heterodoxy. It constitutes the prime device which permits Teilhard to transpose and falsify virtually every traditional conception, beginning with what is (by right) central to his world-view: the idea of man, the inquiring creature who would know both himself and the universe.

What, then, is man? Now, according to the traditional teaching, as it is commonly understood, man is a dichotomous being composed of body and soul. He is thus composed, not of one, but of *two* fundamental elements. Soul and body: these are the constituent principles which unite to make the living man. And this basic dichotomy, let us understand, is none other than the microcosmic exemplification of the primordial duality. What holds true of the cosmos at large holds true for man: both exist through an inscrutable interpenetration or synthesis of spirit and matter.

Soul, then, is the spiritual component of man. But does this mean that soul is spirit, pure and simple? Not exactly. There is in fact a Christian tradition going back to St. Paul which clearly distinguishes the two. According to this teaching, *psyche* (that is to say, soul) is not the same thing as *pneuma*: it is not *spirit* in the strict sense. If it be true, therefore, that man, conceived in the fullest integrality of his being, contains within himself an authentically spiritual factor, then it would appear that there are, not two, but three basic ingredients in the human compound: *corpus, anima,* and *spiritus,* to use the Latin terms. And one arrives thus at a *trichotomous* conception of man, which at first glance seems to contradict the former view.

But despite first appearances—and despite the fact that the issue has at times been hotly debated— the two views are not in reality opposed. They are two ways, if you will, of looking at the soul. The question is whether *pneuma* belongs to the soul (as its essential core), or whether it is to be conceived as situated outside (or "above") the soul. One must realize, in either case, that *pneuma* is in a sense a supra-formal (and hence supra-individual) principle. Spirit is in a way a supra-human element. It is not our soul, but the soul of our soul, one is tempted to say. But the real difficulty, perhaps, lies in the fact that "above the soul"—above the psychic level, in the strict sense—our concepts become somehow inadequate. And this is not at all surprising: if there is indeed such an "above," it could hardly be otherwise.

But these are in any case difficult questions, which we need not attempt to probe too deeply at this point. Suffice it to say that the human soul, understood as the vital and psychic principle within the human compound, depends upon another factor: and that is the *pneuma,* the spirit that animates and enlightens our soul. And whether this *pneuma* be conceived as the spiritual essence of the soul, or whether it be assigned to a higher ontological plane, in either case, soul as we know it—soul as the vital and psychic principle in man—will occupy a certain middle ground. It is a mediating principle, in fact. Situated midway between the spiritual and the corporeal orders of existence, its function is to mediate between the two realms.

This, as one knows very well, is the underlying schema in terms of which the traditional view of man has generally been framed. But what is all too frequently forgotten is that this ontological teaching entails epistemological consequences. When it comes to the question of knowledge, one easily forgets that the psyche plays only a mediating role. We tend to think of knowledge as a "psychic phenomenon." The great fact, however, is that the miracle of knowledge is consummated, not on a psychic, but on a truly spiritual plane. Spirit alone is the primary intellect, the true eye by which we see. The psyche, properly so called, is but a means or a medium. As St. Paul has said, "We now see through a glass, darkly." And let us add that spirit itself is invisible to us, not because it is remote, or because perhaps it does not exist at all, but for the very opposite reason: it is far too near, and far too real, to become a mental object.

*   *   *

As we have noted before, Teilhard fails to distinguish between spirit and psyche, or what amounts to the same, between intellect and mind. Now the act of the intellect is cognition (or understanding, if you will), while the act of the mind is thought; and the two are by no means the same. One might put it this way: thought is the quest of which cognition is the consummation. Thought is a movement; it circles, so to speak, around its object. But cognition is a stasis, a state of vision and of rest. Thought as such, therefore, is not knowledge; at best, it is the occasion of knowledge. But it need not be, and all too often is not. Thought, as we know, can be blind. Thought can become illusory, it can miscarry. But the same cannot be said of the intellectual act, which is an immediate vision, and a certain union with its object.

Now the connection between thought and intellect is extremely variable. Towards one end of the spectrum, thought becomes more or less automatic; it then functions with a minimum of intellectual support. In that state the brain, the computer, runs almost by itself. And this is perhaps what happens most of the time. It happens even in the scientific domain, in scientific research. Yet at crucial moments, when a so-called breakthrough comes about, the balance shifts abruptly: at such times thought ceases to be semi-automatic: it slows down, as it were, almost to the point of stasis. It becomes luminous. On such occasions the phenomenology of our thought changes noticeably; one senses that another factor has come into play.

Thought is a movement, we have said, and cognition "a stasis, a state of vision and of rest." But let us try now to understand this more clearly. The remarkable fact (startling as it may sound) is that cognition does not take place "in time." If it did, it too would be a process or a movement. But as we have said, it is not. Nor could it be. For movement involves dispersion, or a multiplicity of states, whereas the hallmark of cognition is unity. We cannot really perceive a landscape one bit at a time, nor can we hear music successively, note by note. What is scattered in space and time is brought together in the cognitive act. And so the cognitive act cannot be successive, it cannot be a temporal act.

It is no wonder, therefore, that Teilhard confuses cognition with thought: where movement or process has become everything, the die has already been cast. By his radical evolutionism, Teilhard has committed himself to a perspective from which it is no longer possible to understand what cognition is, and wherein it differs from thought.

By the same token, moreover, the radical evolutionist is debarred from any comprehension of what spirit is in its own right, and how it differs from psyche or mind. For it is clear from the foregoing considerations that spirit, too, must somehow escape from the temporal condition; if it did not (if, in other words, it were a process), the same would hold true of the intellectual act. But the remarkable fact, as we have said, is that this act is *not* successive, is *not* temporal. One is forced to conclude, therefore, that spirit as such is not subject to time; it does not disperse into a one-dimensional continuum, as it were. In the expressive language of St. Augustine, spirit is not to be counted among "the things from which times flow." It is not flux, nor does it give rise to flux; on the contrary, spirit is the source of whatever unity, stability and permanence are to be found in the material world. All unity in material things, one could say, is but a reflection of a higher unity which subsists on the spiritual plane.

But there is another fact which we must not forget: spirit, too, belongs to the order of creation. We have not been speaking of the Spirit of God, of the Holy Ghost, the Third Person of the divine Trinity. Spirit (with a small s) is a created and cosmic reality; it constitutes, as it were, the "upper half" (or if you will, the "upper third") of the cosmos taken in its entirety.

We have said that spirit in its own right is not subject to time. But on the other hand, as a part of creation, it also cannot be eternal. It must consequently occupy a middle ground, so to speak, between time and eternity. Now this is what theologians are wont to call "aeviternity"—a difficult notion, to be sure, but one that cannot be avoided. For the very fact of intellection, as we have seen, implies the existence of such a supra-temporal state.

Yet we must also bear in mind that spirit does not simply exist by itself ("in isolation"), but in a certain conjunction with the material world: "In the beginning God created the heaven and the earth." The two belong together; they constitute a totality, a single "organism." Aeviternity and time, therefore, are likewise coordinated; they, too, belong together, like center and circumference of a circle. And as the center is one while the circumference contains a multiplicity of points, so it is with aeviternity and time. Despite their conjunction, the two have opposite characteristics. As St. Thomas Aquinas points out, "Time has before and after; aeviternity in itself has neither before nor after." But he immediately adds a highly significant clause: "Aeviternity in itself has neither before nor after, which can, however, be annexed to it."[11] Here is the crucial point: aeviternity is "orientated" towards time—as center is to circumference, or heaven towards earth.

*   *   *

We are beginning to see that time is by no means as absolute as Teilhard would have us believe. Despite a certain predilection for relativistic terms, moreover, it appears that his handling of the subject is thoroughly Newtonian, and quite naive. Thus he speaks as if everything without exception could be dated in terms of a single cosmic time-scale stretching from negative infinity to the postulated Omega Point, where presumably it must stop. Or does it perhaps stretch even beyond that Point? We are never told. But in any case, up to Omega, at least, everything can be definitively coordinatized in terms of a singe time-coordinate. Yet how do we know that such an all-encompassing time-scale exists? One knows that the theory of relativity began with the simple recognition that time is measured by clocks. It does not actually exist by itself, "in splendid isolation," as the Newtonians imagined. Instead, it is associated with movement, or better said, with moving things: with the things, namely, "from which times flow," in St. Augustine's excellent phrase. One also knows, moreover, in the light of Einsteinian considerations, that "times" do not always flow at the same rate; this happens, for instance, in the case of "times" associated with two clocks in a state of relative motion.

Now what all this shows is that one cannot rightly speak of time without reference to "the things from which times flow." And this means, in particular, that every notion of time is bound to its own ontological plane. If it be true, moreover, even on the corporeal plane, that the multiplicity of things from which "times flow" gives rise to an actual multiplicity of times, how could it be supposed that there exists a single "time" which applies without restriction to the cosmos at large?

But then, as we know, Teilhard has done away with the higher ontological planes; and on that single remaining plane (which perforce coincides with the corporeal) the notion of a globally defined "cosmic time" does indeed become feasible. Yet such a time-scale can only be defined with reference to a determinate cosmic origin (as envisaged in the so-called Big Bang theory), by which the specific times associated with different "world lines" can be calibrated. Ironically enough, however, Teilhard has been generally opposed to the idea of a determinate cosmic origin; he has thus rejected the very thing that is needed to validate his assumption of a universal physical time-scale.

But the deeper question, in any case, is not whether there exists such a universal time-scale on the physical plane, but whether the notion of time applies to the cosmos in its entirety. As we know, time applies, firstly, to the corporeal order. Here one has physical time, or "times," if you will. On a psychological plane, moreover, one also encounters time: "psychological time," let us say. And it is important to note that this kind of time, too, is associated with clocks; biological clocks, presumably, such as our heartbeat or breathing. But these clocks, biological though they be, are yet physical. Psychological time, therefore, derives from the corporeal or physical plane. One could put it this way: the soul is subject to time through its connection with the body. And so, too, when we "sit loose to the body"—as happens in the dream state, or under the influence of drugs and anaesthetics—our time-sense does in fact go off; which means, in practice, that we are able to experience what may seem like minutes or hours in a matter of moments, as measured by physical clocks. And let us not forget, in this connection, the oft-reported "death experience" of perceiving one's entire life unroll before one's eyes within a span of earth-time that can sometimes be checked, and may amount to no more than a second or two.

Now these facts are in line with the traditional doctrine. They suggest that as one ascends from the corporeal to the spiritual plane, time becomes compressed, as it were, and ultimately collapsed into a single point. But we know that such a "point of concentration" must exist: the fact of intellection demands it. Nothing less than this could account for the miracle of knowledge. The stupendous fact is that the apex of our soul is *not* situated in time: it is not thus dispersed. Contrary to Teilhardian belief, man cannot be made to fit into a one-dimensional temporal continuum; he cannot be thus dismembered. Temporal by way of his body, he is supra-temporal by way of his intellectual soul. Thus, in the integrality of his being, he is not a time-bound creature, a thing that "evolves"; for it happens that the very act which makes us human establishes the contrary.

NOTES

1. HE, p. 96.
2. HE, p. 96.
3. *The Mystery of the Mind* (Princeton: Princeton University press, 1975); quoted by E. F. Schumacher in *A Guide for the Perplexed* (New York: Harper, 1977), p. 76.
4. *Man on His Nature* (Cambridge: Cambridge University Press, 1951), p. 256.
5. *Cosmos and Transcendence* (La Salle: Sugden, 1984), pp. 137-142.
6. We have dealt with this question at considerable length in *op. cit.,* chs. 1 & 2.
7. *Mystagogy,* ch. 2; P.G. 91:669C; quoted by Archimandrite Vasileios in *Hymn of Entry* (Crestwood, N.Y.: St. Vladimir's Seminary Press, 1984), p. 67.
8. HE, p. 57.
9. HE, p. 57-58.
10. As Huston Smith has pointed out, "The modern West is the first society to view the physical world as a closed system." See *Forgotten Truth* (New York: Harper & Row, 1977), p. 96.
11. *Summa Theologiae,* I:10; quoted by Ananda Coomaraswamy in *Time and Eternity* (Ascona: Artibus Asiae, 1947), p. 110.

Chapter III

Complexity/Consciousness:
Law or Myth?

Evolution, according to Teilhard de Chardin, is a directed process: it proceeds from the material to the spiritual. The basic idea is simple: "All that exists is matter becoming spirit." But how? That is the question. How do material particles give birth to life, consciousness and intelligence? *Through complexification,* we are told. First there are scattered particles; then come atoms; then molecules; then super-molecules; then cells; then simple multi-cellular organisms; and so on up the evolutive line. And by way of progressive complexification matter gives birth to life, consciousness and thought—in a word, to "spirit." Complexification "is experimentally bound up with a correlative increase in interiorization, that is to say, in the psyche or consciousness,"[1] Teilhard maintains, so much so that consciousness can be "defined experimentally as the specific effect of organized complexity."[2]

This, in brief, is the celebrated Law of Complexity/Consciousness which stands at the heart of Teilhard's system. It constitutes the central pillar, one could say, which supports the entire edifice. It has been put forward "from the phenomenal point of view, to which I systematically confine myself,"[3] and purports to be an empirically verifiable truth.

But is it? The first thing, perhaps, that should give us pause is the obvious fact that consciousness as such is not observable at all, except in ourselves. Each of us, presumably, perceives the world around him, and by reflection becomes aware of the fact that he perceives. We are thus conscious of the outer world, and also conscious of that consciousness, as one might say. But the point is that we are not conscious of someone else's consciousness: it is not for us "an observable." What we do normally observe are *bodies* and *behavior*. And on this basis, by a certain capacity of empathy, we surmise what is going on in the consciousness of another. But marvelous as this faculty may be, it is not infallible, nor is it a means of observation in a scientific sense. Even when it comes to our fellow humans, therefore, it cannot be said that consciousness is an observable— what to speak of molluscs, protozoa or super-molecules!

But if consciousness is not observable, how can it be "defined experimentally as the specific effect of organized complexity"? And if only one side of the postulated equation (or proportionality) can be observed, how can one speak of a scientific law?

Furthermore, to make matters still worse, it turns out that even "complexity" is not in fact a well-defined parameter. For it is not clear, by any means, how one could define the complexity of a physical object in a meaningful way. Could it be defined, perhaps, as the number of elementary particles, or the number of atoms, contained therein? Obviously not, for in that case a pebble would be incomparably more "complex" than an ameba. And yet (presumably for lack of a better idea) Teilhard does introduce this very notion, uncompromising though it be, as a so-called parameter of complexity for "the smallest corpuscles."[4] He is aware of the difficulty, of course, and is careful to point out that this "parameter of complexity" cannot be applied to living organisms: "Once we are past molecules," he explains, "the very hugeness of the values we meet makes any numerical calculation of complexities impossible."[5] But clearly, this is not the reason at all: it is not the quantity of atoms involved which makes the calculation prohibitive—as if one could not count beyond a certain number! No, one can count as far as one wishes—right up to the total number of electrons and protons in the universe. That is not where the problem lies; the difficulty resides in the fact that Teilhard's "parameter of complexity" has not the slightest biological significance and that one has no idea how to define a "parameter of complexity" that does.

But there is yet another problem. Let us suppose that a suitable parameter of complexity can be defined; and let us assume, further, that the consciousness of living creatures, from viruses to man, can be somehow observed and registered on an appropriate scale. And let us suppose, finally, that on the basis of innumerable observations it is found that consciousness is indeed proportional to the complexity of the organisms. Would that settle the matter? Would it constitute a verification of Teilhard's claims?

Not at all. For as we shall presently see, such a state of affairs would accord equally well with the traditional world-view. It turns out, therefore, that the stipulated experimental findings do not adjudicate between the traditional and the Teilhardian positions. And so there is more to the celebrated Law of Complexity than meets the empiricist eye. The fact is that this so-called law harbors a premise of an ontological kind, which can most readily be formulated in negative terms: its affirmation is a denial, and what it denies is the intervention of an immaterial or spiritual factor, a factor which is *not* "the specific effect of organized complexity." To be sure, the doctrine does allow "spirit," *but only on condition that this "spirit" be somehow produced by or extracted from a material substratum.* This assumed "primacy of matter" is the crucial point, the crucial postulate. And for all his habitual equivocation, Teilhard never vacillates on this one central issue. The axiom stands above doubt and above debate: from the start, he is fully determined "to avoid a fundamental dualism."[6] *One* principle, *one* matter or spirit-matter—that is unmistakably his position. If one can speak of "creation" at all under Teilhardian auspices, the new teaching would read: *In the beginning God created the earth.*

But what exactly is wrong with a "fundamental dualism?" Why must the idea be avoided at all cost? It is "at once impossible and anti-scientific," we are told[7], but we are never told *why*. It is strange that an author as prolific and thorough as Teilhard de Chardin should be unwilling to devote even a paragraph to the explication of this essential point. And yet the reason for this neglect is not far to seek: it happens that the rejected notion is *not* impossible or anti-scientific at all. If "impossible" means inconceivable (and what else could it mean?), then Teilhard's first contention is already refuted by the fact that the postulate of a primordial duality has been entertained by the better part of mankind for thousands of years. And as for Teilhard's second claim (that the idea is anti-scientific), even a modest background in matters philosophical should make it clear that this charge is preposterous.[8]

★   ★   ★

It thus turns out that the so-called Law of Complexity is a Trojan horse: something quite unsuspected has been smuggled in under the cover of Science, or of that "phenomenal point of view, to which I systematically confine myself." As happens so often when metaphysics is officially banned, the despised discipline returns by way of the back door.

As we have just remarked, Teilhard has not been able to bring forth a single cogent argument against the traditional dualism. And there can be no doubt that the doctrine remains as viable today as it was in the time of Moses, Plato or the Samkhya cosmologists. The real question, in any case, is whether Teilhard's evolutionist monism stands half as well. Could it not be Teilhard's own Law of Complexity (replete with its inbuilt anti-dualist thrust) that is in fact "at once impossible and anti-scientific"?

The first thing to be observed in this connection is that consciousness cannot after all be conceived as a "specific effect of organized complexity." The claim is fraudulent. Consider, for example, the act of visual perception. The entire optical mechanism is there to translate the "information" contained in an external panorama into a particular "state" of the visual cortex, defined (let us say) by the On or Off positions of a million neurons. So far the process is perfectly familiar and comprehensible to the engineer: this is what also happens, basically, in photography or television. Thus, in the case of photography, for example, the end-product of the entire operation is a piece of paper covered with a fine grid of black and white (or colored) dots. What has been produced is an organized multiplicity of some sort. An actual perception, on the other hand, is something totally different: it is not an organized multiplicity, but a *structured unity*. The passage from the photograph (or the state of the visual cortex) to the actual perception is nothing short of a miracle: the *many* have become *one*.

Let us try to understand this absolutely essential point as clearly as we can: to perceive the picture, it is necessary to take cognizance of a million dots (or a million neurons) *all at once*. But this is something that no conceivable mechanism could accomplish. All that a mechanism, or a biological organ, can do is to transform an input (be it continuous or discrete) into an organized multiplicity of some kind; for what is itself dispersed cannot produce non-dispersion.

It is really as simple as that. What is not simple, on the other hand, is to comprehend (even remotely) that "second fundamental element," as Wilder Penfield has termed it: the element which both programs and reads the cerebral computer. And this is something that cannot but baffle us, for as Sir Charles Sherrington has been forced to admit, the elusive factor "goes in our spatial world more ghostly than a ghost."

There is, however, an important observation to be made: the reason why the element in question (which in traditional parlance is called "the soul") "goes in our spatial world more ghostly than a ghost" is that the element is not itself a spatial entity. This much, at least, we are able to understand: the soul is not a material thing, it is not something that admits extension or can be localized in space. Descartes was wiser, after all, than the scientistic monists when he observed that *res extensa* are not enough; not only thought, but also perception, and in fact all modes of consciousness, demand a supra-spatial principle. And this is of course precisely what the preceding considerations (relating to mechanism and organized multiplicities) have also brought to light.

But Teilhard seems not to have grasped this basic point. If he had, he never could have said that "space-time contains and engenders consciousness,"[9] nor could he have spoken of consciousness as "the specific effect of organized complexity." What space-time contains and can perhaps engender, and what alone can be produced as the specific effect of a spatially organized complexity, is a spatially organized multiplicity. But "spirit," as we have seen, is not a thing of that kind. And so we discover at last that it is in reality the Law of Complexity (and not the *philosophia perennis*) that is "impossible."

★   ★   ★

What the traditional teaching asserts is that consciousness derives, not from the body, but from the soul. And let us not forget: the two are by no means the same! Consciousness, then, is a capacity or power of the soul (a *"pouvoir"* in the sense of the French biologist Maurice Vernet). And as a capacity it is independent of the body. What might be termed empirical consciousness, on the other hand, is obviously "somatic" in the sense that it is conditioned by the body. This empirical consciousness, which we normally enjoy during what is called the waking state, is very much dependent, as we know, upon the body and its "organized complexities." Yet it is nothing other than the realization of a capacity or *pouvoir* which belongs to the soul and has been given from the start. The case is entirely analogous to what happens when a pianist plays upon his instrument: a certain power is actualized. But the point is that neither the latent nor the actualized power belongs to the instrument; it is not the "specific effect" of the piano. After all, the artistry, whether it be in potency or in act, belongs to the artist alone; it does not reside in the hammers or the strings.

And there is another point to be made. Souls do not (nay, *cannot*) evolve; they are created. They come into existence, not by a slow and groping process, but instantly, all at once, in the indivisible moment in which God created the cosmos and its "times." On the other hand, from an empirical standpoint there is indeed an evolution. The concept has a precise and perfectly traditional sense, which corresponds in fact to the etymological meaning of the word: what was there from the start (*sub specie aeternitatis*) "unfolds" itself progressively in time, beginning with its specific moment of birth. And it is to be understood, moreover, that the soul manifests itself by way of the body: it is by way of the body that the soul is born into the temporal world. By way of its own body, let us add; for the connection is far from adventitious.

Our life, then, is an evolution in that sense. We are here to unfold the "talents" that have been inscribed upon our soul. And the same can be said, no doubt, with reference to animals: they, too, have their powers, their specific "talents." Only it must be clearly understood that these differ markedly from our own. It cannot be said that the *pouvoir* of a chimpanzee, for example, includes the composing of symphonies; to think in such terms is to enter straightway into the realm of fantasy. The powers in question are quite specific: they are included, so to speak, in the idea of the given species. Each creature can only act in accordance with its own nature. Thus the latent consciousness in a newborn monkey, for instance, is very definitely a simian consciousness. And that is the reason why the young monkey does not take to the water like a duck; it takes to the trees. Naturalists call it instinct; but by whatever name it be designated, it needs to be understood that the propensity in question is of a *psychic* nature: it belongs to "the second element," to the agent as opposed to the bodily instrument. Instinct is something inscribed in the latent consciousness of the creature.

There is, then, an evolution of individuals; but is there not also an evolution of a given species? Why not? There has obviously been an evolution of mankind. Thus, each of us has been shaped in part by a cultural development going back to remote times. The species, too, is unfolding its possibilities. But always within the limits imposed by its own nature! There is an evolution of individuals, and there is an evolution of species; but there is no transformism, for the very simple reason that nothing can become what it is not.

Everything is contained in that initial capacity, that *pouvoir* of life, which in the case of animals, at any rate, resides in the species. And this capacity is always specific; it includes certain possibilities, and excludes others. There is really no such thing as a universal aptitude, a universal talent: an aptitude is always a fitness for some given function. It is a vector with a magnitude and a direction. Even the rational faculty in man is no exception; it too has its own sphere of operation, outside of which it is powerless.

The *pouvoir* of life does not derive from the body, we have said; it cannot be explained in terms of somatic complexities. Thus, even if it were possible to transmute the body of an ape into human form, the result of such a transformation would not be a man, but only another ape, and a rather sick one at that. For we must remember that the bodily form, with all its complexities, is naturally adapted to the powers of the soul. And that is the reason why beyond a certain point, mutations of structure can only result—not in Darwinian evolution—but in that separation of body and soul which is death.

★   ★   ★

Teilhard himself seems not always to be satisfied with the idea that life and consciousness could be produced simply through the aggregation of particles. It is true that he speaks often enough as though there were not the slightest difficulty in that regard—for instance, when he tells us that "It is the nature of Matter, when raised corpuscularly to a very high degree of complexity, to become centred and interiorized—that is to say, to endow itself with consciousness."[10] At first there are only particles; and then, once a sufficiently high degree of complexity has somehow been attained, consciousness appears upon the scene (as if by magic): that is clearly the message. Yet at other times we are given to understand that the question is not really quite so simple, and that in fact it needs to be assumed that consciousness is there from the start. "We are logically forced to assume," he writes, "the existence in rudimentary form (in a microscopic, i.e., an infinitely diffuse, state) of some sort of psyche in every corpuscle, even in those (the mega-molecules and below) whose complexity is of such a low or modest order as to render it (the psyche) imperceptible."[11]

But why? If it be the nature of Matter "to endow itself with consciousness" when it has attained "a very high degree of complexity," why must it be assumed that some kind of rudimentary consciousness exists even in the simplest of corpuscles? One knows that numerous phenomena (shock-waves, for example) can occur only when a certain critical point or threshold has been reached; how can we be certain that this is not also what happens in the case of consciousness? Why then must one assume that consciousness (or "some sort of psyche") exists already in an electron, or in a gas? Furthermore, if consciousness can be accounted for, or adequately explained, by "a very high degree of corpuscular complexity," why is one "logically forced" to assume that it exists where there is no such organized complexity at all? In fact, how can the "specific effect" exist in the absence of its specific cause? It would seem, therefore, that if one is indeed compelled to postulate "some sort of psyche in every corpuscle," it could only be for the reason that the psyche is *not*, after all, conceivable as the specific effect of organized complexities.

But be that as it may, it is clear in any case that there are not the slightest empirical grounds substantiating the existence of an "infinitely diffuse" psyche or consciousness. Now Teilhard is aware of this difficulty, and has tried to account for it: one assumes the existence of a rudimentary psyche, he tells us, imperceptible though it be, "just as the physicist assumes and can calculate those changes of mass (utterly imperceptible to direct observation) occasioned by slow movement."[12] The reference, of course, is to the relativistic fact that the mass of a particle increases with its velocity by a factor which is exceedingly close to 1 so long as the velocity remains small compared to the speed of light. But in the first place, if "direct observation" means measurement, it is not true that the changes of mass occasioned by slow motion are "utterly imperceptible": they remain in principle "perceptible" right down to the point where quantum effects supervene. And at that point, not only does measurement become impossible, but the relativistic theory itself breaks down; we are then in a domain where no one yet knows what precisely is going on. But what is perhaps still more important, the effect in question (where it does apply) has been predicted on the strength of a rigorous mathematical theory which has been otherwise tested and conclusively verified. If it should nonetheless be true that some of its predictions cannot be put directly to the test, this obviously does not mean that every gratuitous assumption of an unverifiable kind can be passed off as a scientific fact! We need not belabor the point; rhetoric aside, there is absolutely no scientific basis for Teilhard's contention that "some sort of psyche" exists in every corpuscle.

It is questionable, in fact, whether the notion of an "infinitely diffuse" psyche or consciousness makes sense. For as we have noted earlier, consciousness is inherently a power, a certain *pouvoir* of life. It is thus an aptitude for certain specific acts. To speak of an "infinitely diffuse" consciousness, therefore, is very much like speaking of a vector which has neither a magnitude nor a direction; such a "vector" plainly does not exist.

But why does Teilhard make so many assumptions? Why does he make dogmatic statements which turn out to be unsupported, and at times contradictory? What is he really driving at? What is the point of this curious dialectic? It is of course not easy to give a definitive answer to these puzzling questions. But it might not be far amiss to suggest that Teilhard's real concern (and the one thing that he is careful never to contravene) is precisely *the abolition of the traditional dualism*. As we have observed before, this is in fact the hidden thrust of that so-called Law which is central to his theory. One has the impression, at times, that it hardly matters to him whether consciousness springs into existence suddenly, as it were, as a direct result of some fortuitous conjunction of particles, or whether it pre-exists in some rudimentary form. In any case, he seems to vacillate in that regard, and leans now to this, and now to that side of the issue. Yet in either case he denies the traditional dualism; that is just the point. He denies it when he aligns himself (as he seems to, on occasion) with the materialists who delight in explaining everything in terms of "geochemical" processes, and he denies it again when he proclaims some kind of pan-psychism, or a monism based upon a so-called spirit-matter. It seems that just about anything goes, with one notable exception, and that is the traditional teaching. This is the one thing which Teilhard consistently denies.

And for a very good reason: it is the one teaching, too, which is irreconcilably opposed to the postulate of radical evolutionism.

⋆   ⋆   ⋆

But while Teilhard has persistently attacked the very foundations of the traditional teaching, he has also been much concerned to avail himself of some of its principal conclusions. An especially noteworthy case in point is the doctrine of human immortality, which he wishes to appropriate in its most uncompromisingly Christian form. It is not just some universal principle or substance, some amorphous ground, that survives the dissolution of the human compound, but the human person itself, "this man so-and-so"; at times, at least, Teilhard gives us to understand (in conformity with the Christian teaching) that it is truly Peter and Paul who survive.

But the question is whether this orthodox teaching can be maintained within the framework of Teilhard's unorthodox thought. Does it even make sense?

"By death, in the animal," Teilhard writes, "the radial [energy] is reabsorbed in the tangential, while in man it escapes and is liberated from it."[13] Now "radial energy," the mysterious factor which according to Teilhard's theory draws the organism towards higher levels of complexity and consciousness, is obviously but another term for the soul. What Teilhard is saying, therefore, is that at death the human soul detaches itself from the body and continues to exist in another state: it is just the orthodox position, decked out in scientific-sounding terms. Where he differs from the Christian teaching, on the other hand, is in what he has to say regarding the *origin* of this soul: for whereas Christianity insists that the human soul is created by God (created *ex nihilo,* that is), Teilhard is intent upon showing that it has somehow evolved out of the primordial "stuff of the universe." Thus, in his view, the soul comes into existence gradually, through the evolutive process of complexification. In man, moreover, it passes its first critical point and becomes reflective. And finally, at the moment of death, it passes through a second critical point and becomes "detached" from the body. It rises "like a trembling haze that vanishes,"[14] Teilhard tells us poetically. "All around us, one by one, like a continual exhalation, 'souls' break away, carrying upwards their incommunicable load of consciousness."[15]

Now this may very well be true (in some appropriate sense); but how does he know? Is he still speaking from that "phenomenal point of view, to which I systematically confine myself"? Has he actually perceived that "trembling haze"? We are spared such a claim. These things are said from the same ostensibly sober and scientific standpoint from which he speaks about organic evolution, hominization and the rest. But whereas Teilhard's notion of soul or "radial energy" might conceivably have a certain scientific sense when taken in a *bona fide* biological context (where the elusive factor can be investigated by way of its observable effects), it is clear that by the time he speaks of "invisible exhalations" he has altogether departed from the domain of scientific discourse. How, then, does he know? Is this simply a conjecture, a beautiful and perhaps most desirable notion with which to cap his system? Or does he perchance base himself on the authority of Christian tradition, and so, ultimately, on Revelation? But then, in that case, why does he disregard what Christianity has to say on other matters? If the ground of Revelation is solid enough to stand upon when it comes to the soul's end, why not also when it comes to its origin?

But we need not actually concern ourselves with these rather hypothetical questions. If Teilhard has elected to take his stand upon a scientific platform, then his claims are first of all to be judged on that basis. How then, let us ask, does his theory of human immortality stand? And the answer is plain: very badly indeed—so much so, that it could even be argued quite cogently that the notion contradicts his fundamental scientific postulate, the Law of Complexity. For if it be true that somatic complexity begets consciousness as its "specific effect," there must obviously be some nexus, some necessary connection, between these two aspects of the living organism: the corporeal and the psychic. Then death supervenes, and in an instant that "necessary connection" is broken; thought (or consciousness), which just a moment ago rested squarely on the support of brain function, breaks away and floats off, as it were, into outer space. Perhaps it was a blow on the head or a bullet that shattered the physical instrument of thought: everything in Teilhard's system would lead one to the conclusion that this must be the end of thought, the end of consciousness, the end of that "person" who has emerged precisely through the formation of that physical instrument. But no: suddenly, and for no discernible reason, the instrument is no longer needed. The brain ceases to be necessary simply by virtue of its having been shattered.

It is to be noted that the traditional teaching avoids this absurdity. So long as the soul is not created, or brought into existence, through an aggregation of corpuscles, there is no particular difficulty in maintaining that it continues to exist when these corpuscles are again dispersed. It is true that according to the Christian view, the soul is in certain respects curtailed or hampered through the loss of its bodily instrument, which after all was created for its use. Let there be no doubt about it, the body does serve a purpose; it is not just a "prison" of the soul. But it is not the cause of the soul, it is not the source of consciousness, or of the human intellect; and that is the crucial point of difference between the Christian and the Teilhardian anthropology.

According to the traditional view, the soul has a certain independence, a certain autonomy, right from the start. It does not suddenly acquire that autonomy at the moment of death—as if a spiritual agent could be created simply by destroying a physical instrument! Now it is true that in its embodied state the soul sees through the eye, hears through the ear, speaks through the tongue, and thinks through the brain. But *it does not know through the brain,* and that is the essential point. It knows through the intellect, without the intermediary of a corporeal organ. As St. Thomas has expressed it, "The intellect is a faculty of the soul, and the soul is the form of the body; but the power that is called the intellect is not the actualization of any bodily organ, because the activity of the body has nothing in common with the activity of the intellect."[16] And that, to be sure, is precisely the reason why the human soul is able, not only to exist after death, but also to be cognizant (in the sense of pure intellection) in its post-mortem state. As Aristotle had already observed, "There is nothing to prevent some parts of the soul being separable from the body, because they are actualizations of nothing corporeal."[17] Thus, after death, we shall continue to *know,* to *understand* (and perhaps in a much higher degree!), because even here, while still "in the body," we know or understand, not with our brain, but with our intellect. The point is that only those acts which require a corporeal instrument are abrogated at death. And so, too, only those "parts" of the soul which depend upon physical organs for their actualization are affected. From a trichotomous point of view, one could say that the *anima* or *psyche,* properly so called, becomes "absorbed" after death in the purely spiritual part of man, the *pneuma* (which includes the intellect). The *pneuma* as such, on the other hand, is not affected.

The traditional teaching, though it may be based on Revelation, or upon the spiritual experiences of mystics, is nonetheless extremely logical, as we can see. And the more closely it is examined, the more one finds that the pieces fit together with a marvelous and almost mathematical precision. Consider the following: we have observed elsewhere that the act of knowing demands, not an extreme complexity (as Teilhard would have us believe), but just the opposite: for only what is in fact supraspatial and uncompounded could gather up a spatially organized multiplicity into a *bona fide* unity. But by this very same token one also discovers that the intellect is immortal, that it survives, for it is evident that what is perfectly simple cannot be destroyed. Only complexity is vulnerable, and only compounds can be dissolved. And so we find that the tenet of human immortality is altogether consonant with the traditional understanding of the intellectual act. It accords perfectly with every facet of the integral doctrine.

Now the case is very different when this dogma has been cut off from the main body of traditional teaching and grafted into the evolutionist system of Teilhard de Chardin. As we have seen, the resultant theory is plainly discordant. Within the framework of radical evolutionism, the Christian tenet of immortality has become both gratuitous and absurd. Like the farfetched invention of an inept playwright, Teilhard's "discarnate soul" can be nothing more than a *deus ex machina* called forth, as if by fiat, to save a sinking plot. But it does not in fact save the plot; it only adds confusion. It would seem that when Teilhard speaks elsewhere of "the principle of coherence" as the prime criterion of truth,[18] he has first of all condemned his own theory.

*   *   *

Teilhard has always made it a point to present himself, first and foremost, as a man of science. One might be tempted to think that the claim could be tendentious. After all, Carl Jung was no doubt right when he remarked (with reference to Freud) that "Today the voice of one crying in the wilderness must strike a scientific tone if the ear of the multitude is to be reached."[19] And it is clear that neither as a philosopher, nor as a theologian, could Teilhard have had any comparable impact upon society. He needed the prestige and the special charisma of the scientist to captivate his audience, and he knew very well how to capitalize on these assets. And yet nothing that we know contradicts the impression that Teilhard was entirely sincere in his unbounded admiration of science, and in the high estimate which he had formed regarding the scientific worth of his own rather novel ideas. But be that as it may, what we do know is that Teilhard's far-flung speculations about organic evolution, hominization, noogenesis, cosmic convergence and the rest are not in fact scientific, not by any stretch of the imagination! It is a long way from fossils and the skeletal remains of a conjectured Sinanthropus to Point Omega.[20]

One must also remember that Teilhard's renown as a kind of universal scientist has been trumpeted mainly in more or less theological circles. Certainly, in his own field, Teilhard did command the respect of his fellow scientists, as is evidenced by the fact that he was made a member of the prestigious *Academie des Sciences,* and a director in the *Centre National de la Recherche Scientifique.* So far as his wide-ranging theories are concerned, on the other hand, the reaction of scientists has been mixed and generally guarded. On the enthusiastic end of the spectrum mention should be made of Sir Julian Huxley, who has introduced *The Phenomenon of Man* to the English-speaking world with a warm and at times exuberant commendation. Sir Julian goes so far as to say (with specific reference to the Law of Complexity) that "this view admittedly involves speculation of great intellectual boldness, but the speculation is extrapolated from a massive array of fact, and is disciplined by logic. It is, if you like, visionary: but it is the product of a comprehensive and coherent vision."[21] But despite this positive judgment (with which we strongly disagree), the celebrated evolutionist stops short nonetheless of endorsing Teilhard's contention that the book is to be considered "purely and simply as a scientific treatise."[22] The theory may be a bold and disciplined extrapolation, but it is still a visionary venture and not "purely and simply" a scientific doctrine.

As concerns the merits of this venture, scientists have expressed vastly different views. Among the harshest critics one should above all mention Peter Medawar, of Nobel Prize fame, who has given what amounts to a blanket condemnation of the entire Teilhardian theory. In his review of *The Phenomenon of Man,* he has attempted first of all to dispel the stereotyped image of the "great scientist" that had come to surround the figure of Teilhard de Chardin like a nimbus in the eyes of his followers. "Teilhard practiced an intellectually unexacting kind of science," Sir Peter tells us, "in which he achieved a moderate proficiency. He has no grasp of what makes a logical argument or what makes for proof. He does not even preserve the common decencies of scientific writing, though his book is professedly a scientific treatise."[23] Besides objecting to a generally extravagant use of language, involving such literary excesses as "nothing-buttery," Medawar charges that "Teilhard habitually and systematically cheats with words."[24] What he means thereby is that Teilhard "uses in metaphor words like energy, tension, force, impetus, and dimension *as if* they retained the weight and thrust of their special scientific usages."[25] And this is presumably the prime offense against "the common decencies of scientific writing," which Medawar holds against Teilhard de Chardin. Yet there are still other improprieties, not the least of which is the offense of self-contradiction: for example, after having stated that "complexity increases in geometrical progression as we pass from the protozoon higher and higher up the scale of the metazoa," Teilhard goes on to inform the reader that the "nascent cellular world shows itself to be already infinitely complex." Medawar finds this disturbing.

But when he expresses his overall appraisal of the work by saying that "The greater part of it, I shall show, is nonsense, tricked out by a variety of tedious metaphysical conceits,"[26] many have felt that he has gone too far. And to be sure, it is not at all clear what precisely he means by this indictment, and on what basis it has been made. After all, there are those (Nobel laureates included) in whose eyes every facet of metaphysical belief is "a conceit." But this is a question which hardly concerns us here. If Medawar has been too harsh in his overall judgment, the fact remains that he would certainly have recognized *scientific* merit if he had encountered any.

And there is something else that needs very much to be pointed out: in what appears to be his central criticism (i.e., that "Teilhard habitually and systematically cheats with words"), Medawar has no doubt hit the nail on the head. The word "cheat" is of course very strong, and should not be interpreted in its prime sense, which is "to deceive by trickery, to defraud, to swindle"; it should be understood, rather, in its milder sense, which is "to fool" or "to beguile," without any implication of ill intent. What concerns us, in any case, is the fact that a certain systematic misuse of language is to be found throughout the writings of Teilhard de Chardin, and that this does indeed tend to fool and beguile the reader. Medawar has put it very well when he observes that "It is the style that creates the illusion of content."[27] Precisely; and the single most effective and most frequently applied "device" is the abuse of metaphor.

This is what is happening, for example, when at various times consciousness is said to be "a dimension, something with mass, something corpuscular and particulate which can exist in various degrees of concentration, being sometimes infinitely diffuse."[28] And the same thing, of course, is happening when Teilhard speaks of discarnate souls in terms of vapors, exhalations, or bubbles, not to mention "a trembling haze." Thus, in countless passages, he is speaking in terms of metaphors which are sometimes poetic and sometimes scientific-sounding, but always false the moment it is forgotten that they are metaphors. The point is, however, that Teilhard does seem at crucial moments to forget this. And in *The Phenomenon of Man,* at any rate, he forgets it systematically, as it were, by telling us at the outset that he is speaking from a strictly "phenomenal point of view," and that the book is to be read "purely and simply as a scientific treatise." And so the "trembling haze" ceases to be a poetic figure of speech and becomes forthwith a scientific phenomenon. And this is of course precisely what has happened in the eyes of thousands of readers: Teilhard's pronouncements, even of the most poetic and extravagant kind, are received as oracles of Science.

But what is even worse, take away the metaphors and there is no theory left. This is just what Medawar means when he maintains that "It is the style that creates the illusion of content." Teilhard's metaphors are not simply an embellishment or a means to explain some difficult scientific ideas to a nontechnical audience; they are part of the theory. That is what even Sir Julian has failed to grasp when he speaks quite innocently of Teilhard's "genius for fruitful analogy."[29] Analogy with what? With another analogy, perhaps? What is lacking in Teilhard's doctrine are scientific definitions, scientific concepts, which can then perhaps be explained or illustrated in terms of "fruitful analogies."

NOTES

1. PM, p. 301.
2. PM, p. 301.
3. PM, p. 308.
4. MN, p. 21. The fact that this "parameter of complexity" is meaningless above the level of molecules does not deter Teilhard from drawing his so-called "curve of corpusculization," in which the parameter in question serves as an abscissa for "corpuscles" from electrons to man! See MN, pp. 21-25.
5. MN, p. 47.
6. PM, p. 64.
7. PM, p. 64.
8. The point is that science deals with *phenomena;* whereas, the traditional dualism refers to *metaphysical* realities. Neither "matter" nor "spirit" are observables.
9. PM, p. 259.
10. FM, p. 226.
11. PM, pp. 301-302.
12. PM, p. 302.
13. PM, p. 272.
14. HM, p. 190.
15. PM, p. 272.
16. *Opusculum, De unitate intellectus contra Averroistas,* iii; quoted by J. Rickaby, S.J. in *Of God and His Creatures* (Westminster, Md.: Carroll Press, 1950), p. 127n.
17. *De Anima,* II. i. 12.
18. See, for instance, HE, p. 94; CE, p. 130n; and FM, p. 222.
19. *The Collected Works* (New York: Pantheon, 1971), vol. 15, p. 38.
20. It is interesting that Teilhard himself has admitted this, and has in fact repudiated his scientific pretensions in one of his letters, wherein he writes: "I sense how in itself the exploration of the Earth can bring no light, and does not enable us to find any solution to the most fundamental questions of life. I have the impression of moving around an immense problem without being able to penetrate into it. Moreover, as I also observe, this problem appears to wax before my eyes, and I see that its solution is to be sought nowhere but in a 'faith' which goes beyond all experience. It is necessary to break through and pass beyond appearances." (*Lettres de Voyage, 1923-1955,* Edition Grasset, p. 31).
21. PM, p. 16.
22. PM, p. 29.
23. *Mind,* Vol. 70 (1961), p. 105.
24. *Op. cit.,* p. 101.
25. *Ibid.*
26. *Op. cit.,* p. 99.
27. *Ibid.*
28. *Op. cit.,* p. 101.
29. PM, p. 20.

Chapter IV

In Search of Creative Union

There are those who believe that Teilhard has laid the foundations of a new metaphysics supposedly based upon scientific
insights. As Jean Danielou has put it, "He translates the scientific categories into metaphysical categories."[1] Or still more em-
phatically: "He builds a metaphysics as an extension of the science
of his day."[2] Now this presumed metaphysics is none other
than the doctrine of "creative union"; only Teilhard himself
appears to be less certain than his Jesuit confrere that the theory
is in fact metaphysical. "Creative union is not exactly a
metaphysical doctrine," he tells us. "It is rather a sort of empirical and pragmatic explanation of the universe, conceived in
my mind from the need to reconcile in a solidly coherent system scientific views on evolution (accepted as, in their essence,
definitely established) with the innate urge that has impelled
me to look for the Divine not in a cleavage with the physical
world but through matter, and, in some sort of way, in union
with matter."[3] What this means, in plain terms, is that Teilhard
was led to his notion of creative union in an effort to reconcile
the rudiments of Darwinism with his own pantheistic propensities. It is not clear, of course, how a synthesis based upon
Darwinist and pantheistic premises could conceivably result in
"a sort of empirical and pragmatic explanation of the universe."
But be that as it may, let us try, in any case, to discover what
the theory affirms.

Now as one knows, Teilhard alludes to the notion of "creative

union" innumerable times, and yet there are only a few pages
here and there where the matter is dealt with explicitly. One
of these expositions (which happens to be particularly revealing from a scientific point of view) is to be found in the essay
entitled "Human Energy." Written seventeen years after his note
on "Creative Transformation," it can be taken as representing
a relatively mature stage in the unfolding of Teilhard's thought.
It behooves us, therefore, to examine this piece with some care.

Teilhard begins with a statement which underlines the empirical nature of what is to follow: "A principle of universal
value appears to emerge from our outer and inner experience
of the world, which might be called the 'principle of the conservation of personality.' "[4] And what is that principle? "At *a
first stage*," he goes on to say, "the law of conservation of personality only states that the rise of spirit in the universe is an
irreversible phenomenon";[5] or still more succinctly, "Conservation (without regression) of the highest stage of personalization
acquired at each moment by life in the world."[6]

But there is more. "At *a second stage*, the principle of conservation of personality suggests that a *certain amount* of energy,
in the impersonal state, is engaged in the evolution of the universe, and that it is destined to be transmuted entirely into a
personal state at the end of the transformation (the quality of
this 'personal end-product' being moreover a function of the
quantity of 'impersonal' material engaged at the beginning of
the process)."[7] And this explanation is followed by what is
presumably a concise statement of the principle itself: "Conservation (without loss), in the course of the spiritualization
of the universe, of an undefined amount of power or cosmic
'stuff.' "[8]

Obviously this is all very vague. But be that as it may, we
are told in any case that "Under this absolute, *quantitative form*,
the law of conservation of personality is not directly capable
of demonstration, perhaps because it refutes our formal knowledge that we are able to measure the world by 'cubing' it, or
perhaps because we do not yet see how to express the coefficient of transformation from impersonality to personality."[9]

But in the meantime, a far simpler and more prosaic reason
for the stated unverifiability will perhaps have occurred to the
perceptive reader: could it not be that the presumed principle

thus formulated has no scientific content at all?

What mainly concerns us at this point, however, is to eluci-
date whatever *philosophical* sense there might be in these Teilhardian speculations. We are searching, after all, for the
foundations of that evolutionist ontology to which certain theologians are wont to allude.

Let us go on. Unverifiable though it be, Teilhard informs
us that the principle "has nevertheless a use: it states that the
spiritualization taking place in the cosmos must be understood
as a *change of physical state* in the course of which a certain constant is preserved throughout the metamorphosis."[10] For a moment one has the impression that the picture is beginning to
come into focus. But then the realization dawns that we have
not the slightest idea what that certain constant might be. Could
it be the amount of physical energy? Or is it something else?
Why, in any case, are we thus left in the dark?

"Understood in this way," Teilhard goes on, "the conservation of personality in no way implies (quite the contrary) an
'ontological' identity between the unconscious and the self-
conscious. Although subjected to a 'quantic' law, personalization remains in effect essentially an evolutionary transformation, that is to say, continually the generator of something entirely
new. 'So much matter is needed for so much spirit; so much
multiplicity for so much unity. Nothing is lost, yet everything
is created.' This is all that is affirmed."[11]

But the matter is not really quite so simple. A crucial ambiguity (which has been plaguing us all along) has not yet been
definitively resolved. There are two conceptual possibilities,
which need to be distinguished: either matter (or physical energy,
which amounts to the same) is actually transformed into what
might be broadly termed "spirit," or it is not. Now which shall
it be?

In numerous places Teilhard appears to have opted for the first
alternative. One has this impression, for example, when he speaks
of energy "destined to be transmuted entirely into a personal
state," and of a corresponding "coefficient of transformation."
This is always what first comes to mind when Teilhard speaks
of a metamorphosis, or a "change of state." And the same idea,
of course, has been expressed as clearly as one could wish in
the oft-quoted formula: "All that exists is matter becoming spirit."

It is interesting to observe, moreover, that under these auspices the rise of consciousness would presumably be accompanied by a certain diminution of physical energy. And this (at long last!) is something that could in principle be measured, and thus verified. One would not in fact have to know "how to express the coefficient of transformation from impersonality to personality," as Teilhard suggests: the mass or energy defect associated with an irreversible psychogenesis is after all an observable. If "so much energy" is consumed in the production of "so much consciousness" (whatever this may mean), then there is exactly so much less energy in the system after the postulated metamorphosis has occurred. And let us add that if this were found to be the case, Teilhard's principle would unquestionably represent one of the major discoveries in the history of science.

But needless to say, there are no indications whatsoever to suggest that such a mass or energy defect exists. And as we have seen, Teilhard himself has made it a point to inform us that his principle (in its so-called quantitative form) is not subject to verification. It begins to appear, therefore, that we should perhaps adopt the second line of interpretation: matter is not, after all, being transformed into spirit. And this is presumably what Teilhard, too, is suggesting when he declares that "The conservation of personality in no way implies (quite to the contrary) an 'ontological' identity between the unconscious and the self-conscious," and when he adds that the transformation is evolutionary, "that is to say continually the generator of something entirely new." Energy (in the sense of the physicist) would then be strictly conserved, and the so-called metamorphosis would indeed be "a change in physical state," characterized by a certain complexification. Consciousness or spirit, in that case, would be something entirely new, something which does not come forth out of matter by way of a *bona fide* metamorphosis. Is this, perhaps, what Teilhard means when he says that "nothing is lost, yet everything is created"?

But then again, under these auspices, what is to be made of the following statement, which Teilhard has put at the end of the entire discussion: "In a universe where spirit is considered *at the same time* as matter, the principle of the conservation of the personality appears as the most general and satisfactory expression of the invariance of the cosmos first suspected and sought by physics on the side of the conservation of energy."[12] Here Teilhard seems to be leaning once again in the direction of the first alternative. For what else could this statement mean but that matter and spirit are two forms or aspects of a single energy, a single "power or cosmic 'stuff,' " as Teilhard has put it earlier, which is the one thing that is conserved? And this would mean that energy, in its strictly physical manifestation, would be conserved only to the extent that psychogenesis is not taking place, or can be neglected. And it would also mean that there is, after all, an 'ontological' identity between matter and spirit, or "between the unconscious and the self-conscious," contrary to what has been said before.

If we go back to the second interpretation, on the other hand, then Teilhard is saying that a certain aggregation of material particles is required to cause the emergence of spirit ("ex nihilo," as it were). And according to his principle of conservation (at least as it applies to man) this "quantum of spirit" remains in existence even after the aggregate in question has been dissolved. But in that case what Teilhard has enunciated is not a law of conservation, but the very opposite; for to say that something comes out of nothing and remains is to deny that the category in question is "conserved" in the accepted scientific sense of that term. Moreover, it would then have been more correct to say that "So much matter is needed for *the genesis of* so much spirit," inasmuch as spirit, once emerged, no longer requires "so much matter" for its support. And finally, what we would have then is not a monism, a doctrine which speaks of a single "cosmic stuff" within which "changes of state" occur, but a dualism of two irreducible principles, one of which (paradoxically) requires the other in order to emerge.

But perhaps we have still not fathomed the true meaning of Teilhard's less-than-precise affirmations. Could it be that the emergent spirit is neither matter transformed, nor something that emerges in the aforementioned sense, but is to be conceived as the manifestation of something immaterial that was there all along? But in that case the emergence of spirit is neither a transformation nor the creation of something new; and this means that Teilhard would have contradicted himself, not once, but twice.

Yet there is nothing to suggest that Teilhard is in any way disturbed by these ambiguities and apparent contradictions; one has the impression that he wants to have it both ways. He seems habitually to ride the edge of a logical alternative, leaning now to one side, now to the other, without ever committing himself either way.

What are we to make of this apparent confusion? Is it perhaps a mark of unusual profundity, as some have assumed? Or should we perhaps conclude that the law of the excluded middle, too, has become somehow obsolete or superseded in a Darwinistic universe? But fortunately we need not weigh these questions, for it happens that Teilhard himself has made it clear that his theory of creative union has been advanced in a perfectly sober and scientific spirit. It is not meant to be "mystical" in some far-out sense. On the contrary, the theory has been put forward as "a kind of empirical and pragmatic explanation of the universe" and is supposed to constitute "a solidly coherent system." But as we see, it does not, in fact, meet either of these stipulated requirements; and that is just where the difficulty lies.

It is not really hard to understand what Teilhard was attempting to do. He was obviously fascinated with the idea of creative union and charmed by such formulas as *"Deus creat uniendo"* or *"creari est uniri."* As Henri de Lubac has put it, "Such axioms appealed to him and led him to dream of constructing a metaphysics, his own metaphysics, which would be a 'metaphysics of union.' "[13] But it must also be remembered that this close friend and ardent admirer of Teilhard de Chardin concludes his discussion of the subject with the remark: "We must, nevertheless, admit that he did not achieve a perfectly clear and coherent formulation of his thought."[14] In plain words: the truth is that Teilhard's dream of constructing a metaphysics of his own was never realized.

*   *   *

Nonetheless, in view of the fact that the notion of creative union, ill-defined though it be, is obviously central to Teilhard's entire system of thought, it may behoove us to consider the matter at some greater length. There are in particular two sections in the well-known essay *Mon Universe* which need to be closely examined.

"Creative union," so the exposition begins, "is the theory that accepts this proposition: in the present evolutionary phase of the cosmos (the only phase known to us), everything happens as though the One were formed by successive unifications of the Multiple."[15] And as Teilhard goes on to explain, this does *not* mean "that the One is composed of the multiple, i.e., that it is born from the fusion in itself of the elements it associates (for in that case either it would not be something created—something completely new—or the terms of the Multiple would be progressively decreasing, which contradicts our experience)."[16] What is being asserted is simply "that the One appears in the wake of the Multiple, dominating the Multiple, since its essential and formal act is to unite."[17]

Let us remark that this is the kind of statement that has no doubt reassured many orthodox hearts, and has led some interpreters to conclude that Teilhard comes close to being a Thomist. But the point is that one must read on.

"At the lower limit of things," we are informed presently, the so-called law of recurrence "discloses an immense plurality—complete diversity combined with total disunity."[18] It seems to be a settled conviction with Teilhard de Chardin that everything begins in multiplicity and converges towards an ever-greater unity. And yet it is clear that even the most elementary observations disclose just the opposite. The fertilized ovum, which looks like a sphere or tiny globule, divides and subdivides, creating a spherical immensity of cells. Then the blastosphere invaginates, and the cells begin to specialize, thus giving rise to a multiplicity of layers, tissues, and organs. The entire movement appears to be in the direction of increasing multiplicity. And what is death, after all, but the final victory of multiplicity over unity on the organic plane?

It is not without interest, moreover, that one meets a similar spectacle in other domains: in art, or the world of thought, for instance. Here too one can observe what appears to be a pre-existent unity, unfolding a progressively increasing multiplicity from out of itself. Every writer, every creative scientist, every thinker has witnessed this process; it is happening everywhere. We have all experienced it: an idea is born in our mind—at one stroke, we could say; and under the influence of a certain brooding, it swells and breaks up, as it were, into a multiplicity of some kind, which again, by stages and degrees, complexifies further, till it attains its full-blown format. And let us not forget Mozart's testimony to the effect that an entire symphony could first present itself in the form of a single musical idea, conceived all at once, in a flash of inspiration.

The physical universe itself, according to the latest findings, seems to exhibit the same law: it too has sprung out of a single point, as it were, which is moreover inscrutable to science, not because it contains some ultimate particulate multiplicity, but precisely because it contains no particulate multiplicity at all. This is indeed the one thing that we can say with certainty about this "initial singularity": it is not a multiplicity in any sense that physics could understand. Quite to the contrary, we can only conceive of it as a synthetic unity which potentially contains all physical multiplicity within itself, a unity which has given birth to all the multiplicity existing in the external world.

But Teilhard seems to be convinced (no one knows why) that things invariably move in the opposite direction: first multiplicity, then unity.

This is the first premise, in any case; and the second is stranger still: not only do all things begin in multiplicity, but it is unity that unites them. Thus we are told, for example, that "In the first stages in which it becomes conceivable to us, the world has already been for a long time at the mercy of a multitude of elementary souls that fight for its dust in order that, by unifying it, they may exist."[19] But of course the difficulty with this presumed explanation is that it is not in fact conceivable. Even a confirmed Darwinist, we suspect, might find it hard to understand how a "complete diversity, combined with total disunity," could give birth to "elementary souls," which exist by virtue of material aggregates formed under their influence.

But let us go on to the third premise: "Only in man, so far as we know, does spirit so perfectly unite around itself the universality of the universe that, in spite of the momentary dissociation of its organic foundation, nothing can any longer destroy the 'vortex' of operation and consciousness of which it is the subsisting centre." [20] Now this, too, is very strange. How can a "vortex of operation" continue to exist when it is no longer operating on anything? Does not Teilhard himself, as a matter of fact, inform us three pages later that spirit "does not 'hold together', except by 'causing to hold together.'"[21]? But perhaps we are still thinking in somewhat antiquated "immobilist" terms. "In the system of creative union," Teilhard goes on to explain, "it becomes impossible to continue crudely to contrast Spirit and matter. For those who have understood the law of 'spiritualization by union,' there are no longer two compartments in the universe, the spiritual and the physical: there are only *two directions* along one and the same road (the direction of pernicious pluralization, and that of beneficial unification)."[22] But then, what has happened to "souls," those "elementary souls," for example, which supposedly are fighting for the dust of the world? Is it a direction, a vector that is fighting another vector: the future, perhaps, fighting the past? And in the case of the human compound (if such it may be called), how are we to understand what happens at the moment of death? Until just yesterday all the world thought that here, at this fateful juncture, soul and body part company; and even Teilhard spoke of a "vortex of operation" which somehow detaches itself from the material aggregate. Is it a direction, a vector, then, that dissociates itself from another vector? But even then there are *two*: two logical "compartments," just as before, when we still persisted "crudely to contrast Spirit and matter." Or are we to say, perhaps, that body and soul are one and the same thing until death supervenes, at which point the one becomes two? We find it hard to agree with Teilhard when he says with reference to his new theory: "Thus those innumerable difficulties vanish..."[23]

*   *   *

What Teilhard would like to say, but cannot, is that there is Evolution and nothing else. His position is somewhat reminiscent of Heraclitus (and of certain Buddhist philosophers): there are no "things," no substances or natures in the universe, but only movement, only change, only a perpetual *genesis* or becoming. All that exists is flux. Strictly speaking, there is no cosmos even, but only a cosmogenesis. And that is Evolution. But then, this is not really what Heraclitus taught. To be sure, "Everything flows," and this world, with its seemingly solid parts, is in truth "an ever-living fire": but it is a fire "kindled in measure and quenched in measure." That is the crucial point: flux does not stand alone. True to the genius of his race, Heraclitus perceived that the cosmos is subject to measure, that it is bounded by a law. The world moves, but the law remains fixed. There is not only flux or movement, but also a stasis. Not the seeming stasis of a stone "at rest" (which is relative, and in a way illusory), but a stasis that is transcendent, a *logical* stasis, in the truly Greek sense of that term. What we need to realize is that flux and stasis imply one another. And this entails that the phenomenon, the cosmos, the psychophysical reality, partakes somewhat of both. There is that which moves, and that which remains unmoved; in the language of science, there are variables, and there are invariants. And the invariants are essential. In fact, this is just what physics is about; it is a search in quest of invariants. Thus it is not actually the "ever-living fire" as such that matters to the scientist, but the "measures" in which that fire has been "kindled and quenched," to put it in the highly expressive terms of our Greek philosopher.

And these measures derive "from above," that is to say, from the authentically spiritual plane. As we have said in an earlier chapter, the world becomes intelligible by virtue of its spiritual content.

Now it is interesting that Teilhard himself seems at times to be saying exactly the same thing. In *Mon Universe,* for example, he writes that "Nothing in the universe is intelligible, living and consistent except through an element of synthesis, in other words a spirit, or from on high."[24] And again: "'All consistence comes from Spirit.' In that we have the very definition of creative union."[25] Once again we seem to find ourselves momentarily on orthodox ground. And how well he has put it when he goes on to say that "The materialist philosopher, therefore, who looks at a lower level than soul for the solid principle of the universe, grasps no more than dust that slips between his fingers"[26]!

What, then, are we to make of these seemingly orthodox affirmations? Now, to begin with, we need to recall an essential

point: as we have noted in Chapter 2, Teilhard has in effect
rotated the *axis mundi* of the perennial doctrine through ninety
degrees, so as to make it coincide with the stipulated vector
of Evolution. The "above" has thus become the "ahead." But
this means that in Teilhard's theory there *is* no "above," no Spirit
in the authentic sense. There is only Evolution, only directed
flux. There is no room in this "one-dimensional" model for
the category of Spirit. There is past and future, but no metaphysical verticality, no "above," no *bona fide* Spirit. For as we have
seen, Spirit stands on the side—not of flux or evolution—but
of stasis.

And yet Teilhard continues to speak of Spirit. We are told
that "All consistence comes from Spirit," that "everything holds
together from on high."[27] But what does this mean? What can
the phrase "from on high" connote in a one-dimensional universe, a universe of directed flux? Now this is where the "rota-
tion of axes" comes into play: the "above" is henceforth to
be conceived as the "ahead." This, it would seem, is where
Teilhard's main originality lies: the materialists and the Darwinists had never thought of such a thing. They would have
said: "All consistence comes from matter." It never occurred
to them (or perhaps to anyone prior to Teilhard de Chardin)
that the cause of all consistence could lie in the "ahead"—in
a principle of unity yet to be born!

There is, however, a difficulty (as we have also seen): it turns
out that the idea is not in fact conceivable. And is this not
the reason, too, why this pseudo-doctrine has had to be so
much disguised? It would appear that the teaching fully requires all the vagueness, all the ambiguity, all the equivocation
which Teilhard has been able to muster, in order to commend
itself to the impressionable reader. It would never do simply
to proclaim in a loud voice that "All consistence comes from
the ahead."

At bottom, what Teilhard has failed to recognize (and what
persistently plagues him) is that there can be no movement without a corresponding stasis, no evolution, if you will, without
something that does *not* evolve.

★   ★   ★

It is hard to tell whether Teilhard's primary concern was to found a new metaphysics or to impugn the old. But in any case, he does often enough make it a point to attack the traditional metaphysical teaching. We are told, for example, at sporadic intervals, that the old metaphysical categories are "immobilist," that they derive from a pre-scientific world-view, and that they have somehow been rendered obsolete or untenable in the light of modern scientific findings, such as "the discovery of Time." Frequently, moreover, these indictments are made in passing, as if the matter were too obvious, or too well understood, to call for a more careful consideration. Here and there, however, Teilhard does make an effort to deal with these questions at some greater length; and the result is invariably enlightening. Let us see, for example, what he has to say along these lines in his paper "On the Notion of Creative Transformation."

Teilhard begins by reminding us that Scholasticism admits "only two sorts of variations in being"[28]: creation and transformation, namely, conceived respectively as the production of being "out of nothing" and "from potency of the subjacent." And we should perhaps add that this dichotomy belongs not just to Scholasticism (as if it were somehow tied to Latin Christianity and the Middle Ages), but is in fact integral to the Christian tradition as such.

Yet Teilhard is dissatisfied with this doctrine. It is not entirely clear at this point whether he wishes to do away with the traditional idea of creation or wants simply to add a third category to the list. But in any case, he states that "Besides *'creatio ex nihilo subjecti'* and *'transformatio ex potentia subjecti,'* there is room for an act *sui generis* which *makes use* of a pre-existent created being and builds it up into a *completely* new being."[29] And he goes on to explain that "This *act is really creative,* because it calls for renewed intervention on the part of the First Cause."[30]

Teilhard finds it remarkable, moreover, that Scholasticism "has no word to designate this method of divine operation," seeing that it is "conceivable *in abstracto,* and is therefore entitled to a place at least in speculation," and is "probably the only one which satisfies our experience of the world."[31] And he adds: "We should, I believe, have to be blind not to see this: *In natura rerum* (in nature) the two categories of movement separated by Scholasticism (*Creatio et Eductio*) are seen to be constantly fused, combined, together."[32]

Now to begin with, it is by no means the case that *"in natura rerum"* creation and transformation "are seen to be constantly fused, combined, together," for the simple reason that creation cannot be "seen" at all. Only *what happens in time* can be seen or observed in some sense, but the act of creation does *not* take place in time. It cannot because time itself comes into existence by virtue of this act. "God, therefore, in His unchangeable eternity created simultaneously all things whence times flow," to quote St. Augustine again. This, above all, is what we need to bear in mind if we are not to misconstrue the Christian doctrine. It would thus be erroneous, for example, to think that God created the universe six thousand, or twenty billion, years ago—as if that "beginning" in which God created heaven and earth were receding into the distant past with the passing of time; for to think in these terms would be once more to conceive of the creative act as a temporal event. The fact is that "the instantaneous and imperceptible moment of creation,"[33] to use St. Basil's phrase, is "equidistant," one could say, to all times, even as the center of a circle is equidistant to all points on the circumference. Or better said, it is "contiguous" to all times and places, for it constitutes the omnipresent Center where "every where and every when are focused."[34]

Creation, then, is not to be counted among the events that transpire in time, nor is it in any way observable. And on both counts it differs from transformation. For a transformation, obviously, is something that does take place in time and is observable at least in some degree.

Now it is true, certainly, that creation and transformation are somehow joined together; they are in a sense "constantly fused," even as one could say that the center of a circle (or the pencil of its radii, if you will) is "fused" to the circumference. After all, everything in creation hinges upon the creative act. But although creation and transformation are thus fused, they are not on that account the same, even as the center and circumference of a circle are not the same. Scholasticism, then, and the Christian tradition at large, have done well to distinguish the two conceptions.

What Teilhard is driving at, of course, when he insists that the two "are seen to be constantly fused," is that creation and transformation cannot in truth be separated; in reality (*"in natura rerum"*) the two are one and the same, and this is just what the concept of "creative transformation" is meant to express. It supposedly unites once more what Scholasticism has spuriously cut asunder. And that, too, is presumably the reason why Teilhard makes it a point to marvel at the fact that Scholasticism "has no word to designate this method of divine operation"; the implication is that the Thomists were unable to recognize this mode of divine operation because they were blinded by their own mistake.

"There is not one moment when God creates, and one moment when secondary causes develop," Teilhard goes on to explain. "There is always only *one* creative action (identical with conservation) which continually raises creatures towards fuller-being *by means of* their secondary activity and their earlier advances."[35]

What has happened is now clear: Teilhard assumes that creation takes place in time. He seems to think that the traditional doctrine conceives of creative acts as special occurrences which now and then interrupt the normal operation of secondary causes. And he wishes to replace this "discontinuous model" by a continuous one. "Creation is not a periodic intrusion of the First Cause," he tells us; "it is an act co-extensive with the whole duration of the universe."[36]

Now admittedly, creation is not "a periodic intrusion of the First Cause"; of course not. And it is likewise true that in a sense the creative act *is* "co-extensive with the whole duration of the universe," but not in the sense of being continuously spread out over the duration of the cosmos. Quite to the contrary, the act of creation is co-extensive with the duration of the universe in precisely the sense in which this can also be said of the Scholastic *nunc stans* or "eternal now." That is to say, the creative act is co-extensive with all times, not because it has a duration of so many billion years, but inasmuch as it has no duration at all: it is truly an *atemporal* act. It is thus co-extensive with the life-span of the universe, much as the center of a circle is co-extensive with the entire circumference, not by being somehow stretched out or multiplied, but by virtue of being the origin or "source" of the whole structure.

What Teilhard has done is first of all assume that the creative act is both temporal and continuous, and then to fuse the idea of creation and transformation into a single concept of "creative transformation." And this is a perfectly gratuitous step, to say the least. Yet he creates the illusion of presenting an argument (and a rather cogent one at that) by remonstrating against the idea of "periodic intrusions of the First Cause," as if that were the gist of the Scholastic doctrine.

Is this a case of duplicity, or just plain ignorance? We cannot say for sure. We do know, however, that Teilhard was perfectly well aware of the traditional doctrine of "instantaneous" creation, because in fact he refers to it on other occasions.[37] But why then does he not refer to it here, in his paper on "Creative Transformation," where it is crucial? Why, in other words, does he misrepresent the traditional teaching?

The final irony, perhaps, is that the new notion of creative transformation, as Teilhard has formulated it, makes no sense in its own right. It is not actually "conceivable *in abstracto*," as he claims. For to speak of an act "which *makes use* of a pre-existent created being and builds it up into a *completely* new being" is in fact a self-contradiction: clearly so, for to "build up" means to change, to alter in some way. But this entails the idea of continuity, of a *bona fide* metamorphosis or change of state. And this excludes the idea that the end-product is something "completely new." There is a logical contradiction here. And the contradiction remains even after we have been told that "This *act is really creative,* because it calls for renewed intervention on the part of the First Cause." Even a "renewed intervention on the part of the First Cause" cannot "build up" a being into something "completely new"! It would seem that God respects logic, even if some of His creatures do not.

★   ★   ★

In a later work Teilhard makes it a point to attack the Christian doctrine of creation *ex nihilo* as such. He directs his arguments in particular against "its notion of 'participated being,' a lower or secondary form of being gratuitously drawn from 'non-being' by a special act of transcendent causality, 'creatio ex nihilo.'"[38] Now it is needless to say that this notion of participated being is indeed implicit in the Christian concept of creation, and is in fact central to orthodox Christian theology. It will be interesting to see on what grounds Teilhard objects to this immemorial teaching.

"An entirely gratuitous creation, a gesture of pure benevolence, with no other object, for absolute Being, than to *share* his plenitude with a *corona* of participants of whom he has strictly no need—that could satisfy minds that had not yet awoken to the immensity of space-time, the colossal stores of energy and the unfathomable organic articulation of the phenomenal world."[39] That is his first thrust. But why should "the immensity of space-time" or "the colossal stores of energy" contradict, or render implausible, the idea of a gratuitous creation? Is it because the cosmos is so much larger than our "human world"? But Teilhard himself maintains that the cosmos in its entirety has no other *raison d'etre* than to find its completion in God. There is nothing at all unreasonable, then, in the idea that God created the universe, replete with all its immensities, "to share his plenitude with a *corona* of participants of whom he has strictly no need."

Following upon this initial charge, Teilhard veers off into a second arugment, which seems to have little or no connection with the immensities of space-time and energy. "We would suffer deeply," he tells us, "in the honor we pay to being, and the respect we have for God would be insulted, if all this great array, with its huge burden of toil and trouble, were no more than a sort of game whose sole aim was to make us supremely happy."[40] But here again the logic is unclear. Why must it be supposed that the recognition of God's unbounded love and solicitude for His creatures would cause us "to suffer deeply, in the honor we pay to being," or that it would "insult the respect we have for God"? This is all very strange. And in fact, it would seem that so long as we are not totally perverse, the very opposite should be the case: realizing that God has created us "out of nothing," and with no "ulterior motive," simply because He wishes to share His boundless treasures with us, we should rejoice greatly, and should love and respect God all the more. But if it were nonetheless to happen that we "suffer greatly" and feel somehow insulted, what exactly would that prove?

Teilhard himself, perhaps, is not entirely satisfied with the foregoing considerations, for he immediately embarks upon yet another line of attack. "If we could not somehow consciously feel that we cannot 'be of service to God' without God adding something to himself," he goes on to say, "that would most certainly destroy, at the heart of our freedom, the intimate driving forces of action."[41] Now this is something else again: not just hurt feelings, but a kind of paralysis is at stake. Yet it seems questionable, in the first place, that many of us are really quite so "noble" as to spurn the offer of immortal bliss and go on strike, as it were, simply because the prize is in some metaphysical sense gratuitous. Is this the best that Teilhard can do?

His next point is in the same vein: "What use have we for the *selfish* happiness of *sharing* the joy of the supreme Being, when we can dream of the infinitely greater happiness of completing that joy?"[42] But is it not perfectly ridiculous to think that this creature, which according to Teilhard's beliefs, has but recently learned to walk on its hind legs, should fret over conjectured limitations which might conceivably impede its happiness once it has been admitted into the very life of God? We must confess that for our part we find these suggestions absurd and perverse in the extreme.

Teilhard's next argument is stated in the form of a question: "However gratuitous we may suppose Creation 'ex nihilo' to be, is it not inevitably marked in the first place (whatever the theologians of 'participated being' may have said) by an absolute increase of unification, and therefore of unity, in the pleromised real?"[43] Now to begin with, it is unclear what Teilhard means by an "absolute increase of unification," over and above "unification" itself; and we surmise that he employs this curious expression to lend a certain appearance of legitimacy to the next phrase: "and therefore of unity." But be that as it may, what Teilhard is saying, basically, is that unification brings about an increase of unity. But then, this is precisely what the traditional teaching denies. What increases is not unity itself, but the *participation* of unity, or "participated unity," as one could also say. Unity as such, or absolute unity, on the other hand, no less than absolute being, belongs to God alone. And to be sure, there is neither increase nor diminution in God. These are *temporal* notions, after all.

This is what the traditional doctrine has to say on the question;

and whether it be true or false, the position is certainly not illogical. Yet it does quite obviously conflict with the evolutionist claim to the effect that unity as such is born through a process of unification, and that is of course precisely the reason why Teilhard is obliged to attack the doctrine at every turn. The point is, however, that his argument carries no force, for in saying that "an absolute increase of unification" entails an increase of unity, he is doing no more than to reiterate the evolutionist assumption. The argument reduces thus to a *petitio principii*. In plain terms, it begs the question.

We are told next that a new ontology (a "transposition of concepts," as Teilhard calls it) is required at the present stage of human evolution "to justify the ambitions newly emerging in the heart of man."[44] Now it is strange that the justification of ambitions should be deemed sufficient ground for tampering with an immemorial metaphysical doctrine. One might also wonder, moreover, just how new these ambitions are, especially if one recalls that long ago there was reputedly a being, intelligent and powerful, who likewise was said to have cherished vast ambitions—someone, in fact, who desired with all his heart to be "equal to God." But this touches upon another question, which shall need to be dealt with in a later chapter.

We come now, finally, to Teilhard's seventh and last argument: "Philosophically," he writes, "we are still living in an antiquated body of thought, governed by notions of immobility and substance."[45] The implication, of course, is that the Christian doctrine of participated being hinges supposedly upon what Teilhard calls "these two key notions." And he goes on to say that the ideas in question have been "vaguely founded and modelled upon sensorial evidence" which in bygone days could be regarded as "perennial and safe from attack," but has now been discredited through the momentous discoveries of physics. But what exactly does Teilhard understand by the terms "immobility" and "substance"? If he speaks of immobility and substance with reference to pure Being, then it is by no means true that "these two key notions" have been "vaguely founded and modelled upon sensorial evidence." We need but to think of Parmenides, for instance, the apostle of immobility and substance, one could say, who went so far as to deny the reality of motion and change on the grounds that these "sensorial" ideas are incompatible with his ontological conceptions. But be that as it may, what the new physics has in fact discredited is not the presumed immobility or substantiality of pure being, but rather the Newtonian idea of atomic particles: little bits of ponderable matter which were supposed to preserve their self-identity or sameness amidst an ever-changing universe. It is in essence the old atomistic doctrine of Democritus and Leucippus that has been thus disqualified. And it is interesting to note that neither Parmenides, nor Heraclitus, nor Plato, nor Aristotle, nor indeed a single Doctor of the Church, has ever upheld that view. On the contrary, what is sometimes termed the perennial philosophy has always been adamantly opposed to atomism in any of its forms. It was Cartesianism that reintroduced this heterodox ontology, and its subsequent overthrow at the hands of modern physics is thus to be viewed as a step, at any rate, in the direction of the traditional doctrine. Nothing could be more misleading, therefore, than Teilhard's claim that the findings of physics have disqualified the elements of Christian ontology.

After the smoke has cleared, it is thus to be conceded that the traditional doctrine of "participated being" remains unshaken. Reason alone, perhaps, cannot tell whether this doctrine is true. And yet, in the wake of Teilhard's onslaughts, one is more inclined than ever to conclude that the teaching may indeed be "perennial and safe from attack."

NOTES

1. "Signification de Teilhard de Chardin," *Etudes*, vol. 312 (1962), p. 147.
2. *Ibid*.
3. SC, p. 44.
4. HE, p. 160.
5. HE, p. 160.
6. HE, p. 161.
7. HE, p. 161.
8. HE, p. 161.
9. HE, p. 161.
10. HE, p. 161.
11. HE, pp. 161-162.
12. HE, p. 162.
13. *The Religion of Teilhard de Chardin* (New York: Desclee, 1967), p. 196.

14. Op. cit., p. 200.
15. SC, p. 45.
16. SC, p. 45.
17. SC, p. 45.
18. SC, p. 46.
19. SC, p. 46.
20. SC, p. 47.
21. SC, p. 50.
22. SC, p. 51.
23. SC, p. 51.
24. SC, p. 57.
25. SC, p. 49.
26. SC, p. 49.
27. SC, p. 50.
28. CE, p. 21.
29. CE, p. 22.
30. CE, p. 22.
31. CE, pp. 22-23.
32. CE, p. 23.
33. *Hexaemeron*, I.6.
34. Dante, *Paradiso*, XXIX.12.
35. CE, p. 23.
36. CE, p. 23.
37. For example, in HE, p. 239.
38. SC, p. 180.
39. SC, pp. 180-181.
40. SC, p. 181.
41. SC, p. 181.
42. SC, p. 181.
43. SC, p. 181.
44. SC, p. 181.
45. SC. p. 182.

Chapter V

The Omega Hypothesis

It was no doubt one of Teilhard's most cherished convictions that the cosmos as a whole is somehow converging towards an Omega Point. He felt that cosmic evolution must have a term, and that this "end" can only be conceived as a point or center of universal convergence. And he seemed to believe, moreover, that this conclusion could be established, or rendered plausible, on purely scientific grounds. One has the impression, in fact, that in his eyes "the discovery of Omega" looms as the ultimate recognition of a unified science, a science which has itself converged to that "ultra-physics" of which he sometimes speaks.

Yet, epoch-making as it may be, the scientific recognition of an Omega Point as the ultimate term of cosmogenesis was for Teilhard but the first major step towards an even more momentous discovery: the realization, namely, that "the Omega Point of science" coincides in reality with Christ. What appears to the eye of science as a universal center of attraction and confluence is in reality none other than the cosmic Christ of St. Paul; that is the second major finding to which Teilhard lays claim.

It hardly needs pointing out that this twofold discovery (or conjecture, as the case may be) is absolutely central to Teilhard's thought. What is not clear, on the other hand, is what exactly Teilhard has in mind when he speaks of a "convergent" universe. Now the primary sense of the word is spatial: "to converge" means to come together at a point. Are we to understand, then, that the cosmos in its entirety will eventually draw together and collapse into a single point, a single center of gravitational attraction? This is one of those questions which Teilhard does not answer with a simple "yes" or "no." The fact is that he speaks of convergence in a number of different senses, which in his mind seem to be somehow equivalent or fused. And while for the most part, certainly, he speaks in metaphor, he does also on occasion employ the term unmistakably in its primary spatial sense.

There can be no doubt that "the gravitational model" played an important role in Teilhard's thought, as he himself admits when he alludes to "the curiously seductive power that the phenomenon of gravity exerted on my mind while I was still very young,"[1] and when he tells us that "by its gravitational nature, the Universe, I saw, was falling—falling forwards—in the direction of Spirit as upon its stable form."[2] In those days, moreover, there was nothing scientifically impossible in the idea of a universal gravitational collapse. Or better said, the new scientific cosmology which discloses an exactly opposite picture was just in its nascent stage. It began, as one may recall, in 1913 with Slipher's experimental discovery of receding galaxies, and received its theoretical foundations in 1917 with Einstein's formulation of general relativity. But it was not until 1930 or thereabouts that the idea of an expanding universe came to be more widely appreciated, and not until 1965 that the so-called Big Bang model gained a compelling status following the dramatic discovery of the "cosmic fireball radiation" by Arno Penzias and Robert Wilson. It was thus some ten years after the death of Teilhard de Chardin that the notion of a gravitationally convergent universe was definitively ruled out and replaced by the opposite conception, the idea of an exploding universe.

Teilhard himself, however, began at some point to shift from a purely gravitational notion of cosmic convergence to something more sophisticated, and considerably less clear. "This was no longer universal 'attraction' gradually drawing around itself the cosmic Mass," he tells us, "but that as yet undiscovered and unnamed power which forces Matter (as it concentrates under pressure) to arrange itself in ever larger molecules, differentiated and organic in structure."[3] By now the idea of convergence has changed; it has apparently become "complexification," in the physical sense of particulate aggregation. "Beyond and above the *concentration-curve*," we are told, "I began to distinguish the *arrangement-curve*. . . ."[4] But does this mean that the earlier idea of a cosmic "concentration-curve" has now been scrapped? Teilhard does not say that. In fact, he seems still to be attracted to the first notion, and continues to allude to it here and there. This is the case, for instance, when (in 1942) he delivers himself at considerable length on the so-called "cone of time." As we shall have occasion to see, the geometry of that imagined cone clearly implies the old idea of universal confluence. And as if to settle the matter, Teilhard goes so far as to speak of "a growing awareness of the convergent nature of Space-Time" as "the event that characterizes our epoch."[5]

One can say in retrospect that he could not have been more wrong, for as we have just noted, the truly epochal discovery of astrophysics which was coming to light at the time is that the universe was born in a stupendous explosion and has been literally flying apart ever since. But these developments had not yet caused much of a stir outside astrophysical circles. Meanwhile it is evident that the notion of cosmic convergence in the primary sense of gravitational collapse continues to play a role in Teilhard's speculations.

*   *   *

But it is henceforth accompanied by other conceptions, as we have said, the first of which is again physical and distinctly spatial: an "irresistible 'Vortex'" which spins into itself, always in the same direction, the whole Stuff of things, from the most simple to the most complex; spinning it into ever more comprehensive and more astronomically complicated nuclei,"[6] as Teilhard tells us in graphic terms. And this cosmic movement of complexification, this "structural torsion," as he calls it, is said to result in "an increase (under the influence of interiorization) of consciousness, or a rise in psychic temperature, in the core of the corpuscles that are successively produced."[7]

What this affirms, of course, is nothing else than Teilhard's celebrated Law of Complexity/Consciousness; only this time the dual process of complexification and interiorization has been explicitly conceived as the manifestation of an "as yet undiscovered and unnamed power," which presumably resides in the heart of Matter.

But once again there are difficulties. Quite apart from the fact that the stipulated "power" remains admittedly undiscovered, one does know in any case that matter as such has a universal tendency to move precisely in the reverse direction: from the complex to the simple. There is a well-founded law of entropy which affirms that a system of particles under the action of physical forces will tend to move towards a homogeneous state, a state of equilibrium: from order to disorder, as one can also say. There are no grounds, moreover, to suppose that this law is somehow abrogated within a living organism. Now it is true, of course, that living organisms tend to complexify during the ascending curve of their life-cycle and that they maintain a stupendous degree of order; but they do so by ingesting energy from their environment. That is just why we need to eat and to breathe; it takes energy to maintain order. And in the process of maintaining its own order, the organism inevitably causes a corresponding disorder in the environment. We have reason to believe, therefore, that when it comes to the total system (organism plus environment), the law of entropy is by no means violated. Or better said, it is not violated at all (neither within nor outside the organism), because it only applies to complete systems. And this means that it is indeed the universal tendency of matter as such to fall into disorder; the phenomenon of life does not alter this fact.

There are two positions, then, which can be assumed. One can say, in the first place, that life is a statistical accident, the result of an initial improbability of astronomical magnitude perpetuating itself, so to speak, through metabolic devices; and this of course amounts to the classical Darwinist position. Or else one can conjecture that life is the manifestation of a vital principle, a special kind of energy, if you will, which is by no means the same as that physical energy which (as Einstein has shown) is the equivalent of matter. And this is what not a few biologists have maintained, and what Teilhard himself seems to be saying when he speaks of an as yet undiscovered power, or of such mysterious things as his so-called radial energy. Only in that case the relationship between life and matter is not one of evolution (of matter gradually transforming itself into life), but of a ceaseless struggle between two alien principles which are tending in opposite directions. The forces of life, then, are engaged in mortal combat, as it were, with an obstreperous element upon which they have fastened, and which for a time they dominate, only to be vanquished at last and forced to withdraw, presumably, into their native habitat.

These are the two conceptual possibilities, basically, which the law of entropy leaves open to us. And each in its own way contradicts Teilhard's assumption of an evolutive universe in which "the fundamental property of the cosmic mass is to concentrate upon itself, within an ever-growing consciousness, as a result of attraction and synthesis."[8] Teilhard is aware of the difficulty, moreover; for he immediately goes on to say that "In spite of the appearance, so impressive as a factor of physics, of secondary phenomena of progressive dispersion (such as entropy), there is only one real evolution, *the evolution of convergence,* because it alone is positive and creative."[9] But this is no argument at all: what Teilhard is doing is to deny the universal validity of the entropic law just because it is incompatible with his own assumptions about "real evolution." We are asked, in other words, to give up a basic law belonging to the most exact science on the strength of conjectures, for which there is no evidence at all.

What is also strange is that after having postulated the existence of a universal tendency on the part of matter "to concentrate upon itself," Teilhard informs us a few pages later that "The whole cosmic Event may be reduced in its essence to one single vast process of arrangement, whose mechanism (that is, the use of effects of Large Numbers and the play of Chance) is governed by statistical necessity."[10] This is strange, we say, for to speak of the play of chance is to deny implicitly that the phenomenon in question is due to an innate tendency. Thus, for example, if a chimpanzee were let loose at the keyboard of a typewriter, it would be quite appropriate to conceive of the print-out in statistical terms. And if it should happen that one discovers an English sentence or two of simian authorship, one would be justified in concluding that the creature must have been pounding away for immense stretches of time. But the situation is obviously different in the case of a human typist.

The typist, one might say, has a tendency to produce English sentences. And so the production of these sentences is no longer a statistical phenomenon; it has nothing whatsoever to do with "the play of chance." Now the same logic, exactly, applies to that vast process of arrangement which Teilhard envisions; here, too, the notion of pure chance is opposed to the idea of innate tendency.

Teilhard himself, moreover, seems at times to realize that his theory of universal convergence does not sit well with the findings of science. We are told, however, that it is science, and not his own theory, that is at fault. By the analytical nature of its methodology, Teilhard maintains, science is constrained to look always in the wrong direction, as it were: "By following science, we have gone no further than *the extreme lower limits of the real,* where beings are at their most impoverished and tenuous,"[11] he tells us; "what we have been doing is to advance in the direction in which everything disintegrates and is attenuated."[12] But this postulate, too, does not help Teilhard's cause. For in the first place, the charge is inaccurate, seeing that science, for all its categorical limitations (which Teilhard is always willing, in other contexts, to overlook), is nonetheless oriented in the direction of unity. What else is a scientific law, after all, than a certain mode of unity? But if it should still be true that science is incapable of grasping the higher unities, how then could it ever arrive at the recognition of Omega, the highest unity of all?

Teilhard's reply to this obvious objection is ingenious in the extreme: science, he maintains, "by the very impotence of its analytical efforts, has taught us that in the direction in which things become complex in unity, there must lie a supreme center of convergence and consistence, in which everything is knit together and holds together."[13] It would seem, however, that one needs to be "touched with evolutionist grace" to understand how an epoch-making scientific discovery could be grounded in nothing more than impotence.

*   *   *

But be that as it may, we need yet to consider a third mode of cosmic convergence (or better said, perhaps, a third aspect or dimension of the Teilhardian cosmo-convergence), that is, the psychic aspect. We encounter this notion, for example, early in *The Phenomenon of Man*, when Teilhard informs us that "All the rest of this essay will be nothing but the story of the struggle in the universe between the unified *multiple* and the unorganized *multitude*: the application throughout of the great *Law of complexity and consciousness*: a law that itself implies a psychically convergent structure and curvature of the world."[14] Yet in place of an explanation as to what all this means, and how a psychic convergence and cosmic curvature follow from "the great *Law*," we are only told at this juncture that "We must not go too fast."

Later in the book, however, Teilhard gives us to understand that the phenomenon of psychic convergence begins to take place in the human domain, after the evolutive trajectory has crossed "the critical point of reflection." The idea seems to be that a reflective or human-type consciousness is centered, or ego-centered, as one could also say; it has somehow the capacity, and indeed the tendency, to relate everything to itself. And so, metaphorically speaking, it gathers up the universe, or a certain small portion thereof, at any rate, and concentrates it upon a single point, a single psychic center. There is, then, a "psychic convergence" in that sense.

But the first and perhaps most obvious difficulty with this notion is that there is not just one universal cosmic convergence of that kind, but a vast number, rather, of such psychophysical happenings: one for each reflective center or conscious human being. If one wishes, nonetheless, to speak of a single psychic convergence, at least on a planetary scale, one needs therefore to introduce or postulate some appropriate notion of a collective psyche; and that is of course where Teilhard's noosphere comes into the picture.

The basic idea is that human socialization gradually gives birth to a super-organism, replete with a psyche of its own, which is the noosphere. And this happens, moreover, in compliance with "the great Law." Thus we are told, for example (in *Mon Universe*), that "The unification that is being developed so intensely in our time in the human spirit and the human collectivity is the authentic continuation of the biological process that produced the human brain. That is what creative union means."[15]

This is the picture, as Teilhard has drawn it innumerable times. And we certainly cannot agree with Henri de Lubac when he writes that "We should not attach too much importance to what we are told about this 'super-organism,' that it will be made up of all human individuals just as the biological individual is made up of cells. Here again, there is no more in this biological language than an analogy, whose shortcomings were recognized by Père Teilhard himself."[16] Now it is true enough that "The individuals that enter into the composition of such a super-organism are not conceived as ceasing to be so many reflective, personal centers."[17] Teilhard himself has made this perfectly clear when he tells us repeatedly that collectivization, in the authentically organismal sense, "differentiates" and "super-personalizes" the human cells, and that the entire process is converging towards a "centered system of centers." But this does not mean that Teilhard has retracted his biological claims; how can he? It is obviously the only quasi-scientific basis which could allow him to speak of a super-organism, an organic noosphere, and an eventual psychic convergence of planetary proportions. It might even be suggested that this is precisely the motivation behind his Law of Complexity; it is the only thing that could lend an appearance of scientific validity to his views regarding the future of mankind. At any rate, it is abundantly clear that in Teilhard's eyes the idea of a biologically founded noosphere was not just an analogy, whose shortcomings he recognized. If that were the case, he would obviously be deceiving us when he declares (with reference to his usual biological argument): "We cannot, therefore, fail to see that of all living things we know, none is more really, more intensely, living than the noosphere."[18] In a word, on this crucial issue, as on certain other matters, it would seem that Henri de Lubac is trying rather desperately to tone down what his Jesuit confrere has said.

But let us go on. The great event which Teilhard needs to postulate is the formation within the noosphere of a unique center, or center of centers: "The existence ahead of us," to put it in his own words, "of some critical and final point of ultra-hominization, corresponding to a complete reflection of the noosphere upon itself."[19] This is what present-day humanity is supposedly straining to bring to birth; this is what all the stress and anguish is about. What is at stake "is no longer the simple isolated reflection of an individual upon himself," Teilhard tells us, "but the conjugate and combined reflection of innumerable elements, adjusting and mutually reinforcing their activities, and so gradually forming one vast mirror—a mirror in which the universe might one day reflect itself and so fall into shape."[20] And this event, presumably, will be that psychic convergence of the world which "the great Law of Complexity implies," or enables us to foresee.

Psychic convergence, therefore, is thought to go hand in hand with the convergence of complexification, so much so that Teilhard leaves us with the impression that the two are not just complementary aspects of a single process, but actually one and the same thing. Thus, almost immediately after telling us about the "complete reflection of the noosphere upon itself," and in the same breath, as it were, Teilhard goes on to say that "We no longer have in the universe nothing but that heart-breaking entropy, inexorably reducing things (as we are still constantly being told) to their most elementary and most stable forms: but, emerging through and above this rain of ashes, we see a sort of cosmic vortex within which the stuff of the world, by the preferential use of chances, twists and coils upon itself ever more tightly in more complex and more fully centered assemblies."[21]

And the passage closes, incidentally, with the following inimitable statement, which in a way may be left to speak for itself: "A world that is in equilibrium upon instability, because it is in movement: and a world whose dynamic consistence is increasing in exact proportion with the complexity of its arrangements, because it is converging upon itself in as many sidereal points as there ever have been, as there are now, and there ever will be, thinking planets."[22]

*   *   *

One of the most remarkable features of Teilhard's theory of the noosphere is the fact that he actually conceives of it as a spherical envelope or aura stretching around the planet Earth. At an earlier stage in the unfolding of his ideas he had come to think of the so-called biosphere as a "living membrane stretched like a film over the lustrous surface of the star which holds us."[23] And then, later, he discovered that "There was something more: around this sentient protoplasmic layer, an ultimate envelope was beginning to become apparent to me, taking on its own individuality and gradually detaching itself like a luminous aura. This envelope was not only conscious, but thinking, and from the time when I first became aware of it, it was always there that I found concentrated in an ever more dazzling and consistent form, the essence or rather the very soul of the Earth."[24]

There is every indication that Teilhard means this to be more than just poetry, or the account of a subjective experience. And in fact the spherical-membrane idea occurs often enough in what is purportedly a scientific context. It is clearly in evidence, for instance, when Teilhard tells us that "Under the combined force of the multiplication (in numbers) and expansion (in radius of influence) of human individuals on the surface of the globe, the noosphere has for the last century shown signs of a sudden organic compression upon itself and compenetration."[25]

It must be remembered, however, that the noosphere is supposed to be a *psychic* principle: it is made up of reflective consciousness, or as Teilhard also says, of thought. And for this very reason it cannot be conceived as a corporeal entity, a thing that occupies space; we already had occasion to touch on this point in an earlier chapter. Consider the visual perception of a landscape, for instance. If we suppose that the landscape, as it presents itself to the observer in consciousness, were itself extended in space (presumably within the brain), then it could possess no more unity than a photograph, which consists, after all, of a few thousand scattered dots. It is evident that the metaphor of psychic convergence—of a spatial multiplicity being gathered into a single center—would not apply. One of the inalienable characteristics of reflective consciousness, therefore, is that it is *not* extended, and thus *not* situated in space.

Or again (to approach the question from another direction), by what conceivable experiment or operational procedure could one actually localize a given element of consciousness? Just how does one measure the coordinates of a mental image, or determine its diameter? Only a little thought is needed to persuade oneself that there actually are no such procedures; there cannot be. It is obvious, on the other hand, that a thing which exists in space can be spatially localized; it has coordinates which can in principle be ascertained, at least to within a certain approximation. It follows, then, that consciousness (or what amounts to the same, its content) is not a thing of that kind. It is nothing but foolishness, and an abuse of metaphor, to speak of consciousness or thought as though it were a spatial entity.

Are we then to believe that when Teilhard speaks of the noospheric envelope as a spherical membrane, which "gradually detaches itself like a luminous aura" from a sentient protoplasmic layer, he is speaking only in metaphor? It would be hard to admit this. Teilhard himself, moreover, provides compelling evidence to the contrary. Consider, for instance, the following statement from *The Phenomenon of Man,* which occurs in a pivotal section introducing the Omega concept: "Because it contains and engenders consciousness, space-time is necessarily *of a convergent nature.*"[26] We are explicitly told, here, that space-time *contains* consciousness. And not only does Teilhard affirm this misconception, but he uses it as a premise. His thought (which as usual is more implied than expressed) appears to be as follows: because consciousness exists in and is engendered by space-time, and because in its reflective state consciousness concentrates a certain spatio-temporal content upon a center within itself, therefore space-time concentrates itself upon a center. A certain "in-folding" of space-time upon itself takes place. And following upon the expected "complete reflection of the noosphere upon itself," which is tantamount to the formation of a unique center of centers, that in-folding will take the form of a convergence of space-time, a convergence directed towards that supreme center. And that is why Teilhard goes on to say (with reference to space-time) that "Accordingly its enormous layers, followed in the right direction, must somewhere ahead become involuted to a point which we might call Omega, which fuses and consumes them integrally in itself."[27]

What has happened, apparently, is that Teilhard has in the end become duped by his own metaphors. We need not actually concern ourselves with the noosphere and its presumed self-reflection; to see what is going on it will suffice to consider the cognitive act by which we come to know the familiar things in space and time. Now it is quite clear that nothing actually happens to space, or to space-time, by virtue of this act. Space-time does not develop some mysterious curvature simply because I contemplate a field or a mountain. Nor does some bit of space compress itself and slip into someone's psyche. There are actually no "radii" of space or space-time converging to a point. There is the cognitive act (which is admittedly a miracle)—but there is no such thing as a convergence of space-time to a psychic center. It is an illusion which Teilhard has deftly conjured up; he is clearly a master at this.

⋆　　　⋆　　　⋆

It appears, in any case, that the Teilhardian notion of a convergent space-time applies supposedly to space-time in its totality. "Caught within its curve," Teilhard explains, "the layers of Matter (considered as separate elements *no less than as a whole*) tighten and converge in Thought, by synthesis. Therefore it is as a cone, in the form of a cone that it can best be depicted."[28] It is not simply a question of isolated regions detaching themselves from the rest of the cosmos, but of a universal convergence to a single Apex. And this means, in particular, that matter "as a whole" becomes eventually spiritualized. Teilhard says so repeatedly: for example, when he speaks of consciousness becoming "co-extensive with the universe,"[29] and of "a flux, at once physical and psychic, which made the Totality of the Stuff of Things fold in on itself, by giving it complexity, carrying this to the point where that Stuff is made to co-reflect itself."[30]

Yet at the same time one knows full well that our planet will eventually become uninhabitable, and that terrestrial life will cease. All these organic complexities, which are said to have evolved out of primordial matter in the course of millions of years, will be broken down again, and will disappear, leaving the Earth every bit as inanimate and barren as it was at the start. And if there be other planets in the universe, moreover, on which life has evolved, one can say with scientific certainty that the same fate awaits them all.

Now it is obvious that this fact is not propitious to Teilhard's theory. It poses a formidable problem, of which Teilhard, of course, was not unaware. "We cannot resolve this contradiction between congenital mortality of the planets and the demand for irreversibility developed by planetized life on their surface by covering it up or deferring it," he tells us quite rightly; "we have finally to banish the spectre of Death from our horizon."[31] But just how is this to be done? How does one "banish the spectre of Death"? Teilhard's proposed resolution of the impasse is as follows: "Is it not conceivable," he says, "that Mankind, at the end of its totalization, its folding-in upon itself, may reach a critical level of maturity where, leaving Earth and stars to lapse slowly back into the dwindling mass of primordial energy, it will detach itself from this planet and join the one true, irreversible essence of things, the Omega Point?"[32]

But actually this supposition raises more difficulties than it resolves. One might wonder, for example, what happens to men and women who have died before mankind has reached "a critical level of maturity." And if it be true that the souls of the "prematurely deceased" have been able to survive, what further need is there for the conjectured critical point? What has happened, moreover, to the Law of Complexity, which had given us to understand that the psychic is so closely tied to cerebral complexities that the two are virtually inseparable? If consciousness is really "the specific effect" of complexity, how can the two part company?

It is hard to avoid the impression that in trying to escape from the difficulty occasioned by the mortality of planets, Teilhard has been forced to back away from his evolutionist monism to a position that comes perilously close to the traditional dualism. Somewhere along the "evolutive trajectory" he has to admit a certain separation between body and soul, or matter and spirit, which seems hardly compatible with the idea that the two are simply different aspects, or states, of one and the same thing. When all is said and done, the phenomenon of death and survival can only be conceived as a parting of the way; there is something that moves on, and something that is left behind. And in a rather poetic letter, which Teilhard wrote in 1917 from the Front, he goes so far as to suggest that "in a way, the whole tangible universe itself is a vast residue, a skeleton of countless lives that have germinated in it and left it, leaving behind them only a trifling, infinitesimal, part of their riches."[33] The same idea, moreover, is to be found in some of Teilhard's latest compositions; it is clearly in evidence, for example, when he alludes to "this rain of ashes," above which the cosmic vortex "twists and coils upon itself ever more tightly in more complex and more fully centered assemblies," a passage which was written only four years before his death.

What, then, is Teilhard's definitive position? It is not certain, of course, that there is one. All that one can say is that in a number of of places he gives us to understand (in a rather indirect manner, to be sure) that some portion of terrestrial matter gets caught up in the vortex of complexification, and having crossed a certain threshold, becomes permanently transformed into thought, while the remaining portion gets swept away by the downward current of entropy.

But how does this square with the notion of a single Apex, and with the idea that "the Totality of the Stuff of Things" folds in upon itself? What will happen to the less fortunate portion of matter which ends up in the current of "that heartbreaking entropy"? Will it, too, become eventually "hominized"? Teilhard does not actually say so. And yet, when he speaks of a spiritualized mankind "leaving Earth and stars to lapse slowly back into the dwindling mass of primordial energy," he does seem to suggest, however faintly, that the "mass of primordial energy" (by which he presumably means the amount of physical energy in the universe) is gradually diminishing, and may eventually be reduced to zero. Are we then to suppose, perhaps, that the lapsing Earth and stars will all be somehow recycled, so that every particle in the universe will eventually be complexified and hominized? Is there to be eventually a single ascending vortex without any compensating "rain of ashes"? And what about the notion, implicit in all of this, that the formation of a human soul, or its departure from the body, is associated with a certain mass defect: if that be the case, why are we not told of this momentous fact in unequivocal terms? And why has no such effect been observed?

But let us not belabor the point. There is every reason to believe that the amount of matter (or better said, physical energy) within the cosmos is strictly conserved; the most exact of our sciences guarantees this. We are left, therefore, with only two conceivable alternatives: one can say, with the materialists, that there is no such thing as soul and immortality; or one can admit the traditional dualism. But Teilhard wants to have it both ways: he wants to have soul and immortality on an essentially materialistic basis. It is small wonder, therefore, that he finds the going tough.

★   ★   ★

Enough has been said regarding the Teilhardian notion of cosmo-convergence to show that the theory is not by any means well founded. It is astonishing that Teilhard could have seen fit to promulgate these rather nebulous and incoherent speculations in dogmatic terms as a scientific truth, when in fact there is actually not a shred of evidence to support an hypothesis of that kind: "the evidence that Science provides"[34] exists nowhere except possibly in Teilhard's unusually fertile imagination. As George Gaylord Simpson, the well-known evolutionist and friend of Teilhard de Chardin, has pointed out in his review of *The Phenomenon of Man*, the Omega doctrine has no basis in scientific fact. "One cannot object to the piety and mysticism of his book," he goes on to say, "but one can object to its initial claim to be a scientific treatise, and to the arrangement that puts its real premises briefly, in part obscurely, as a sort of appendage after the conclusions drawn from them."[35] The fact is that Teilhard has promulgated his private mystical theories under the colors of Science, and amazingly enough, countless individuals, including many who should certainly know better, have been taken in.

The question remains, of course, how Teilhard's doctrine stands from a theological point of view; must it be admitted that "one cannot object to the piety and mysticism of his book"? Now on this score, too, there is much to be said; indeed, it is a question which will concern us for the remainder of this monograph. The problem has many aspects, which shall need to be dealt with successively, starting with what is no doubt the crucial issue: Teilhard's identification of Omega with Christ.

To begin with, it could certainly be argued that inasmuch as the so-called "Omega Point of science" has turned out to be fictitious, it makes no further sense to ask whether that nonexistent Point can be identified with Christ. And yet it will not be without interest to observe how Teilhard goes about to conceive of the Incarnate Lord in terms of his postulated cosmology.

"In a Universe of 'Conical' structure," we are told, "Christ has a place (the apex!) ready for Him to fill, where His Spirit can radiate through all the centuries and all beings."[36] Now to begin with, the "apex" of such an imagined "cone of Time" could be neither a *place* (i.e., a spatial locus), nor an *event* (i.e., a point of space-time), for the reason that it must clearly be situated outside the space-time continuum, on its "boundary," so to speak. Nothing whatsoever, therefore, can be "located" at that apex, in a physical sense. Nor is it conceivable that a physical entity could somehow be moved into that apex: in fact, the only possible way to get there from within the space-time continuum would be to wait till "the end of time," when all the so-called world-lines will merge in that singularity.

We must understand, moreover, that Teilhard is definitely speaking of the Incarnate and Risen Christ; he is not speaking of the Logos as such, the eternal and "pre-cosmic" Word of God. It is questionable, in fact, whether Teilhard *ever* conceives of Christ in such a purely transcendent sense. But be that as it may, his present meaning is beyond doubt; what Teilhard is telling us is that by virtue of His Incarnation and Resurrection Christ has positioned Himself at the apex of the postulated Time Cone. But this actually makes no sense at all: for as we have just seen, it is certainly not by entering into space-time that the imagined Omega Point is to be reached. And indeed, to do so would be to move exactly in the wrong direction.

Nor can it be said, by way of rejoinder, that Teilhard conceives of these matters in some high and exclusively mystical sense which does not answer to scientific analysis; for it is the whole point of his theory, after all, to amalgamate theological and scientific insights. We are perfectly within our rights, then, to take him at his scientific word.

Teilhard goes out of his way, as a matter of fact, to stress the physical and supposedly scientific nature of his Christological speculations. "Starting from the evolutive Omega," he tells us for example, "at which we assume Christ to stand, not only does it become possible to conceive Christ as radiating *physically* over the terrifying totality of things, but what is more, that radiation must inevitably work up to a maximum of penetrative and activating power."[37] But here again Teilhard misses the mark. For it is a basic and quite elementary fact of physics that velocity vectors point into the future. And this implies that the postulated Apex (if it existed) would be the one Point from which no radiation whatsoever could penetrate into the universe (let alone "work up to a maximum of penetrative and activating power"). Christ would thus have positioned Himself at the worst possible spot!

Nor does it make any more sense when Teilhard speaks of the Ascended Christ as having been "raised to the position of Prime Mover of the evolutive movement of complexity-consciousness."[38] For nothing could be more obvious than that a Prime Mover, if he exists at all, must be there from the start. A Prime Mover who takes up his post, so to speak, in the middle of the evolutive process is an absurdity. Or are we perhaps to suppose that there was another Prime Mover at first, who was later "relieved" by the Risen Christ? It is difficult to understand how such ideas could ever have been taken seriously.

Teilhard is theologically right, no doubt, when he speaks of the cosmic Christ as a universal Center of attraction and influence—of "radiation," if you will. But he evinces an astonishing lack of theological comprehension when he suggests that this radiation is *physical*. Though it be true that Christ assumed a physical body, it must be said that His "radiation" is nonetheless spiritual: it is in fact the Holy Ghost. This is indeed the "fire" which Christ came "to cast upon the earth" (*Luke* 12:49); and let no one say that the Spirit of God is a "physical radiation"!

★   ★   ★

The fact is that Christianity knows nothing of a convergent universe in the Teilhardian sense. It does not envision a conical space-time presided over by an Apex at which all the world-lines are supposed to meet at the end of time; such an idea, obviously, would have been quite foreign to the mind of the Fathers. And yet there is an element in the traditional conception of God and world which is nonetheless akin to Teilhard's Apex: Christianity, too, knows of a mysterious point, if you will, where God and cosmos are said to meet.

Now, it needs to be observed, in the first place, that contrary to a certain popular misconception the God of Christianity is not transcendent in an exclusivist sense; He is not really an "extrinsicist God," as Teilhard charges, a God who supposedly resides somewhere beyond the clouds. We need to understand quite clearly that according to the authentic Christian conception, God is not only transcendent, but immanent as well. For as St. Thomas Aquinas has explained, "Since God is the universal cause of all being, in whatever region being is to be found, there must be the divine presence."[39] Yet not as an object, not as a "thing"!

But then, if God is present everywhere, how can there be a single "point of contact," as it were, between God and world? Is it possible, in other words, to conceive of a single omnipresent Point? Now as every mathematician will readily understand, it is not only possible, but quite easy to do so; what is needed (if we may be excused for the use of technical jargon) is a "vertical dimension," orthogonal to space-time, and an extended metric which is degenerate in that vertical direction. One can then conceive of the vertical lines or "radii" as converging to a single Point, whose distance to all points of space-time is precisely zero.

What is surprising, however, is that this "model" is perfectly orthodox; unlike Teilhard's conical apex idea, it is *not* foreign to the mind of the Fathers. The conception is in fact integral to Christianity, and indeed, it is archetypal, as one could say. A single observation may suffice to make this clear: the "model" which we have described in such abstract and seemingly artificial terms is visibly exemplified, for all to see, by the "vault of heaven," and by the dome in sacred architecture, which may be thought of as a replica of that vault. Here, in the cathedral of God or the basilica of man, we can actually behold the ascending radii soaring upwards, high above the ground on which we stand, and converging above our heads to a central point, at which the august figure of the Pantocrator can be imagined or perceived. The faithful, moreover, even the simplest among them, understand full well that the "distance" from this plane of earth to where Christ stands is not to be measured in meters or miles; it is a spiritual distance, which the "pure in heart" can cover in a trice.

There is, then, according to Christian conception, a Point

"from which Heaven and all Nature hang," to use Dante's expressive words. "Here every where and every when are focused," the poet goes on to say; for indeed, wherever we may be, and whatever the moment of cosmic history, we find ourselves confronting that Point. It does not fluctuate, it does not move. The world moves, but that Point remains ever fixed; for it is in truth "the pivot around which the primordial wheel revolves."[40]

Now this is the authentic Omega Point, one could say, the "Omega Point of theology," to be sure—for as we have seen, no other is in sight. That Point, however, is not the Apex of Teilhard's imagined cone: *not the conjectured end of the universe, but its ever-present Center.*

And there is more; there is a *bona fide* Christological connection here, as we shall presently discover. Let us go on; the doctrine is marvelous indeed! That one fixed Point, the true Center of the world, turns out to be hollow, as it were; it is a Gate. And this, too, we can behold, if not in the vault of heaven, then at least in the dome of every traditionally constructed basilica: it is there as a small round aperture, in fresco or mosaic depiction, perhaps. And this, let us remark, is also presumably what monastic tonsure is primarily meant to convey; it is no accident, after all, that the Cross was set atop of Golgotha ("which by interpretation means 'skull'").

Now it is beyond dispute that this conception of a universal Center and Gate is to be found not only in Christianity, but in virtually all the metaphysical traditions of mankind.[41] What is special to Christianity, on the other hand, is the concept of the Incarnation: the idea that Christ, the eternal Word of God, descends into the world (by way of this Gate) in order that men may, *in Him,* ascend into the Kingdom of God (again by way of this same Gate). It is in this sense that Christ said: "I am the door." (*John* 10:9). Or still more clearly: "And I, if I be lifted up from the earth, will draw all men unto me." (*John* 12:32). Now, to be "lifted up from the earth" means ultimately to ascend into Heaven through that mysterious "opening": that "narrow gate" or "eye of the needle," no less, through which the "rich man" could not pass. This is the passage out of this world, the veritable Passover. And luckily for the followers of Christ—luckily for all men!—this is not a matter of waiting several million years till the cosmos at large will (hopefully) have completed its evolutive trajectory. Happily this is not how the matter stands; the authentic Passover is in fact to be accomplished in a single instant—in "the twinkling of an eye," as it has been said. For it is a journey, if you will, not *within* terrestrial time, but out of it; a journey, not into the distant future, but into the Eternal Now.

NOTES

1. HM, p. 33.
2. HM, p. 28.
3. HM, p. 33.
4. HM, p. 33.
5. FM, p. 96.
6. HM, p. 33.
7. HM, p. 33.
8. CE, p. 87.
9. CE, p. 87.
10. HM, p. 51.
11. SC, p. 28.
12. SC, p. 30.
13. SC, p. 34.
14. PM, p. 61.
15. SC, p. 82.
16. *The Religion of Teilhard de Chardin* (New York: Desclee, 1967), p. 208.
17. *Ibid.*
18. AE, p. 288.
19. AE, p. 290.
20. AE, p. 288.
21. AE, p. 290.
22. AE, p. 290.
23. HM, p. 32.
24. HM, p. 32.
25. AE, p. 291.
26. PM, p. 259.
27. PM, p. 259.
28. FM, pp. 91-92 (italics added).
29. PM, p. 309.
30. HM, p. 82.
31. FM, pp. 126-127.
32. FM, p. 127.
33. HM, p. 194.
34. HM, p. 91.

35. *Scientific American,* April, 1960; p. 206.
36. FM, p. 98.
37. HM, p. 94 (Teilhard's italics).
38. HM, p. 94.
39. *Summa Contra Gentiles,* III.68.
40. *Paradiso,* XXVIII.41, XXIX. 12, and XIII.11, respectively.
41. See, for instance, A. K. Coomaraswamy, *Selected Papers* (Princeton: Princeton University Press, 1977), vol. 1, pp. 415-544; vol. 2, pp. 220-230.

Chapter VI

The God of Evolution

There has been much debate over the question of Teilhard's theological orthodoxy. The first thing to be done, of course, is to ascertain precisely where Teilhard stands on the basic issues; and this, as we know, is not an easy task. "Imprecision or contradiction in definition is one of the constant problems in the study of the Teilhard canon,"[1] observes George Simpson. It is hardly surprising, therefore, that opinions have varied greatly as to what, exactly, Teilhard did say regarding the nature and attributes of God.

To be sure, he exhibits pantheistic tendencies. But just how far does he go in that direction? There are those (like the Dominican Guerard de Lauriers, for instance) who maintain that Teilhard espoused "a veritable metaphysical monism," a monism "so radical that it removes being"[2]; whereas other theologians (such as Henri de Lubac) are given to pleading the case of Teilhardian orthodoxy. "Père Teilhard, one need hardly say, believed in God," writes de Lubac in answer to de Lauriers; "but he believed also, and affirmed, that, transcending the world, 'God could dispense with the world,' that he was self-sufficing; that the inevitability that we see in the world is only 'a consequence upon the free will of the Creator.' That in itself is enough to dismiss the accusation."[3]

But in fact it is not: for it happens that elsewhere Teilhard flatly contradicts these orthodox-sounding affirmations which his distinguished confrere has adduced. Thus, in an essay entitled

"Suggestions for a New Theology," for instance, Teilhard makes it a point to reproach the traditional doctrine precisely for its belief in the absolute self-sufficiency of God: "God could, it appeared, dispense with the universe,"[4] he charges. His point is that this time-honored belief has now become outmoded and needs to be given up. Or again, in one of his latest works he goes so far as to say that "In truth, it is not the sense of contingence of the created but the sense of the mutual completion of the world and God which gives life to Christianity."[5] We are told, in other words, that just as the world has need of God, so also God has need of the world: a far cry, indeed, from the position that "God could dispense with the world."

Nor does the case stand any better when it comes to the stipulated "free will of the Creator." Here, too, de Lubac seems to forget that Teilhard has often enough expressed himself on the opposite side of the issue. He does so, for example, in one of his very early compositions (dated 1919) when he asks: "In making God personal and free, Non-being absolute, the Creation gratuitous, and the Fall accidental, are we not in danger of making the Universe *intolerable* and the value of souls (on which we lay so much emphasis!) inexplicable?"[6] One can hardly fail to sense how much of Teilhard's later theological thought is implicit in this interesting sentence, written when Teilhard was just a few years out of the seminary (he was ordained in 1912).

Which brings us to another question: the "evolution" of Teilhard's theological beliefs. To be sure, the Teilhardian writings, spread out as they are over a period of some forty years, do exhibit a certain development of ideas. So far as theological questions are concerned, moreover, there is an unmistakable drift in the direction of increasingly unorthodox positions. And as a matter of fact, Teilhard himself alludes with evident satisfaction to a certain falling off from the traditional Christian outlook. Thus, in *The Heart of Matter* (written five years before his death) he speaks condescendingly of an earlier phase during which he was supposedly still under the influence of certain traditional conceptions, or subject to "those odd effects of inhibition," as he puts it, "that so often prevent us from recognizing what is staring us in the face."[7] Moreover, it was during this stage preceding his final "emancipation" that Teilhard composed his most nearly orthodox pieces: the principal works which are unfailingly cited by de Lubac and others as proof of Teilhard's theological innocence. "I can see quite clearly," Teilhard tells us (looking back upon these early years), "how the inspiration behind 'The Mass on the World' and *Le Milieu Divine* and their writing belong to that somewhat self-centered and self-enclosed period of my inner life."[8]

Yet we must not make too much of this presumed evolution of Teilhard's theological thought. For already in some of his earliest writings, as we have seen, he had expressed distinct misgivings concerning fundamental tenets of orthodox theology, such as the absolute freedom of God and the gratuitous nature of creation. It is clear that the seeds of divergence were there from the start. Only it would appear that Teilhard was somewhat less sure of himself in his younger years, and not as free in the expression of his more heterodox views. There is also evidence of a certain lingering orthodoxy which may have coexisted somehow with his less-than-orthodox opinions, and which at times came to the fore in passages of rare beauty. Are these to be counted, perhaps, among those "odd effects of inhibition" to which, in his later years, Teilhard alludes? All that we know for certain, in any event, is that Teilhard did become progressively less orthodox, and more radical in the expression of his beliefs.

★   ★   ★

Every theologian worthy of the name has conceived of God as immutable. It is only the created thing, the creature, that is subject to transformation. "They shall be changed," says the Psalmist, "but thou art the same." (*Ps.* 101:27, 28). Not that God remains somehow fixed, like a stone. The point, rather, is that God is not at all affected by time. His Being, unlike our own, is not spread out, as it were, over a temporal continuum. How could it be? How could the Author of time be subject to change? "Before Abraham was, *I am*" (*John* 8:58): not "I was," but "I am." Clearly, by this quite startling use of the present tense, Christ has proclaimed a great truth: He has given us to understand that the "I am" which He declared to the Jews is in truth none other than the *"ego sum qui sum"* which God had previously declared unto Moses from the Burning Bush (*Ex.* 3:14). It betokens a mode of Being beyond the pale of time, a mode which belongs to God alone. And let us by all means observe that this is not simply a matter of speculative interest, but a truth that is vital to the Christian Faith. For as St. Augustine has pointed out,[9] there is indeed a connection between the pronouncement of *John* 8:58 and the dire warning sounded in *John* 8:24: "If ye believe not that I am [*ego sum*], ye shall die in your sins."[10]

It will be of great interest, therefore, to see what an "evolutionist theology" has to say on that point. Where exactly does Teilhard stand? Does he submit to the orthodox view that God is "above time," that He is immutable? It would be quite absurd to claim that he does; not, at any rate, after he had freed himself from "those odd effects of inhibition" which in his earlier years had supposedly prevented him from seeing the light. For as Teilhard himself tells us with reference to that transitional period of comparative orthodoxy, "I failed to understand that as God 'metamorphized' the World from the depths of matter to the peaks of Spirit, so in addition the World must inevitably and to the same degree 'endomorphize' God." And by way of further clarification, he adds: "As a direct consequence of the unitive process by which God is revealed to us, he in some way 'transforms himself' as he incorporates us."[11]

Here, in this late work (*The Heart of Matter*, 1950), it does indeed appear that Teilhard has cast off all his "inhibitions." He goes out of his way, in fact, to make his unorthodox point with the utmost clarity. "All around us, and within our own selves, God is in process of 'changing,' " he declares; "his brilliance increases, and the glow of his coloring grows richer."[12] This is no doubt what three years later he referred to as "the mutual completion of the world and God which gives life to Christianity." Not just the world, but God, too, is changing, and becoming more perfect; that is obviously the message. "I see in the World a mysterious product of completion and fulfillment for the Absolute Being himself,"[13] Teilhard tells us. Never mind that Christ Himself declares unto us: "Be ye perfect, even as your Father in heaven *is* perfect" (present tense, once again!); perhaps this Gospel teaching belongs to an earlier phase of human evolution, antedating Darwin and "the discovery of Time." In any case, we are now told dogmatically that "the Absolute Being" is not yet fully perfect, that God Himself depends upon Evolution for His "completion and fulfillment"—as if this fact alone would not suffice to render "the Absolute Being" less than absolute!

It must not be supposed, moreover, that when Teilhard seems to attribute change or transformation to God, he is in fact referring only to the human nature of Christ, or to His Mystical Body. For if that were the case, why would he speak of God and "the Absolute Being," instead of Christ, or the Pleroma? Granting that Teilhard is not much given to sharp theological distinctions, it must nonetheless be assumed that he knows very well how to distinguish between two clearly distinguishable ideas when he wants to. What is perhaps still more to the point, however, is that the conception of a mutable or "evolving" God is entirely in line with Teilhard's rejection of the traditional Christian doctrine concerning creation and participated being, and with his famous theory of "creative union" which is supposed to replace these "antiquated" ideas. Thus, when he tells us that "There is ultimately no unity without unification,"[14] the implication is clear: this can only mean that God Himself has no other unity than that which is given to Him by way of the evolutive process. And so, too, God's unity is not yet complete: He too must await "the end of the world" when all shall be fulfilled.

By this time Teilhard has manifestly repudiated the position expressed earlier in "The Mass on the World" when he wrote that "The world travails, not to bring forth from within itself some supreme reality, but to find its consummation through a union with a pre-existent Being."[15] Or are we perhaps to suppose that even in this seemingly orthodox affirmation there is a hidden implication to the effect that the pre-existent Being becomes somehow enlarged by virtue of the anticipated union? This too is conceivable; for it will be recalled that in 1919 (four years before "The Mass on the World") Teilhard had already expressed reservations relating to the traditional conception of participated being. Yet we must also remember that according to his own testimony it was only much later that he came to realize what he took to be the full truth: the idea, namely, that just as God "metamorphized" the world, "so in addition the

World must inevitably and to the same degree 'endomorphize' God." By his own admission he was prevented during his earlier years from recognizing this presumed reciprocity between God and world by virtue of a certain adhesion to the traditional outlook from which he had not yet emancipated himself.

This does not mean, of course, that Teilhard was ever fully orthodox in his theological beliefs. From the start it had been his tendency to conceive of God more or less exclusively as "the Evolver," and in a distinctly unorthodox sense at that. In an early essay ("The Modes of Divine Action in the Universe," 1920), for example, he maintains that "God's power has not so free a field for its action as we assume: on the contrary, in virtue of the very constitution of the participated being it labours to produce...it is always obliged, in the course of its creative effort, to pass through a whole series of intermediaries and to overcome a whole succession of inevitable risks—whatever may be said by the theologians, who are always ready to introduce the operation of the *'potentia absoluta divina'* (the absolute power of God)."[16] Teilhard seems to assume that the conception of God's omnipotence was the invention of overzealous theologians, forgetting that the idea is thoroughly biblical: "He spake, and it was done; he commanded, and it stood fast," declares the Psalmist (*Ps.* 32:9). Nothing, in fact, could be more strange to Christianity than the notion of a God who "labours to produce," and who "is always obliged" to take chances. One sees that even at this comparatively early stage in the unfolding of his theological ideas, Teilhard had already begun to deviate from the orthodox position. The Absolute had become relativized, one could say, and diminished in relation to the universe. It seems that from the outset Teilhard was bent upon blurring the fundamental distinction between God and world. It is not even clear any longer whether God is indeed the Creator of the universe; for we are told that "Properly speaking, God *does not make:* He *makes things make themselves*."[17] Thus, true to his evolutionist assumptions, Teilhard conceives the creative act as a temporal process in which the creature has its share. What he gives us is basically the Darwinist picture, only with the additional proviso that behind the scenes there is a God capable of exerting a certain influence. But not enough of an influence, it would seem, to interfere substantially

with the Darwinist workings of the evolutive process; for as
we have seen, Teilhard is careful to point out that "God never
acts except evolutively."[18] And this is a matter of paramount
importance in his eyes: it is a basic principle, in fact, which
"seems to me to be necessary, and all that is necessary, to mod-
ernize and give a fresh start to Christianity."[19] What is needed,
it seems, is a theology in which God has been essentially demoted
to an accessory of Evolution.

But the final "breakthrough" was yet to come. Teilhard had
long believed that God "metamorphizes" the world; but it was
only in the closing years of his life that he came to realize the
converse of this truth: namely, that the world, too, acts upon
God, that it must "inevitably and to the same degree 'endomorphize' God." At this point the Teilhardian God ceased to be
simply "the Evolver," and became at least in part a product
or resultant of the evolutive process.

*   *   *

"I see in the World a mysterious product of completion and
fulfillment for the Absolute Being himself": it is no wonder
that the Roman censors, who in 1948 examined the given man-
uscript, found this statement heretical. Yet obvious and undeniable as this may be, the point has nonetheless been disputed
by theologians of a liberal kind. Teilhard's erudite editor, for
instance, has taken it upon himself to argue (in a lengthy footnote) that the censured Jesuit was right all along; the idea that
God Himself is somehow completed by a transfigured world,
he maintains, is indeed perfectly orthodox. Even de Bérulle,
we are told, has said as much. But what exactly did this venerable author say? Here is the passage:

> God the Father, who is the fontal source of the God-
> head... produces two divine Persons in himself. And the Son,
> who is the second producing Person in the Godhead, con-
> cludes his productiveness in a single divine Person. And this
> third Person, who does not produce anything eternal and un-
> created, produces the incarnate Word. And this incarnate
> Word... produces the order of grace and of glory which
> ends... in making us Gods by anticipation... This completes
> God's communication in himself and outside himself.[20]

This is the excerpt from *Les Grandeurs de Jesus* (1623) which is supposed to legitimize Teilhard's contention to the effect that God " 'transforms himself' as he incorporates us." But it happens that this passage (which is as beautiful as it is orthodox) actually proves the very opposite. For in affirming that the Holy Spirit "does not produce anything eternal and uncreated," de Bérulle implies that the Triune God is Himself "eternal and uncreated"; and being eternal and uncreated, there can be no question of any change, transformation or evolutive increase. Inasmuch as God is eternal, He is exempt from the condition of time; and being uncreated, He is *ipso facto* exempt from any conceivable effects of "creative union." The "production," therefore, to which de Bérulle alludes, beginning with the Incarnation, refers to "the order of grace and of glory." Here, and here alone, time enters the picture: there is an evolution, if you will; something is being transformed and perfected. Yet what is undergoing these transformations, what suffers change, is not God, but the creation: it is *we* who must grow, it is *we* who must be made perfect, "even as your Father in heaven *is* perfect." And that, too, is the reason why de Bérulle distinguishes between the communication of God "in himself and outside of himself." The order of grace and glory, for all its splendor, is yet to be counted as something "outside" of God. Christianity insists upon this point: even in the beatified state the boundary between the creature and God is not obliterated. There is a marvelous union which defies imagining, but not an identity. And it is this seemingly fine distinction that differentiates Christian orthodoxy from pantheism in any of its forms. This is all very basic; and surely both Teilhard and his zealous editor should have understood and acknowledged what the Church has always affirmed.

The fact is that from a theological point of view Teilhard has not a leg to stand on; and for this reason alone it was expedient that he present his theological speculations in a scientific garb. In fact, the credentials of Science were needed on two counts: first, to disqualify the old theology, and secondly to validate the new. The choice, as Teilhard repeatedly suggests, is between a pre-scientific theology which is no longer tenable, and a new outlook consonant with the latest discoveries. Like Freud, Jung, and other influential figures of our time, Teilhard makes it a point to present himself as an empiricist, a man of science. It is clear that he does not wish to be perceived as a theologian in the established sense. The image he projects is that of a pioneer. Unmistakably he presents himself as the inaugurator of a brand new theology—a scientific theology, no less, which is no longer bound by the old rules or subject to censure on the strength of traditional norms. "Before all creation, proclaims the Scholastic, the Absolute existed in its fullness," he declares; the point being that his own doctrine is fundamentally different: "For us who are simply trying to construct a sort of ultra-physics, by combining the sum of our experiments in the most harmonious way, the answer to the problem is not so positive. From the empirical point of view there is no pure act but only a final term to which the serial bundle that envelops us is converging."[21]

Yet the fact remains that Teilhard does ceaselessly theologize— for the simple reason that he speaks of God. And in so doing, he clearly departs from "the empirical point of view" to which he pretends to confine himself, for nothing could be more obvious than that the idea of God is *not* an empirical notion. It is out of the question, therefore, that Teilhard's quasi-theological speculations could be validated on empirical grounds.

Let us add that Teilhard is right, of course, when he claims that "from an empirical point of view there is no pure act" (only it would have been more accurate to say that the question has no empirical sense in the first place). But not only is there no pure act: it happens that "from an empirical point of view" there is also no such thing as "a final term to which the serial bundle that envelops us is converging." For indeed there is actually not the slightest empirical evidence in support of Teilhard's Omega hypothesis. From the start the celebrated Omega Point was nothing more than a quasi-theological notion, masquerading in scientific dress. Teilhard has been less than candid with his readers in that regard, as even his friend George Simpson has pointed out. He misleads us when he speaks of "combining the sum of our experiments"—as if by some scientific calculation, too formidable for laymen (and theologians) to grasp, the expert "ultra-physicist" could infer the existence and properties of the stipulated Omega Point! Is it a case of conscious deception, then? Or can one suppose that these baseless claims have been put forward in good faith by an individual incapable of distinguishing between scientific fact and poetic flights (which would come down to Medawar's point that "before deceiving others he has taken great pains to deceive himself"[22])?

This is always the unanswerable question. What is clear, on the other hand, is that the postulated Omega Point had been earmarked from the start to serve as the god-term of Teilhard's speculative system. From the beginning Teilhard had invested that imagined entity with a plethora of quasi-divine attributes, thinly disguised in a scientific-sounding terminology. Knowingly or unknowingly, as the case may be, he fabricated a kind of scientific fantasy which came more and more to bear the imagined features of "the cosmic Christ." The great task, now, was to build a full-fledged theology around this purportedly scientific Omega.

But of couse this could not be done without violence to the orthodox position. It was therefore necessary first of all to undermine the authority of the theological tradition; and here, too, as we have noted before, the credentials of Science come into play. And again spuriously: for there *are* no empirical grounds on which to dispute theological propositions. Hence too there can be no actual argument: it is all a matter of suggestion, of innuendo. We are told, for example, that so long as men believed in "a static world" it was possible to think of the Creator as "structurally independent of his work"; but today, on the other hand, in an evolutive universe, "God is not conceivable (either structurally or dynamically) except insofar as he coincides with (as a sort of 'formal' cause), but without being lost in, the center of convergence of cosmogenesis."[23] One is hard pressed, of course, to comprehend what exactly it could mean to say that God coincides with Omega "without being lost" therein: one would think that if two terms coincide there is an end of the matter. But be that as it may, we are told in effect that the old theology is somehow tied to a static conception of the universe and needs therefore to be abandoned, now that we have discovered that things are actually in a state of evolutive flux. This is the suggestion, the innuendo. But let us recall, in the first place, that the idea of universal flux was obviously familiar, not only to Heraclitus, but to many of the Greek and Latin Fathers who nonetheless staunchly believed in a "structurally independent" God. There is not even the slightest logical conflict, moreover, between the idea of a transcendent, eternal, and immutable God, and a world that is in a state of perpetual flux, or if you will, of evolutive progression. Thus, no matter how irrefutable and scientific these presumed insights into the nature of the universe might be, Teilhard's implicit claim to the effect that they rule somehow against the tenets of orthodox theology is patently false. Once again we are being misled.

★   ★   ★

As Teilhard himself admits, his doctrine is pantheistic.[24] Indeed, the die was cast the moment he rejected the Judeo-Christian idea of creation, with its implied conception of participated being; and Teilhard knows it. "Since God cannot be conceived except as monopolizing in himself the totality of being," he tells us, "then either the world is no more than an appearance—or else it is in itself a part, an aspect, or a phase of God."[25] The alternative is logically indisputable, despite the fact that "appearance" could of course mean many things: the Hindu *maya*, for instance, as popularly conceived. From a Christian perspective, on the other hand, the world is not simply an "illusion," or a kind of "cosmic dream"; it is rather "a lower or secondary form of being gratuitously drawn from 'non-being' by a special act of transcendent causality," as Teilhard has rightly pointed out. And this in fact amounts precisely to the notion of "participated being" which (as we have seen in Chapter 4) he castigates and categorically rejects. Now the logical consequence of this step is clear: by the aforementioned alternative it implies that the world has become "a part, an aspect, or a phase of God." Thus, in Teilhard's eyes, God has become "the Whole."

To be sure, this is a rather popular and enticing conception nowadays: Teilhard may be right when he speaks of a mounting "passion for the Whole."[26] What is more, the idea has of late received considerable support from scientific quarters. One must remember that after more than two centuries of unmitigated Newtonian materialism science has at last discovered that "The whole is more than the sum of its parts"—which is indeed a giant step forward. An entirely new Weltanschauung has emerged. As David Bohm has put it:

> One is led to a new notion of unbroken wholeness which denies the classical idea of analyzability of the world into separately and independently existing parts. . .Rather, we say that inseparable quantum interconnectedness of the whole universe is the fundamental reality, and that relatively independently behaving parts are merely particular and contingent forms within this whole.[27]

And from here it is but a small step to a holistic pantheism. Having come to realize that there is an "organic whole" which cannot be conceived simply as an aggregate of particles, and that in the final analysis it could even be said that there *are* no particles, what could be more natural for individuals of a scientistic bent than to jump to the conclusion that the biggest conceivable "Whole" could be none other than God?

But the fact remains that the stipulated identification is incompatible with the Christian position. Nor, for that matter, is it concordant with the traditional tenets of the East— notwithstanding all that Fritjof Capra has said on that score.[28] For whatever differences of metaphysical outlook there may exist between Christianity and the Oriental doctrines, both agree nonetheless that God is infinitely more than the universe, no matter how holistically the latter might be conceived.

There is a sense, of course, in which one can legitimately speak of Deity as "the Whole"; God is indeed "the Whole" insofar as He is conceived "as monopolizing in himself the totality of being," to put it in Teilhard's phrase. But He becomes the "cosmic whole" only on condition that one has rejected (or failed to grasp) the crucial distinction between absolute and contingent being. And this is decidedly unorthodox: for in one way or another this distinction has been sharply drawn within every major traditional school, be it in the East or in the West.

This fact is perhaps more easily discernible in the case of Christianity; yet even in the Oriental traditions it is clearly in evidence. One needs but to recall, for instance, the celebrated Upanishadic verse which can be rendered as follows: "That is full, this is full; from that fullness, this fullness is derived; taking fullness from fullness, fullness alone remains." Here is an

explicit distinction between the two "pleromas": the divine and
the cosmic. There is God, the divine "fullness," we are told;
and there is that second "fullness," which can be none other
than the holistic universe, that "unbroken wholeness" to which
modern science has begun to awake. But the two must not
be confounded; and though in some mysterious and perhaps
ultimately inscrutable manner the second is said to have sprung
from the first, the Upanishad (and all theology) affirms that
"fullness alone remains."

This time-honored distinction between the divine and the
cosmic plenum is also guaranteed by another fundamental conception which Christianity likewise holds in common with the
Oriental traditions: the idea, namely, that God is the Architect
or Lawgiver of the universe.[29] For this notion entails that the
cosmos, in all its "fullness," is still a bounded thing, a finite
entity. God Himself has "measured" it, and in so doing has
fixed the very bounds by virtue of which it exists; He has "set
His compass upon the face of the deep," as we read in the
Book of Proverbs.[30] On the other hand, there is no one to
"measure" God: in sharp contrast to the cosmos, God Himself
is absolutely unbounded. He is thus "infinite" in the strict sense
of that term. And this, too, is no doubt the reason why God
is not in the least "diminished" through the creative act: it is
the reason why "fullness alone remains."

Such is the perennial doctrine; and it is of great interest to
note that recent findings of a scientific nature have (quite unex-
pectedly) begun to point very much in the same direction. The
first major step in that regard was the startling recognition that
the cosmos at large is indeed bounded in all of its dimensions:
it has turned out to be finite in its spatial magnitude, in its
duration, and in the total amount of energy which it contains.
We are told, in particular, that our universe came into existence
some twenty billion years ago—a fact which has been acutely
embarrassing to the atheists. But that is not all. For as we have
noted earlier (in connection with the so-called anthropic principle), it happens that the fundamental physical constants which
control every phase and every aspect of the cosmic process have
been "fine tuned," as it were, to the very values which they
must have if the cosmos is to admit life and the phenomenon
of man. But if this circumstance is not simply an "accident"

(whatever that might mean), it does surely suggest the perennial notion of a divine Lawgiver—"higher and other than the
world-tree, time and forms"[31] as the *Svetasvatara Upanishad*
proclaims.

Yet Teilhard, as we have seen, stands on the other side of
the issue. Oblivious of the aforementioned findings (which admittedly had not yet fully come to light), and in defiance not
only of Christian tradition, but of the perennial metaphysical
wisdom of mankind, he has opted in favor of holistic pantheism. And he goes so far as to claim that "Ultimately, our thought
cannot grasp anything but the Whole, nor, when it really comes
to the point, can our dreams entertain anything but the Whole."[32]
Moreover, if there be any doubt as to which "whole" or "fullness" Teilhard is alluding to, the following passage will make
this abundantly clear:

> Thus, from the patient, prosaic, but cumulative work of scien-
> tists of all types, there has spontaneously emerged the most
> impressive revelation of the Whole that could possibly be
> conceived. What the ancient poets, philosophers and mystics
> had glimpsed or discovered (primarily by intuition), what
> modern philosophy demands, more rigorously, in the order
> of metaphysics, science of today has brought within our
> grasp. . .[33]

Only it needs to be said that this is actually *not* what the wise
men of old "had glimpsed or discovered"—not, at any rate, so
long as one pays these "poets, philosophers and mystics" the
courtesy of taking them at their word. For it is clear that the
cosmic plenum—that "unbroken wholeness" to which David
Bohm alludes—is by no means "higher and other than the
world-tree, time and forms": after all, that cosmic plenum *is*
"the world-tree," or at least an aspect thereof. It is just that
Teilhard, along with so many contemporary popularizers of ancient metaphysical lore, has failed to distinguish between "this
fullness" and that other, to put it thus.

To be sure, God "monopolizes in himself the totality of being";
and this is precisely the import of the biblical *ego sum qui sum*.[34]
But that "being" is absolute: it is "pure being," one could also
say, Being that is not subject to any conditions or bounds. It
is also true that such Being cannot be grasped: it eludes us by

the very fact of being unconditioned. And this, too, has been recognized by the wise. "What, then, can I do?" exclaimed St. Augustine. "What that existence is, let Him tell, let Him declare it within; let the inner man hear, the mind apprehend that true existence. . ."[35] And Meister Eckhart observes: "I have no doubt of this, that if the soul had the remotest notion of what Being means, she would never waver from it for an instant."[36]

God, then, is not the cosmic whole; He is indeed "higher and other than the world-tree. . ." We must not forget that the cosmic whole, however vast it may be, is nonetheless conditioned; if it were not, it would not in any sense be "cosmic," nor would science have anything to say about it. And therefore, contrary to Teilhard's ontological surmise, the cosmos as a whole, no less than its parts, remains "a lower or secondary mode of being."

★   ★   ★

As we have noted earlier, Teilhard's postulated Omega had been earmarked from the start to serve as the god-term of his system. Not that God reveals Himself to us through that (real or imagined) Center—a notion which of course would be perfectly orthodox; after all, the cosmos is a theophany, as St. Paul has said. What Teilhard is driving at, rather, is something more: in an evolutive universe, let us recall, "God is not conceivable (either structurally or dynamically) except insofar as he coincides with. . .the center of convergence of cosmogenesis." Teilhard is adamant on the point: "In future only a God who is functionally and totally 'Omega' can satisfy us."[37] This identification, presumably, is what it takes to transform "the Father-God of two thousand years ago" into an up-to-date "cosmogenesis-God."[38]

In Teilhard's system God has become "totally Omega" by an act of definition: "God can only be defined as a *Center of centers*,"[39] we are told.

But why? Why should all other conceptions of Deity be ruled out? After all, our forefathers conceived of God in so many ways! As we learn from Dionysius, they thought of Him as Being, Life and Intelligence; as Wisdom, Reason and Truth; as Power, the Great and the Small; as Peace and as Holiness. There

is in fact no end to His "divine names." But one needs also
to realize that God is beyond every name and conception, "that
while He possesses all the positive attributes of the universe
(being their universal Cause), yet in a stricter sense He does
not possess them, since He transcends them all. . ."[40]

The truth, strictly speaking, is that God cannot be "defined":
for to define is to limit, to set bounds; but who can "measure"
God? How can the Infinite be circumscribed? And that is why
"those who cling to the objects of human thought"[41] delude
themselves when they theologize, and why only "the poor in
spirit" can enter into the Presence of God.

But Teilhard insists not only that God can be defined, but
that this can only be done in one way: "God can only be defined as a *Center of centers*." And he goes on to say that "in
this complexity lies the perfection of His unity."[42] Teilhard's
ever-helpful editor, moreover, fearing perhaps that the reader
might find this hard to grasp, has supplied the following eluci-
dation: "The more God *is,* the more power He has to center
and perfectly personalize. Consequently unchangingness belongs
no less to the richness of an infinite complexity supremely unified than to an essential simplicity." Spoken like a true disciple!
"The more God *is*": the very phrase takes one's breath away.
But then, once God has been *defined* as "a Center of centers"
He has evidently ceased to be absolute and transcendent, and
has become in effect tied to the cosmos. After all, a center
(whether of centers or of anything else) cannot be conceived
apart from the system whose center it is.

Such a "cosmogenesis-God," to be sure, can no longer be
immutable. As a Center of centers He too is subject to change,
He too must "evolve"; and such "unchangingness" as is said
to belong to "the richness of an infinite complexity supremely
unified" could only come about at the end—as the culmination
of the entire cosmogenetic process.

At the same time, however, Teilhard cautions us that "We
must be careful to note that under this evolutive facet Omega
still only reveals *half of itself.*"[43] And he goes on to explain:

> While being the last term of its series, it is also *outside all
> series.* Not only does it crown, but it closes. Otherwise the
> sum would fall short of itself, in organic contradiction with
> the whole operation. When, going beyond the elements, we

come to speak of the conscious Pole of the world, it is not enough to say that it *emerges* from the rise of consciousness: we must add that from this genesis it has already *emerged;* without which it could neither subjugate into love nor fix in incorruptibility. If by its very nature it did not escape from the time and space which it gathers together, it would not be Omega.[44]

But what does this actually mean? If "the other half" of Omega "has already emerged from this genesis," this would seem to imply that it, too, has evolved. All of Omega, then, would be a product of cosmogenesis. But perhaps Teilhard means to imply that there is a transcendent kernel, as it were, something which has existed from the start and presumably constitutes the very heart of Omega. Is that perhaps the entity which "by its very nature" escapes from time and space? But then in what sense could this term (which is supposed to be "outside all series") be said to have "already emerged from this genesis"? Surely the phrase "already emerged" implies a preceding "immersion"; and this would seem to rule out the idea that "the other half" of Omega could "by its very nature" escape from time and space.

The problem is that Teilhard wants God to be both the Evolver and that which ultimately evolves; and he is obviously finding it hard to formulate this questionable idea in a clear and logically consistent way. He wants Omega to be ever-present ("outside all series"), and he also wants this same Omega to be the term of evolution ("the last term of its series"). And he apparently essays to accomplish this by partitioning Omega; what is supposed to be the supreme unity has been somehow split in half. And not until the end of time, presumably, when the cosmogenetic process of creative union will have reached its term, can Omega be absolutely one; only then will the two "halves" come together, as it were; only then will God Himself be whole!

"The more God *is*...": it now appears that the Christ who "was before Abraham" must correspond to a lesser degree of being. The biblical "I Am" turns out to be misleading: God should rather have said "I Shall Be." And would it not also have been more accurate if Christ had said: "I and my Father *shall be* one"?

We are beginning to see that the new theology is quite unlike the old: the transition from "the Father-God of two thousand years ago" (the God of biblical Revelation, that is) to a "cosmogenesis-God" is more radical than one might think. It is a big step from "the living God of Abraham" to a God defined as a "Center of centers," a God who is "functionally and totally 'Omega'."

*   *   *

The new theology revolves around the Incarnate Christ. But of course the figure of Christ, too, has undergone a change: it has been transformed into a kind of cosmic Christ, clothed with the body of the universe. And most importantly, it has become an evolving Christ, a Christ who is strangely dependent upon the cosmogenetic process. As Teilhard tells us dramatically (in an essay completed just a month before his death):

> It is Christ, in very truth, who saves,
> —but should we not immediately add that at the same time
> it is Christ who is saved by
> Evolution?[45]

One wonders, moreover, how this cosmogenetic Christ is related to God the Father—or are we naive even to ask? Has not "the Father-God of two thousand years ago" been given up? It is hard to tell just how much of Christian theology we are still permitted to presuppose. Is there actually anything left of *ad intra* theology: of the Trinitarian doctrine?

Teilhard himself has little to say on this crucial issue. Rarely does he touch upon the subject, and only in passing, as it were; but when he does consider it, he is at pains to look at even this question from an evolutive point of view. We are told, for example, that the trinitarian nature of God "is manifestly the essential condition of God's inherent capacity to be the personal (and, in spite of the Incarnation, the transcendent) summit of a universe which is in process of personalization."[46] We are not told, however, why it is necessary to postulate the existence of *three* transcendent Persons in order to account for the production of a single "personal summit of the universe." But be that as it may, the statement is no doubt reassuring to many souls. It is one of those occasional nuggets of near-orthodoxy which someone like Henri de Lubac might well hold up as proof of theological rectitude. Yet the matter is not really quite so simple. Teilhard has made other statements, too, which bear upon the issue. Consider, for example, the following passage which is central to his argument in *The Phenomenon of Man:* "If the world is convergent and if Christ occupies its center, then the Christogenesis of St. Paul and St. John is nothing else and nothing less than the extension, both awaited and unhoped for, of that noogenesis in which cosmogenesis—as regards our experience—culminates."[47] Now in the first place it must be recalled that there is not just one "Christogenesis of St. Paul and St. John," but actually two: there is the eternal procession of the Son, the Word that was "in the beginning"; and there is the human birth of Christ, when "That which was from the beginning" (*1 John* 1:1) "became flesh, and dwelt among us" (*John* 1:14). Which "Christogenesis," then, is Teilhard referring to? It obviously could not be the eternal procession of the Logos: only a "cosmic Christogenesis" could conceivably be envisioned as an "extension" of the natural evolutive process. But then, what about the *ad intra* Logos doctrine: does Teilhard accept the idea of the eternally-begotten Word? One has ample reason to believe that he does not; and as a matter of fact, Teilhard himself implies as much in a passage which it behooves us to consider well:

> In the first century of the Church, Christianity made its definitive entry into human thought by boldly identifying the Christ of the gospel with the Alexandrian Logos. The logical continuation of the same tactics and the prelude to the same success must be found in the instinct which is now urging the faithful, after two thousand years, to return to the same policy; but this time it must not be with the ordinating principle of the stable Greek kosmos but with the neo-Logos of modern philosophy the evolutive principle of a universe in movement.[48]

Now it was of course St. John, the Beloved Disciple, who identified Christ with the Logos; and one is struck by the fact that Teilhard evidently conceives of this momentous step as a kind of philosophical conjecture. The adjective "Alexandrian" is there to emphasize the local and time-bound nature of this Johannine teaching, which was supposedly tied to the now-antiquated conception of "the stable Greek kosmos." The obvious implication is that St. John was attempting (as best he could) to adapt the religious ideas of nascent Christianity to a rather primitive and pre-scientific Weltanschauung. And now that we have at last discovered the true contours of the universe, we are not only entitled but obligated to employ "the same tactics" in order to achieve a better and perhaps definitive formulation of the Christian truth. The message is clear: Teilhard himself is the new Apostle who has now overruled St. John by identifying Christ with "the neo-Logos of modern philosophy—the evolutive principle of a universe in movement."

We are not concerned at the moment with the blatant impiety and indeed impertinence of this arrogation. What alone concerns us at this point is the fact that Teilhard has evidently rejected the New Testament Logos doctrine. And at the same time, of course, he has implicitly rejected the traditional Christian concept of Revelation—which now leaves him virtually free to do as he will.

★   ★   ★

What interests Teilhard almost exclusively is the Incarnate Christ, the Christ who has supposedly become coincident with Omega: "It was in order that he might become Omega that it was necessary for him, through the travail of his Incarnation, to conquer and animate the universe."[49] It is hardly clear, of course, what it could possibly mean to speak of an Incarnation now that Christ has been identified with "the neo-Logos of modern philosophy." Just when and where, one wonders, did this "neo-Logos" take birth? Considering the utter incongruity of such a postulated event, one is not surprised to learn that "like the Creation (of which it is the visible aspect) the Incarnation is an act co-extensive with the duration of the world."[50]

It does not seem to bother Teilhard (or his numerous followers) that this is not at all what Scripture has taught, and what Christendom has believed for some two thousand years. He seems to take it for granted that his credentials as a "scientist" give him *carte blanche* to "readjust the fundamental lines of our Christology,"[51] to put it in his own words.

But let us go on: what is it that Teilhard is telling us? Are we to believe, perhaps, that Christ descended into the world at the beginning of time to clothe Himself in its particles, its plasmas, or its primordial slime? Teilhard does not openly commit himself on this point. The idea of a "descent" is obviously not to his liking; and yet, if there is no pre-existence—no "descent," therefore—how can one speak of an Incarnation at all? At times Teilhard does seem to succumb to this logical demand; for example, when he tells us that "the Redeemer could penetrate the stuff of the cosmos, could pour himself into the life-blood of the universe, only by first dissolving himself in matter, later to be reborn from it."[52] Yet elsewhere he seems to rule out the pre-existence of Christ: "if God wished to have Christ," he tells us, "to launch a complete universe and scatter life with a lavish hand was no more than he was obliged to do."[53] The implication is clear: there was no pre-existence, no Christ "before ever the world began." It was not within God's power "to have Christ" without first "launching" a universe. So, too, we read in *Mon Univers:* "God did not will individually (nor could he have constructed as though they were separate bits), the sun, the earth, plants, or Man. He willed his Christ;—and in order to have his Christ, he had to create the spiritual world, and man in particular, upon which Christ might germinate."[54] Here again the implication is that God did not and could not "have his Christ" prior to the cosmogenetic process—which is of course a far cry from what Teilhard had told us earlier, when he spoke of Christ as "first dissolving himself in matter, later to be reborn from it." But be that as it may, where there is no pre-existence—no Christ who could truthfully say "before Abraham was, I am"—there can be no Incarnation either: the very idea demands a supra-cosmic antecedent.

But then it is always possible to use the old word for a new idea. By a certain abuse of language, one can speak of the Incarnation as "the visible aspect" of Creation (evolutively conceived): only it happens that this, too, does not make any sense. For if the Incarnation is indeed "co-extensive with the duration of the world," then by this very token it is no more and no less "visible" than the cosmogenetic process as such. Under these auspices the Incarnation has become indistinguishable from cosmogenesis, in the Teilhardian sense of that term. Rhetoric aside, what Teilhard has done is to get rid of the idea: he has "universalized" the concept right out of existence. In his system, the Incarnation has become simply cosmogenesis: it has become the birth of galaxies, of stars and planets and protein molecules. As one might have predicted, the concept has been swallowed up by what is actually (as von Balthasar has pointed out) "the only category of thought" in Teilhard's intellectual arsenal: the problematic idea of universal evolution.

For Teilhard it is an unquestionable truth that "Nothing can enter into the universe that does not emerge from it"[55] —which seems to rule out the possibility that anything can enter in the first place. Not even Christ: "For Christ to make his way into the world by any side-road would be incomprehensible," we are told. Yes, it *is* incomprehensible to a thoroughgoing evolutionist, simply because such an individual denies that there is anything above or beyond the universe. To those who believe in the reality of an absolutely transcendent God, on the other hand, the idea is not incomprehensible in the least. And in fact, this is just what Scripture declares, and what Christians have always believed: Christ did "make His way into the world"— not, indeed, by a "side-road," but by a mysterious eschatological path which He was again to retrace at the Ascension, when He returned to His super-celestial Abode, clothed in the transfigured flesh of His humanity. It is a path which can be discerned by men of spiritual sight (*John* 1:51), but only up to a certain point, beyond which the Way is obscured to human vision as if by a cloud (*Matt.* 24:30, 26:64; *Rev.* 1:7). There is a mysterious "opening" that leads out of this world (as we have said before), a "narrow gate" through which it is hard to pass. And indeed, only He who descended by this Way is able to pass through and enter into the supra-cosmic realm that lies beyond this Gate (*John* 3:13). The true Way, therefore, and the veritable Gate, is Christ: "I am the way," Christ said; and again, "I am the door." (*John* 14:6, 10:9).

But for Teilhard "Nothing can enter into the universe that does not emerge from it"; there is no path—no "side-road," as he says somewhat contemptuously with reference to this time-honored and scriptural idea—there is no Way and no Gate that leads into or out of this universe. And so, what he misleadingly calls "the Incarnation" can be nothing more than an "ascent from plurality" which is co-extensive with the entire history of the universe. "That is why the Incarnation of the Word was infinitely painful and mortifying," he tells us, "so much so that it can be symbolized by a cross."[56]

       ★   ★   ★

Even though "creation, incarnation and redemption are not facts which can be *localized* at a given point of time and space,"[57] Teilhard assures us that "it is nevertheless true that all three can take the form of particular *expressive* facts. . .These historical facts, however, are only a specially heightened expression of a process which is 'cosmic' in dimensions."[58] Thus, in Teilhard's eyes, the birth of the Redeemer is but "a specially heightened expression" of a universal cosmic process that is going on throughout the universe. But in that case one might well ask what it is that distinguishes the "historical" Christ? If it be true that Jesus of Nazareth came into existence by the same evolutionary path which (according to the Darwinists) has been traversed by us all, why should he be unlike other men? Why should he have been singled out, as it were, "to become Omega"? Are we to suppose, perhaps, that he was accidentally endowed with a bigger brain?

Be that as it may, Teilhard seems in any case to concur with the judgment of Christianity that by His Resurrection the Incarnate Christ became *kyrios,* Lord of the world: "It marks Christ's effective assumption of his function as the universal center,"[59] Teilhard affirms. One wonders, of course, what "Resurrection" could mean to an evolutionist, and for that matter, how (under such auspices) it can be imagined that a deceased person could become a universal center. And as one might surmise, these are questions which do not seem to interest Teilhard particularly, and on which he does not care to shed much light. When it comes to such matters it would appear that he is perfectly content to invoke the authority of Christian tradition as a sufficient guarantee that his assertions are true. In Teilhard's eyes, apparently, Catholic tradition is something to be used when it serves one's purpose, and cast aside when it does not.

The Resurrection, then, is a fact: "It marks Christ's effective assumption of his function as the universal center." Now this statement (rightly understood) is of course entirely orthodox. But the next sentence, already, is not: "Until that time," Teilhard goes on to say, "he was present in all things as a soul that is painfully gathering together its embryonic elements." Not at all: "until that time" Christ was indeed present in all things, but not "as a soul that is painfully gathering together its embryonic elements" (whatever this less-than-felicitous expression might mean). As the Logos, the eternal Word of God, Christ has always been "present in all things," that is to say, immanent in the universe; this is not something that has come to pass at a particular moment of cosmic history. The immanence of God is a metaphysical fact which does not coincide with the Incarnation. Nor does it have anything to do with a pre-human "soul," or with a painful "gathering together of embryonic elements." What Christianity teaches is that Christ assumed a soul when He assumed a body: and this happened when Mary conceived—and not a moment before! And so, too, the Word became—not a plasma, or a fish, or a reptile—but a man. And this alone, let us observe, implies that the Incarnation is *not* "co-extensive with the duration of the world"; for no one, least of all a Darwinist, would maintain that men have existed ever since the world began.

Teilhard conceives of Christ as "the leading shoot" of the evolutive tree, the central shoot whose roots extend back "into the furthest limits of the past,"[60] the lowest state from whence all things, according to the evolutionist dogma, must take their start. We are to think of Him as having concentrated within Himself the primordial sap of the universe, the very sap which also flows in our veins. He has gathered together in His own consciousness "the whole mass of passions, of anticipations, of fears, of sufferings, of happiness, of which each man represents one drop."[61] Now this vision (which is not without its strong poetic and mystical appeal) is correct so far as it goes. According to orthodox Christian doctrine, Christ does recapitulate within Himself "the hopes and fears of all the world." In a sense He contains each and every one of us within His ample soul, in that Sacred Heart which burns in boundless love. And it is also true that His human roots, so to speak, extend backwards to the very beginning of our race. But we must not forget that Christ has a "double parentage": He is both the Son of God and the Son of Man. As Son of Man—or on His mother's side, as one might say—His ancestry traces back into the distant past, and conceivably (if the transformists are right) to the very birth of the universe. And yet His true stature cannot be measured in these terms; the crucial fact which distinguishes the Incarnate Christ from all other men is that "I and my Father are one." (*John* 10:30). This is what Christianity has always taught, and it is precisely this confession that makes us Christian in the order of faith.

But then, how can this central theological fact be understood in evolutionist terms? One must not expect too much. The "God of Evolution" can only be a truncated God: one arrives at the new theology by way of certain deletions, beginning with the absolute transcendence and infinity of God. It has always been recognized that God is in a sense the universal goal, the universal point of attraction upon which the creation is centered, and to which it tends as to its final term. But no one prior to Teilhard de Chardin had ever imagined that this single recognition could serve as a sufficient basis upon which to erect an entire theology: no one had thought that God could actually be *defined* as a "Center of centers."

★   ★   ★

Along with the absolute transcendence of God Teilhard has lost the idea of divine immanence. Necessarily so; for as C. E. Rolt has astutely observed (in his commentary on Dionysius), "The Godhead's Transcendence and Immanence are ultimately the same fact."[61] But there is no room for this profound metaphysical fact in Teilhard's evolutionist scheme. Where God has been defined as a Center of centers or conceived as a holistic totality of cosmic existence there can be no transcendence (even though on occasion Teilhard still avails himself of this term); and so, too, there can be no divine immanence, in the authentic metaphysical sense. What has happened is that transcendence has disappeared while immanence has become confounded with Incarnation.

Teilhard thinks that God cannot be immanent in the universe

without becoming incarnated. He goes so far as to say that "to create is for God to unite himself to his work, that is to say in one way or another to involve himself in the world by incarnation."[62] This, presumably, is what it means for God to become "endomorphized" or "Christified." And this is supposedly an ongoing process: God is becoming progressively more "united to his work," more immanent and incarnate in the universe.

What Christianity teaches, on the other hand, is that from the start God has been fully immanent in creation. Symbolically speaking, the cosmos has never been without its fixed Center, its "point of contact" with God. And since the beginning of time Christ, the eternal Logos, has presided over the universe, which was created *in Him, through Him,* and *unto Him,* as St. Paul has said.[63] But we must also bear in mind that there has been a certain falling away from that primordial center and dominion: there has been a Rebellion and a Fall, as we learn from Scripture. The original harmony and coherence of creation have become compromised. Not that the primordial Center has disappeared: it is there exactly as before. Only *we* have exited, as it were. In the symbolic language of the Old Testament, mankind has departed from the Garden of Eden, and from the Tree of Life which stands in its midst.

Meanwhile the cosmic Center remains within all things. But though the Center is "within," the creature is "without"; and that is where the entire problem of existence lies. It is this externality that makes room for "distance"; and what is the Fall but an estrangement from God? God is ever present, to be sure; but the problem is that we are far away. "Thou art within, but I was without," laments St. Augustine.

In terms of this perennial symbolism we can now begin to understand what Christ has accomplished by His Incarnation. One could perhaps put it this way: the Center has swelled, as it were, and has entered the cosmos. It has begun to take possession of the world. We have strayed from the Center, and the Center is now pursuing us to the ends of the earth. And this expansion, this growth, began when a Virgin conceived and bore a Child: "and they shall call his name Emmanuel," *God with us* (*Matt.* 1:23).

God had always been *within,* as we have said; but He had

not been "with us." This is the miracle of Bethlehem: "The Word became flesh and dwelt among us." Not that the Word came to dwell within the flesh as in a tabernacle; for indeed, as the universal Center Christ had always been present within all things. No, the Word did not simply *enter* flesh: it *became* flesh, as St. John declares. That is the Mystery. And that is why the body of the Incarnate Christ is unlike any other body, and why His actions, too, have a universal significance and an unlimited efficacy. What distinguishes the man Jesus from all other men is that Jesus is God: He is both man and God, to be precise.

This (as we have indicated before) is the crucial point of which we must never lose sight: everything hinges upon this one supreme Christological fact. It is the reason why certain events which, historically speaking, took place two thousand years ago, have transformed the world, and why, as Mersch has well said, "In their supreme efficacy they continue to be the principle that acts in all human events."[64] By His divinity Christ has always been the Center of the universe; but by His Incarnation He became the Head of a transfigured humanity. One should not forget, however, that "If the Saviour is Head through His humanity and in His humanity, He is such only by reason of His divinity."[65]

The Word "became flesh." Let it be said, however, that Christianity does not envisage this act as an evolutive process, but as a gratuitous intervention on the part of God. It is Christ who of His own free will took up human flesh, as it were, in order to breathe His Spirit into that flesh and transfigure it. And historically speaking, this redemptive and deifying Act was accomplished in stages, beginning with the Annunciation, and ending with the Ascension of the Risen Lord. Christianity perceives this entire sequence as a radical break in the natural course of events; it marks a new beginning, the advent of a new creation.

It is true that St. Paul envisions the Risen Christ as the Center of creation, as Teilhard has often reminded us. But not in the sense that a new Center has been formed, or that a hitherto vacant Apex has been occupied. Not at all: by His Ascension the Risen Lord has assumed in His human or theandric form a position and a prerogative that He had always held by virtue of His divinity. And for this reason, too, there can be no dispute as to "which Christ" St. Paul is referring to when he declares that "In Him all things consist" (*Col.* 1:17): whether this refers to the eternal Word or to the Risen Lord. One could say that it refers to both, for the two have now become forever joined. "It is clear," as Mersch observes, "that according to the Apostle, Christ's primacy as Head is the continuation of His primacy as Word, and that these two prerogatives of excellence mutually explain each other."[66]

Let us also point out that the entire cycle of "sacred history" ending with the Ascension of Christ does not entail the slightest change or transformation in the nature of God. The world does not "endomorphize" God, as Teilhard imagines. In His divine nature Christ has suffered no change: neither increase nor diminution. All the changes that have taken place pertain solely to His *human* nature. And let us be careful to add that from the moment of the Resurrection that human nature, too, has passed beyond all change. It has accomplished the Passover. As the Church teaches in her symbolic formula, "He is seated at the right hand of God the Father Almighty"—an image which surely conveys a sense of stasis, of invulnerability to change.

What has been transformed, and has ultimately passed beyond the possibility of further change, is the human nature of Christ, which has become eternally united to God. And that, of course, is the true purpose of the Incarnation: *God became man in order that man might become God*, to repeat the great patristic formula. *In Christo* all men can "become God." But we must be careful to understand this in the sense in which it is meant: both halves of the formula are elliptical. Thus, in the first place, God did not "become man" in the sense of suffering a transformation, as we have said before. His "taking flesh" is an act of giving, an act of bestowing Himself upon a lesser nature without suffering the slightest diminution, let alone "increase." And so, too, "becoming God" does not mean that man shall give up one nature and assume another, but that he shall become the recipient, through grace, of what the Bible has termed "the glory" of God. What Christianity proclaims is an eternal participation in the Life of God—but not an identity.

*   *   *

Despite all that is implied by the ideas of Immanence and Incarnation, the God of Christianity remains the Transcendent, the Incomprehensible, the Absolute which brooks no familiarity. Nothing can bridge or narrow this gap; and the nearer man draws to God, in fact, the more acutely he becomes aware of Him as the One who forever surpasses his reach.

By the same token, moreover, it can also be said that the faith of a Christian is not founded upon any calculation: it is worlds removed from a "philosophical" conviction. The Christian does not believe in God because he has become persuaded that the universe has an Omega Point, or that there must be Someone to drive evolution to its ultimate end. Presumably he does not hold any such convictions at all; and if perchance he did, he would recognize them to be woefully inadequate as a foundation for his religious beliefs. Faith is a divine gift which man can only receive through an act of humility: we need what the Gospel terms "poverty of spirit." It might not be too much to say that we come to believe in the God of Christianity in the degree to which we have ceased to believe in anything else. God cannot be simply one certainty among many—He must ultimately be *the only certainty.*

But this is obviously not the characteristic attitude of Teilhard de Chardin. As he himself admits in a most illuminating passage:

> If as a result of some interior revolution, I were to lose in succession my faith in Christ, my faith in a personal God, and my faith in spirit, I feel that I should continue *to believe* invincibly *in the world.* The world (its value, its infallibility and its goodness)—that, when all is said and done, is the first, the last, and the only thing in which I believe.[67]

The fact is that Teilhard wants only as much of God as he is able to fit into his evolutionist scheme. He claims to need the Incarnate Christ for the purposes of evolution: Christ is there to drive the wheels of progress, and to consummate the evolutive ascent. Teilhard beholds Him as the Omega Point of the universe: he envisions a Christ who fronts the cosmos, but not the Christ who "was before Abraham," the eternal Logos, the Second Person of the Holy Trinity. Teilhard does not know that notwithstanding what he exuberantly terms "the discovery of Time and Space," the universe is as nothing before God, and that even the Pantocrator (if for a moment He could be separated from the eternal Logos) would be as nothing too.

Teilhard claims to have found a cosmic use for the Incarnate Christ; but despite certain expressions of theological courtesy, it is plain that he has no need for God the Father. He believes "invincibly" in the goodness of the world, forgetting (as Christ has taught us) that "the Father alone is good." Teilhard seems to lack the essential precondition for true Christian faith: a naturalistic and utilitarian rationalism stands always in the way. His real faith lies elsewhere, as he himself admits. Despite many a Christian sentiment and pious phrase, it appears that the world has gained precedence over God in his thought and in his heart.

It is hardly surprising, therefore, that Teilhard's theology is not only truncated, but thoroughly secularized. His great ambition is to bring God into coincidence with the world, evolutively conceived. "When all is said and done," Teilhard's God—the much-trumpeted "God of Evolution"—can be nothing more nor less than "the first, the last, the only thing in which I believe."

NOTES

1. *Scientific American*, April 1960, p. 204.
2. "La demarche du Père Teilhard de Chardin," *Divinitas,* vol. 3 (1959), p. 227.
3. *The Religion of Teilhard de Chardin* (New York: Desclee, 1967), p. 195.
4. CE, p. 182.
5. CE, p. 227.
6. HM, p. 219.
7. HM, p. 52.
8. HM, p. 52.
9. *In Joannis Evangelium,* 38:10. See *The Nicene and Post-Nicene Fathers* (Grand Rapids: Eerdmans, 1974), vol. 7.
10. It is strange that the *ego eimi* of the Greek text (or *ego sum* of the Vulgate) should have been rendered by the phrase "I am he" (as it has in so many English translations). Not only is this obviously incorrect, but the effect of this mistranslation is to obscure the metaphysical sense. One can only surmise that the metaphysical sensitivity of Christians has not always been up to par.
11. HM, pp. 52-53.

12. HM, p. 53.
13. HM, p. 54.
14. SC, p. 184.
15. HM, p. 129.
16. CE, p. 31.
17. CE, p. 28.
18. CE, p. 160n.
19. CE, p. 160n.
20. Quoted in HM, p. 79n.
21. HE, p. 70.
22. *Mind*, vol. 70 (1961), p. 99.
23. CE, p. 239.
24. See, for instance, CE, p. 171, where Teilhard extols "Christian pantheism."
25. SC, p. 180.
26. CE, p. 65.
27. D. Bohm and B. Hiley, "On the intuitive understanding of nonlocality as implied by quantum theory," *Foundations of Physics*, vol. 5 (1975), pp. 96, 102; quoted in *The Tao of Physics* (New York: Bantam, 1977), p. 124.
28. Capra claims that the new physical Weltanschauung agrees substantially with the mystical outlook of China and India. He has argued the case in *The Tao of Physics*, a book which despite its serious and in part rather technical content has been something of a "best-seller" for years.
29. Capra seems to be under the impression that this is a specifically Western or Judeo-Christian concept. Yet it can be readily demonstrated that the idea is equally Vedic. In fact, as Ananda Coomaraswamy has pointed out, the much-abused term *maya* stems from the verb root *ma*, which means "to measure, mete out, mark off." To affirm that the world is *maya*, therefore, is to say that it is a measured or bounded thing. And to be sure, it is God who bestows or imposes these cosmic bounds. As the *Svetasvatara Upanishad* declares (verse 4:10):
    One should know that Nature is *Maya*,
    And that the Mighty Lord is the *Mayin*.
30. "With His ray He has measured heaven and earth," says the Rig Veda (VIII:25:18). We have treated this question at some length in *Cosmos and Transcendence* (La Salle: Sugden, 1984), Chapter 3.
31. *Svet. Up.*, 6:6.
32. CE, p. 58.
33. CE, p. 63.
34. See *Cosmos and Transcendence*, pp. 48-51.
35. *In Joannis Evangelium*, 38:10.
36. *Meister Eckhart* (C. de B. Evans, trans., London: Watkins, 1924), vol. I, p. 206.
37. CE, p. 240.
38. CE, p. 202.
39. HE, p. 68.
40. *Dionysius the Areopagite* (C. E. Rolt, trans., London, SPCK, 1940), p. 193.
41. *Ibid.*, p. 192.
42. HE, p. 168.
43. PM, p. 270.
44. PM, pp. 270-271.

45. HM, p. 92.
46. CE, p. 158.
47. PM, p. 297.
48. CE, pp. 180-181.
49. SC, p. 54.
50. SC, p. 64.
51. CE, p. 139.
52. SC, p. 60.
53. CE, p. 32.
54. SC, p. 79.
55. SC, p. 60.
56. SC, p. 60.
57. CE, p. 135.
58. CE, p. 135.
59. SC, p. 164.
60. SC, p. 61.
61. *Dionysius the Areopagite,* p. 184n.
62. CE, p. 182.
63. *Col.* 1:16. Here again it happens that the first of these three prepositions (Gk. *en*) is generally mistranslated. Presumably the terms *en autoi, di autou,* and *eis auton* are meant to indicate that the Logos is the paradigmatic, the efficient, and the final cause of the universe, respectively.
64. Emile Mersch, *The Whole Christ* (Milwaukee: Bruce 1938), p. 125.
65. Mersch, op. cit., p. 127.
66. Op. cit., p. 141.
67. CE, p. 99.

Chapter VII

Biblical Fall and Evolutionist Ascent

Christianity speaks of a primordial perfection and a subsequent Fall; now it is hardly surprising that this biblically founded doctrine has not been well received in evolutionist circles. Teilhard has surely a point when he writes that "The principal obstacle encountered by orthodox thinkers when they try to accommodate the *revealed* historical picture of human origins to the present scientific evidence is the traditional notion of original sin."[1] Only let it be said at once that what actually militates against the orthodox position is not "the present scientific evidence," but simply the evolutionist dogma, for which there is no evidence at all.

We must remember, too, that the biblical account admits of numerous interpretations, ranging from the more or less "historical" to the highly allegorical. Not that Scripture is ambiguous in the ordinary sense, or that theological tradition has not yet been able to ascertain the one true meaning of the *Genesis* tale: a single truth is being reflected on a number of existential planes, and this is what at once explains and justifies the multiple lines of interpretation.

Teilhard alludes to "the jealous maintenance, as a dogma, of strict monogenism (first one man, and then one man and one woman), which it is in actual fact impossible for science to accept."[2] Now it is debatable whether the biblical "monogenism" can be legitimately interpreted as an "actual fact" in the sense of empirical science. But even if one should maintain that Adam

133

and Eve were people more or less like ourselves who lived long
ago in the valley of the Euphrates, the resultant "picture of
human origins" would still not be in conflict with any established fact. When it comes to the actual origin of man (or for
that matter, of any other species), we find ourselves (scientifically) in a realm of conjecture, of untested hypothesis. There
are no instruments of perception which could enable us to pick
up the decisive event; and as Teilhard himself admits by his
"law of automatic suppression," one cannot even expect to find
a fossil record of the first progenitors.

This line of criticism, then, leads nowhere; and Teilhard knows
it. Thus, in his essay entitled "Fall, Redemption, and Geocentrism," he veers away almost immediately from the paleontological argument and begins to talk instead about "the collapse
of geocentrism." In his eyes that "collapse" signified the emergence of what he terms the evolutionist point of view; "The
fact was," he tells us, "that in consequence the seeds of decomposition had been introduced into the whole of the Genesis
theory of the Fall."[3] But here again Teilhard is moving too
fast. Logically speaking, it is a very long way from Copernicus
to Darwin; so much so that it is difficult to see any clear connection between the respective doctrines. What is perhaps still
more to the point, however, is that in the light of twentieth
century physics one can no longer say that Copernicus was
right and Ptolemy wrong. All that one can legitimately claim
is that the Copernican coordinate system leads to simpler laws
of planetary motion (which, incidentally, is precisely what Copernicus himself did claim). What has actually collapsed is not
so much geocentrism as it is the capacity of civilized man to
perceive more in Nature than mere extension and measurable
magnitudes. It is our ability to read the cosmic icon that has
deteriorated virtually to the point of collapse. And this, to be
sure, has introduced "the seeds of decomposition," not only
into the Genesis account of the Fall, but into the entire biblical
world-view: but this is another question.

*   *   *

Christianity teaches that the Fall of Adam has affected the
whole of mankind with the condition of Original Sin; and Teil-

hard finds this hard to accept. "It is impossible to universalize the first Adam," he tells us, "without destroying his individuality."[4] Apparently Teilhard believes that Adam could not have had an effect upon the whole of mankind so long as we conceive of him as a *bona fide* person. And this leads him to suppose that Adam is not a person, but some kind of principle: "Strictly speaking, there is no first Adam," he declares. "The name disguises a universal and unbreakable law of reversion or perversion—the price that has to be paid for progress."[5]

But before concerning ourselves with "the price that has to be paid for progress," it might be well to ask what all this entails with reference to the Incarnate Christ: would not the second Adam have to suffer a corresponding fate? If "It is impossible to universalize the first Adam without destroying his individuality," would not the same hold true of the Redeemer? After all, the two cases are analogous: "For as by one man's disobedience many were made sinners," St. Paul apprises us, "so by the obedience of one shall many be made righteous." (*Rom.* 5:19). If the first of these facts is inconceivable, would not the second be inconceivable too? In other words: if Teilhard is right when he says that "Strictly speaking, there is no first Adam," would it not follow by the same token that there is no second Adam as well?

Obviously Teilhard cannot admit this; it would be fatal to the Omega theory, and to his entire program. He is forced, therefore, to forestall this objection: "The case of the second Adam is completely different," he assures us. But why? "There is, it is clear, no lower center of divergence in the universe at which we could place the first Adam,"[6] he goes on to say. Now from a scientific point of view, this is no doubt correct; only it happens that exactly the same holds true, *mutatis mutandis*, with reference to the second Adam. Not only can it be said that the stipulated Omega Point does not exist, but it turns out (as we have also noted before) that if it did, it would be entirely unsuitable as a locus of the Risen Christ. Scientifically speaking, therefore, the case for the second Adam is not a whit more promising than for the first.

The real point, however, is that in both instances the biblical account is not to be interpreted on the level of scientific discourse. Let us not forget that "The first man Adam was made

a living soul; the last Adam a quickening spirit." (*1 Cor.* 15:45).
But what has science to say about such matters? The problem,
therefore, lies not with the biblical teaching, or with scientific
theory, but with the scientistic claim that whatsoever eludes
the net of science is *ipso facto* unreal. It is this scientistic postulate which forces Teilhard to conclude that "It is impossible
to universalize the first Adam without destroying his individuality," and it is this same prejudice which again causes him
to imagine that Christianity will collapse unless one can discover an "Omega Point of science" to serve as a platform for
Christ.

Yet, oddly enough, Teilhard himself admits occasionally that
the biblical and the scientific world-views correspond to different
levels of vision. "We cannot retain both pictures without moving alternately from one to the other," he tells us. "Their as-
sociation clashes, it rings false. In combining them on one and
the same plane we are certainly victims of an error in perspective."[7] Precisely; only in Teilhard's eyes this means that the biblical Weltanschauung belongs to the realm of fantasy. At best
it constitutes a myth which (in this day and age) needs to be
somehow "demythologized" and transposed into a scientific key.
And that is of course what his own theological speculations
are intended to accomplish: it is the reason, for instance, why
Teilhard does not rest content until he has convinced himself
(six pages later) that Creation, Fall, Incarnation and Redemption
—'all four of these events'—are somehow "co-extensive with
the duration and totality of the world." He is not in the least
embarrassed to interpret this time-honored teaching in alien
terms; when it comes to his own fusion of biblical and scientific notions, he seems no longer to feel that such an associa-
tion "clashes," and that it "rings false."

But let us get back to Teilhard's polemics against the traditional conception of Paradise, the first Adam, and Original Sin.
Teilhard is aware, of course, that these biblical notions can be
understood on more than one level (although he apparently views
these various options as so many rival theories—which in principle they are not). Thus there is, first of all, the "literal" interpretation, which situates the Garden of Eden upon this earth
and regards Adam as having been endowed with a body more
or less like our own. And as we have seen, Teilhard objects

to this view because it appears to him to be tantamount to a monogenism which can be ruled out on scientific grounds. Having thus disposed of this particular option (as he seems to believe), he then goes on to consider certain versions of what he terms the "Alexandrian explanation." Broadly speaking, these allegorical interpretations conceive of Paradise as a "higher state," and of Adam (before the Fall) as incomparably more spiritual than we. According to this view Adam was endowed with virtually god-like faculties which we no longer possess, and with a kind of body which differs markedly from our own. And then came the Fall. It hardly matters whether we conceive of this primordial event as an internal disintegration, or as a descent into a lower world and subsequent "encrustation." The point, in either case, is that the Fall entails an effective loss of these higher spiritual endowments. Let us understand it well: according to Christian teaching, it is this primordial catastrophe —and not a Darwinist ascent—that is responsible for the human condition as we know it today.

No wonder that Teilhard is displeased. The doctrine is obviously a thorn in his side, a "theory" which needs at all cost to be disproved or discredited. But just how is this to be done? What are Teilhard's arguments? In a late essay he has summarized his objections in the form of three concise statements.

His first point is that "The whole of the extra-cosmic part of the story has 'an arbitrary and fanciful' ring. It takes us into the realm of pure imagination."[8] But what Teilhard apparently fails to realize is that *any* affirmation regarding ultimate realities (be they "first" or "last") will perforce appear to some degree fanciful and imaginary—by the very fact that these realities cannot be subject to the conditions of our phenomenal world. And one is tempted to add that when it comes to the fanciful and imaginary, Teilhard is hardly the one to cast the first stone.

"Secondly, and much more seriously," he goes on to say, "the *instantaneous* creation of the first Adam seems to me an incomprehensible type of operation—unless the word simply covers the absence of any attempt at explanation." Now this is a question which we have already examined at considerable length and disposed of (in Chapter 4).

Which brings us to the third point: "Finally, if we accept the hypothesis of a *single, perfect* being put to the test *on only one* occasion, the likelihood of the Fall is so slight that one can only regard the Creator as having been extremely unlucky." But in fact one can only regard this statement as being extremely inept—if for no other reason than that it makes no sense whatsoever to speak of "likelihood" with reference to a unique event, one that can be "put to the test on only one occasion."

And these are the grounds upon which Teilhard has taken it upon himself to impugn two thousand years of Christian tradition!

★   ★   ★

The plain fact is that an evolutionist Weltanschauung does not admit a primordial state of perfection. One way or another, therefore, Teilhard was obliged to rid himself of the first Adam. In the end we are told that "Adam and Eve are images of mankind pressing on towards God;"[9] this banality is all that remains.

But what about the idea of Original Sin—is this to be jettisoned too? One has the impression that Teilhard would like to very much, but cannot, for the simple reason that this would also knock out the idea of Redemption, which is obviously central to Christianity. Yet he does the next best thing: instead of discarding the concept of Original Sin, he recasts it in strictly evolutionist terms. And this suffices to remove the sting of the ancient doctrine.

Teilhard is quite right on that score—the idea of sin has indeed become taboo in the modern world. "Whenever we try intellectually and vitally to assimilate Christianity with all our modern soul," as he puts it, "the first obstacles we meet always derive from original sin."[10] In Teilhard's eyes "It clips the wings of hope" and "drags us back inexorably into the *overpowering* darkness of reparation and expiation."[11] The fault, however, lies not with the dogma as such, but supposedly with the antiquated form in which it has been expressed. This form, we are told, "represents a survival of obsolete static views into our now evolutionary way of thinking. Fundamentally, in fact, the idea of Fall is no more than an attempt to explain evil in a fixed universe."[12]

Let us then consider what becomes of Original Sin once we

have liberated ourselves from "obsolete static views." In an evolutionary cosmos, a universe in process of creative union in Teilhard's sense, evil is to be conceived, basically, as a certain resistance on the part of "the multiple" to unification. "Since its gradual unification entails a multitude of tentative probings," Teilhard explains, "it cannot escape (from the moment it ceases to be 'nothing') being permeated by suffering and error."[13] Evil, then, is tantamount to disorder, and disorders arise from a statistical necessity. We are told that it is "absolutely inevitable that local disorders appear," and that "from level to level, collective states of disorder result from these elementary disorders (because of the organically interwoven nature of the cosmic stuff)." And finally: "Above the level of life this entails suffering, and, starting with man, it becomes sin."[14]

There it is; but even a cursory look at the new doctrine should give us pause. Why, first of all, should disorder turn into sin on the human level; why speak of "sin" in place of disease, error or imperfection? And surely there is a difference! The very fact that there is no such thing as sin below the level of man should suffice to make this clear. The point, of course, is that sin presupposes the idea of responsibility, of an agent capable of exercising moral judgment. In a word, it presupposes a knowledge of right and wrong, and a freedom of choice.

There may be a connection between sin and disorder, inasmuch as sinful acts may tend to produce disorderly states. Yet what ultimately counts, from an ethical point of view, is not the physical effect of an action (say the "disorder" to which it may give rise), but the *intention behind the act:* the same physical act, therefore, may on occasion be good, bad or indifferent, depending on what was in our heart when we acted.

In Teilhard's theory, on the other hand, evil has in effect been identified with disorder; it becomes essentially a thermodynamic quantity: basically, it becomes entropy. But the point is that while evil may indeed be a cause of disorder (even as "death is the wages of sin"), the two are by no means the same. Death as such, for example, is not a sin, nor is it an evil (as St. Paul has likewise taught us, when he exclaims: "Oh Death, where is thy sting?"). In a word, by transposing the basic conceptions of Christian ethics to a scientific plane—to the level of statistical mechanics, no less—Teilhard has robbed the key terms of their authentic meaning. In his eagerness to reduce the essentials of Christian teaching to the preconceived categories of evolutionist dogma, he has laid the foundations of a scientistic pseudo-ethics which not only falsifies ethical doctrine, but opens the door to all kinds of monstrous possibilities. It is not by accident, for example, that Teilhard advocates various technological interventions aimed at promoting what he conceives to be further strides in the direction of "anthropogenesis" or "cerebralization"—not excluding mandatory surgery!

But these are matters which shall need to be considered in their proper place. Let us go on now to examine how Teilhard justifies his fundamental ethical stand. His first point is as follows: under the new auspices "The evidence of science is necessarily, and always will be, respected, since the experiential background of dogma coincides with that of evolution."[15] The implication, of course, is once again that the traditional view does *not* respect "the evidence of science," which is to say that it has been falsified by certain scientific findings. But this charge is clearly preposterous: what are these momentous findings? Is it perhaps the Darwinian theory? It is no wonder that Teilhard has elected to make his point by innuendo, as it were.

The second presumed advantage of the new theory, we are told, is that "The problem of evil disappears." True enough. It is a modest appraisal, in fact; for on closer examination one finds (as we have seen) that not only the problem, but the very idea of evil, has disappeared. But let us follow Teilhard's argument: "In this picture," he goes on to say, "physical suffering and moral transgression are inevitably introduced into the world not because of some deficiency in the creative act, but by the very structure of participated being: in other words, they are introduced as the *statistically inevitable by-product* of the unification of the multiple. In consequence they contradict neither the power of God nor his goodness."[16] Now, to begin with, if moral transgression is inevitable, if it comes about by force of necessity, how then can one speak of sin? Or to put it another way: the very concept of moral transgression presupposes the idea of human freedom, the possibility, in other words, of *not* transgressing. But perhaps this is said from the now antiquated point of view; perhaps, in an evolutionist universe, the concept of morality is no longer tied to the postulate of human freedom.

But even if one were to redefine the idea of moral good along Darwinist lines, so that morality becomes simply a matter of using one's brain as best one can to minimize disorder, it would still be true that disorders exist, and that they constitute a deficiency. And so the problem remains how an all-powerful and benevolent God could have created such a less-than-perfect world. Teilhard pretends that the impasse has been resolved by the circumstance that in his theory, "physical suffering and moral transgression" have become statistically inevitable (whatever that might mean). But so far from solving the problem, this does no more than deny the omnipotence of God. After all, an occurrence can be truly inevitable (whether in a "statistical" or any other sense) only so long as God lacks either the will or the power to stop it. What Teilhard is saying, therefore, when he speaks of a "statistically inevitable by-product," is that even God is powerless in the face of these statistical disorders. Now this might be considered by some a debatable point. What is not debatable, however, is that Teilhard contradicts himself when he goes on to maintain (with reference to these same "inevitable" disorders) that "They contradict neither the power of God nor his goodness."

It goes without saying that a "problem of evil" exists only so long as we believe in the absolute power and goodness of God. One does not solve it, therefore, by denying these premises, nor of course does one do so by contradicting oneself. Teilhard is mistaken, moreover, when he intimates that this question of theodicy poses an insuperable difficulty for the traditional doctrine. On the contrary; it is only after the problem has been spuriously transposed, Teilhardian style, onto what may be aptly termed a purely natural plane, that it becomes truly intractable. Teilhard himself, by the narrowness of his scientistic premises, has rendered it insoluble.

★   ★   ★

What Teilhard has failed to grasp is that evil is not caused by natural processes, but by personal agents. It stems, not from the material, but from the spiritual pole of creation. Teilhard is looking in the wrong direction when he seeks for the origin of evil in the resistance of "the multiple" to unification. Now it is true that evil can be conceived as a resistance or an opposition of some kind; the point is, however, that it is a *willful* resistance, a *willful* opposition. What evil resists or opposes, moreover, is not the creative act, but the created order. It attacks the primordial world, the pristine universe as it issues from the hand of God.

We must recall, once again, that the world was not created *in* time, but *with* time. It was thus created in that supra-temporal "beginning" of *Genesis* 1:1, or "instantaneously," as one can also say. And this alone entails that the creative act is irresistible. "He spoke, and it was done; He commanded, and it stood fast." Not one by one, in temporal sequence, as some imagine, but *omnia simul,* all at once. Who, then, could oppose this Act?

It follows by the same token, moreover, that the creation as such must be perfect. If there is nothing that can impede or thwart the divine creative will, how could anything be amiss? And Scripture too confirms this when it apprises us of the fact that God beheld the new creation and saw that it was "good."

What, then, has happened? What has gone wrong? For it is obvious that the world in which we find ourselves is indeed very far removed from a state of perfection. And man, too—we ourselves!—are exceedingly imperfect. One sees thus that there *must* have been a Fall.

We have said that evil is caused by personal agents; and we need now to consider more closely what this means. The great fact (which is so often overlooked) is that God created not only natures (or "things," as we say), but also *persons.* What, then, is a person? one may ask. And surprisingly, this question cannot really be answered; it turns out to be badly posed. For as Richard of St. Victor has very astutely pointed out, the person answers, not to the question "What?", but rather to the question "Who?".

Christian theology teaches us, moreover, that the mystery of personhood is rooted in God. Because God is a Person (or Three Persons, to be more exact), man can be a person too—by reflection, so to speak. "And God said, Let us make man in our image, after our likeness." (*Gen.* 1:26). We must not fail to observe that here God speaks of Himself in the plural form—which indicates, in the light of Trinitarian doctrine, that the reference is indeed to the divine *hypostases* or Persons.

There is something godlike, therefore, in personhood; or better said, in a person, whoever he or she may be. Only one must remember that the person is not by any means the individual, as we commonly suppose. Individuality, one might say, is a mask. It is woven out of a multiplicity of attributes which belong, not to the person, but to his nature. And a nature, let us recall, is common to many beings: it belongs to the species, as the Scholastics would say. But every person is unique; he is one of a kind—except that in this instance one cannot speak of "a kind" at all. We sense this uniqueness at times (be it in ourselves or in someone else), and at such moments we begin to know the person. Yet we never quite succeed: the person remains a mystery, a profound enigma—as indeed befits an image of God.

Now it might seem strange that evil should arise precisely from what is most godlike within creation. Yet it is perhaps not quite so strange after all; for as Georges Florovsky has well said, "The human fall consists precisely in the fact that man limits himself to himself, that man falls, as it were, in love with himself. And through this concentration on himself man separated himself from God and broke the spiritual and free contact with God. It was a kind of delirium, a self-erotic obsession, a spiritual narcissism."[17] And it is not really hard to understand that this separation from God should have proved to be not only disastrous, but actually fatal.

From this point of vantage, moreover, one is able in principle to resolve what Teilhard refers to as "the problem of evil." The crucial fact is that personhood implies freedom. In the order of creation, of course, this freedom is a certain power derived from on high: it is a bounty bestowed by God, and of all gifts perhaps the most precious. For it is only in the fullness of this God-given freedom that the creature is able, *Deo volente,* to attain union with God. But this very freedom also entails an element of risk, for it entails the option of refusing the divine mandates, of opposing oneself to God's will. And therein lies the origin of evil: at its source evil is nothing but a willful opposition to God, a kind of disobedience or rebellion. Now we must understand, furthermore, that God, having once bestowed the incomparable gift of freedom, does not take it back. He does not revoke this freedom, even when it is put to ill use. Strangely enough, it is rather his own power which God relinquishes, as it were, in the face of the rebellious creature. As Vladimir Lossky has beautifully expressed it:

> God becomes *powerless* before human freedom; He cannot violate it since it flows from His own omnipotence. Certainly man was created by the will of God alone; but he cannot be deified by it alone. A single will for creation, but two for deification. A single will to raise up the image, but two to make the image into a likeness. The love of God for man is so great that it cannot constrain; for there is no love without respect. *Divine will* always will submit itself to gropings, to detours, even to revolts of *human will* to bring it to a free consent: of such is divine providence, and the classical image of the pedagogue must seem feeble indeed to anyone who has felt God as a beggar of love waiting at the soul's door without ever daring to force it.[18]

What more can one say? This, perhaps, is as close as we can come to resolving the so-called problem of evil; and to anyone "who has felt God as a beggar of love waiting at the soul's door" it will suffice.

★   ★   ★

It may be enlightening at this point to recall an ancient exegetical tradition, already known to and approved of by St. Augustine, which interprets the story of Adam and Eve in anthropological terms. As Meister Eckhart writes in his *Liber parabolarum Genesis,* "The saints and theologians generally interpret what is written in the third Chapter symbolically (*parabolice*) and understand by the serpent the sensual nature (*sensitivum*), by the woman the lower mind (*inferius rationale*), but by the man the higher reason (*superius rationalis*)."[19] And he goes on, a little later, to explain from this point of view what has happened in consequence of Original Sin: "But after the highest power of the soul had lost its connection to and aspiration towards God (*adhaesione et ordine a deo*) through the commission of sin—'But your iniquities have separated between you and your God' (*Isaias* 59:2)—all the powers of the soul, the lower mental as well as the sensual, were successively cut off from the higher reason and its hegemony. . ."[20] In a word, the

hierarchic structure of the human compound came undone. As
St. Thomas Aquinas also writes:

> By the sin of our first parent original justice was taken away,
> by which not only were the lower parts of the soul held
> together under the control of reason, without any disorder
> whatever, but also the whole body was held together in sub-
> jection to the soul, without any defect. Therefore, when origi-
> nal justice was forfeited through the sin of our first parent,
> just as human nature was stricken in the soul by the disorder
> among the powers, so also it became subject to corruption,
> by reason of disorder in the body.[21]

The picture that emerges is exceedingly clear. So long as man
lived in his primordial state of innocence, he remained close
to God and fully integrated. From a trichotomous point of view
one can say that his spirit was united to God, his soul was
united to his spirit, and his body was united to his soul. And
thus bound together, he was one being, one theomorphic organism. But by the Fall he became disunited, fragmented as
it were. It was a kind of rebellion: the spirit rebelling against
God (through "disobedience"), the soul against the spirit (through
self-love and concupiscence), and the body against the soul
(through inertia). And in the wake of this rebellion, this veritable revolution, a certain reversal of the natural order took place.
As Vladimir Lossky says (with reference to the original order
and its subsequent inversion):

> The spirit must find its sustenance in God, must live from
> God; the soul must feed on the spirit; the body must live
> from the soul—such was the original ordering of our im-
> mortal nature. But turning back from God, the spirit, instead
> of providing food for the soul, begins to live at the expense
> of the soul, feeding itself on its substance (what we usually
> call "spiritual values"); the soul in turn begins to live with
> the life of the body, and this is the origin of the passions;
> finally, the body is forced to seek its nourishment outside,
> in inanimate matter, and in the end comes on death. The
> human complex finally disintegrates.[22]

It is interesting to ask, in this connection, whether what we
generally take to be the human body might not actually correspond to those "coats of skins" which God is said to have

made for Adam and Eve following upon their transgression (*Gen.* 3:21). We know, at any rate, that some of the Fathers (notably St. Gregory of Nyssa) have speculated along these lines. Could it be that the true (and primordial) body still exists, concealed beneath that "outer shell," that *annamayakośa* or "sheath made of food," as it is called in the Vedantic literature, which is to be shed at the moment of death and is destined to disintegrate? These are matters, in any case, into which we are ill-equipped to probe, and on which the Church, in her wisdom, has refused to make any definitive pronouncements.

Suffice it to say that by virtue of the Fall something in man has become subject to death. And that something, moreover, is not simply the body. We must not say (as did certain Platonists) that the body dies in its entirety while the soul remains fully intact. For without doubt the Fall has affected the soul as well: it too has undergone a profound transformation. In a sense it has become split in two; and it scarcely matters whether or not we call the one "real" and dismiss the other as a mere appearance or phenomenal superimposition. The fact remains that something of ourselves has become mortal, and that the catastrophe of death affects not only our body, but our psyche as well.

In Pauline language one can say that in consequence of the Fall we have become split into an outer and an inner man, a spiritual and a carnal being. It is the latter, moreover, which on the whole has waxed throughout history, and in the mass of humanity is still on the increase. So much so that in modern times it has become virtually impossible for countless men and women to realize that they are *more* than a purely carnal being: our spiritual nature has for the most part become almost totally eclipsed. And this in itself explains, moreover, why the typical man of today has almost no conception of the Fall, and why the notion of Original Sin strikes him generally as an abhorrent fantasy, fabricated by morbid or infantile theologians. It explains why "Whenever we try intellectually and vitally to assimilate Christianity with all our modern soul, the first obstacles we meet always derive from Original Sin." No wonder; one can have no sense of Original Sin without some awareness, however dim, of the pristine purity, and no conception of the Fall without at least some inkling of a higher antecedent. And these are just the perceptions which have grown exceedingly faint, especially in the more "civilized" and sophisticated portions of mankind.

If it be true, therefore, that a Fall has taken place, then it is not surprising in the least that man should subsequently find it hard to conceive of his pristine state. One must expect, in fact, that not only his own primordial nature, but the entire spiritual order will have receded from his field of vision. Teilhard is surely right when he points out that "There is not the least trace on the horizon, not the smallest scar, to mark the ruins of a golden age or our cutting off from a better world."[23] But he is quite mistaken when he supposes that this in itself renders the biblical doctrine implausible; for as the preceding considerations have made clear, it is exactly what the teaching would lead us to expect. Nothing, in fact, can be more reasonable than to suppose that the expulsion from Paradise is not so much a change of place as it is a certain fall into oblivion, a certain reduction in the cognitive possibilities effectively open to man. Is this not ultimately where the problem lies? We have lost our spiritual sight. As St. Paul said to the Corinthians, "The natural man [*psychikos anthropos*] receiveth not the things of the Spirit of God: for they are foolishness unto him: neither can he know them, because they are spiritually discerned." (*1 Cor.* 2:14).

We must understand that this natural man, this carnal or outer man, came into existence by way of the Fall. Prior to the Fall there was only one man, and now there are, as it were, two. The Fall, as we have seen, can be understood as a disintegration, in the most literal sense. And out of this disintegration there has emerged the outer man, who could also be called the ego-centered man. He represents so to speak the *anima-corpus* compound cut off from its spiritual source. He is the *psychikos anthropos* or "psychic man" inasmuch as his life is centered upon the psyche (as distinguished from spirit or *pneuma* in the Pauline sense). Now this is of course the man we are all familiar with; the spiritual man in us has become to a large extent eclipsed, as we have observed before. And it is this outer man, let it be said, that is investigated by our sciences and lauded by the humanists. He is all "our modern soul" can envision. Seyyed Hossein Nasr is no doubt right when he maintains (with reference to the contemporary scene) that "There has never been as little knowledge of man, of the *anthropos*."[24] What we know, and alone are able to know, through our so-called scientific means (or through what Teilhard is pleased to call "the phenomenal point of view, to which I systematically confine myself") is no more than the natural man, the outer man. These are among the means accessible to the *psychikos anthropos,* and what they reveal are certain modalities of that same *psychikos anthropos.* Under these auspices we can have no knowledge of the spiritual man, nor can we know "the things of the Spirit of God." It is interesting, moreover, that St. Paul distinguishes between "receiving" and "knowing": not only are we incapable (on this level) of any spiritual knowledge, but we cannot even receive the higher teaching with an open and unprejudiced mind, let alone with faith. In a word, it is the innate tendency of the *psychikos anthropos* to be profane and thoroughly secular in his Weltanschauung. No wonder, therefore, that Teilhard, who obviously exults in "our modern soul," should find it imperative to reinterpret and fundamentally recast the spiritual teachings of Christianity.

★   ★   ★

But there is something more to be said. One can see, in the light of what has gone before, that the Fall is to be conceived not only as a primordial event, but also, to some degree, as an ongoing process. As Frithjof Schoun has observed, "This drama is always repeating itself anew, in collective history as in the life of individuals."[25] Understandably so: having once become destabilized on account of the primordial Fall, man has a continuing propensity to become more and more alienated from his spiritual source. By virtue of Original Sin it has become his natural tendency to draw away from the primordial Center. And the further he moves in a centrifugal direction, the more readily he falls prey to what might be termed the fatal attraction of the periphery. As Christ has told us, the more spiritually impoverished a man becomes, the more he forfeits "even that which he has." (*Mark* 4:25).

Yet to the outer man, this loss appears generally as a distinct gain—until the point is reached when this descending movement ends in catastrophe. As the spiritual man wanes, the carnal man waxes and extends his dominion over the face of the earth (for a time); there seems to be a certain compensation, a kind of inverse ratio between the two. It is no wonder, therefore, that to the carnal man the pageant of history should present itself on the whole as an ascending trajectory. Blind to the spiritual world (as St. Paul informs us), he does not behold the treasures he is leaving behind; as with Esau, it pains him not to give up his birthright for a mess of pottage.

There is an accelerating human drift away from the Garden of Eden, and from the Tree of Life which grows in its midst—but the *psychikos anthropos* perceives it not. He is facing the periphery, one could say, and what he sees is the periphery rising up, as it were, and looming ever larger before him. And is this not what Teilhard's much-trumpeted "discovery of Space and Time" actually signifies from a higher point of view? As we learn from the traditional ontologies, the conditions of space and time apply mainly to the cosmic periphery—to this corporeal world, which constitutes the lowest tier in the edifice of creation.[26] This is indeed the Heraclitean realm of perpetual flux where "All things flow" and universal transformation rules supreme. Is it any wonder, then, that along with Space and Time the idea of Evolution, too, should loom large in these latter days?

Meanwhile the disintegration of the *anthropos* continues at an increasing pace. Originally there was one man, as we have said, and then, by virtue of the primordial Fall, there were two. But it happens that the *psychikos anthropos* is himself disintegrating. First of all, to be sure, he has become divided into the conscious and the unconscious parts of himself, a dichotomy which mirrors, as it were, the primordial split. But the process of disintegration does not stop there; in the memorable words of George Herbert: "Oh, what a thing is man! How farre from power, from settled peace and rest! He is some twentie sev'rall men at least each sev'rall houre."

Who does not know this? Who does not recognize that in our contemporary civilization, especially, dispersion has become the order of the day?

There are also contrary forces, of course, which promote human integration on various levels. And above all there is yet the religious factor, which not only integrates on a psychic plane, but in varying degrees connects us to the spiritual world. Religion is the great force which opposes the continuing Fall: it is truly a *re-ligare*, a "binding back." Yet one knows that on the whole the religious influence has waned. As is often said with reference to the modern West, we find ourselves in a post-Christian era. And while we cannot perhaps foretell what the future has in store, we know that since the demise of the Middle Ages the influence of Christianity upon Western society has obviously suffered a drastic decline. The human mass, one could say, is no longer connected—no longer "tied back"—to the spiritual Center; and so it is free at last to follow its centrifugal bent without hindrance. This is what the great modern movement is all about. From an authentically Christian point of view the spectacle of human evolution, in the contemporary sense, is but the ongoing Fall, perceived through the eyes of "liberated" man.

NOTES

1. CE, p. 36.
2. CE, p. 36.
3. CE, p. 37.
4. CE, p. 39.
5. CE, p. 41.
6. CE, p. 41.
7. CE, p. 47.
8. CE, p. 193.
9. CE, p. 52.
10. CE, p. 79.
11. CE, p. 70-80.
12. CE, p. 80.
13. CE, p. 195.
14. CE, p. 195.
15. CE, p. 196.
16. CE, p. 196.
17. *Collected Works,* Vol. III (Belmont, Mass.: Nordland, 1976), p. 85.
18. *Orthodox Theology* (Crestwood, N.Y.: St. Vladimir's Seminary Press, 1978), p. 73.
19. *Die Lateinischen Werke* (Stuttgart: Kohlhammer, 1965), Vol. I, p. 602. This line of interpretation, incidentally, throws much needed light on the teachings of St. Paul (so unpopular nowadays) relating to the position of the woman *vis-a-vis* her husband and the Church as given in Chapter 11 of First Corinthians.
20. Op. cit., p. 612.
21. *Summa Theologiae* I-II, Qest. 85, Art. 5.
22. *The Mystical Theology of the Eastern Church* (Crestwood, N.Y.: St. Vladimir's

Seminary Press, 1976), p. 128.
23. CE, p. 47.
24. "Contemporary Man, Between the Rim and the Axis," *Studies in Comparative Religion,* Vol. 7 (1973), p. 116.
25. *Light on the Ancient Worlds* (London: Perennial, 1965), p. 44.
26. See, for instance, Huston Smith, *Forgotten Truth* (New York: Harper & Row, 1967), pp. 37-59.

Chapter VIII

The Idea of Progress

If the French Jesuit has actually inverted the Christian doctrine—if he has deftly turned it upside down—we must not forget that given the contemporary climate of thought, he did not in fact have very far to go. Teilhard is no isolated thinker, and not nearly as unprecedented as some have imagined. He stands rather at the head of an advancing front, at the crest of the very movement that has ushered in the modern age.

Let us consider that movement.

Surprisingly, perhaps, the roots of modernity trace back to the great era of Scholasticism. Notwithstanding the unquestioned orthodoxy of its illustrious teachings, it was actually the genius of the thirteenth century that gave birth to what later came to be called "rationalism." As some had forewarned, the Scholastic enterprise was not without peril: from the outset there was the danger that it could give rise to an overvaluation of human rationality—of discursive thought, if you will—which in time would prove fatal to the Christian faith.

One must remember that reason, too, has its limitations; it does not simply coincide with intellect, or with intelligence as such. For all its apparent prowess, it constitutes but one particular mode of knowing, a mode which moreover is secondary or derivative. Discursive thought represents after all an indirect way of knowing, a knowing "by reflection," as we say. Thought as such belongs in fact to the psychic plane, to the level of the *psychikos anthropos*; and so, too, it does not cover the entire ground of knowing, as we are prone to suppose. To be sure, the spiritual man in us has also his cognitive means. And as we learn from St. Paul, it is only by way of these higher and indeed god-like faculties that we shall be able, *Deo volente,* to know "the things of the Spirit of God."

Now the great Scholastics, of course, understood this perfectly well. They did not idolize human rationality, nor were they ignorant of the fact that the spiritually integrated man can readily dispense with syllogisms. They knew, moreover, how to combine reasoning with spiritual contemplation; in their hands argument could serve as a catalyst of intellection in the true sense. But unfortunately this spiritual art has not been passed on to the bulk of their disciples; it is mainly the more external and contingent aspects of Scholasticism that have been transmitted to posterity—the mere instrument, if you will. And it may be the very perfection of this instrument which contributed to the subsequent decline of spiritual vision; after all, the "letter" does have a tendency to "kill."

The fact is, in any case, that no sooner had the great masters passed from the scene than signs of decadence and disintegration began to appear. Already in the fourteenth century we discern the rise of a sterile but yet ostensibly Christian rationalism—a rationalism that was fast losing touch with the realities of the spiritual order—accompanied, as one would expect, by a movement towards skepticism and philosophical doubt. No longer was reason regarded as the handmaid of a higher intellectual faculty, a power in us that needs to be awakened through grace and a certain spiritual art. And this was the fatal step: reason declared its own autonomy.

More than any other factor, we believe, it was the birth of rationalism that brought the Middle Ages to a close; and clearly, it was a fall. As Seyyed Hossein Nasr has observed, "Renaissance man ceased to be the ambivalent man of the Middle Ages, half angel, half man, torn between heaven and earth. Rather, he became wholly man, but now a totally earthbound creature."[1]

It would take us too far afield to trace even the principal stages of this fateful "evolution"—for indeed, the full transition did not come about all at once. Instead, we would like to draw attention to one particular concept which emerged quite early in the course of that development and began immediately to play a decisive role: the idea, namely, of "progress." Given the conditions of the post-medieval world, this is an essential notion; our post-Christian civilization demands it. Once Heaven was closed and man had become reduced to "a totally earthbound creature," a substitute was needed, an Ersatz that could somehow take the place of the spiritual quest. Progress, then—the specifically modern concept of a future collective utopia—replaces the quest for God, and ultimately becomes confounded with that quest. In other words, while the idea of progress is initially conceived in predominantly secular terms, a stage is eventually reached at which the veneration of Progress blossoms forth into a mysticism of sorts, a "religion of the future" that claims to fulfill and supersede all the religions of the past.

Now this is manifestly the point at which Teilhard de Chardin enters upon the scene. For the moment, however, what concerns us is simply the fact that futurism and a cult of progress are inevitable once the world has become flattened out in the collective imagination and there has been an effective loss of verticality. As Huston Smith has put it:

> The consequence for hope was obvious: if being has no upper stories, hope has no vertical prospect. If it is to go anywhere—and hope by definition implies a going of some sort—henceforth that "where" could only be forward or horizontal. The extent to which the modern doctrine of progress is the child, not of evidence, as it would like to believe, but of hope's élan—the fact that being indispensable it *does* spring eternal in the human breast and, in the modern world view, has no direction to flow save forward—is among the undernoted facts of history.[2]

★   ★   ★

Before the end of the eighteenth century the so-called Christian humanism of an Erasmus had given way to the secular humanism of Rousseau. It was an unavoidable transition; the Renaissance alliance between neopaganism and Christianity had been precarious at best, and was bound to disintegrate. In retrospect one can see that the sixteenth century was indeed an age of contradiction, and the presumed union of hellenistic and Christian culture little more than a fake. One needs but to look at the art of the period—an art which for all its genius no longer knew how to distinguish between Aphrodite and the Virgin, or between Apollo and Christ.

But the rise of secular humanism, with its truncated Weltanschauung, its "liberated" ideologies, and its naive cult of progress, constitutes only half the picture; this cultural transformation was complemented by another development of the utmost importance, namely the rise of modern science. It is not altogether surprising that there should have been an evolution of that kind. After all, what Huston Smith has said about hope must apply to the sphere of knowledge as well: if "Being has no upper stories," then knowledge, too, "has no vertical prospect." Once man has become, as it were, "a totally earth-bound creature," science as we know it becomes indeed the only authentic and feasible form of knowledge. No wonder, then, that there has been a veritable explosion in that domain.

Yet the birth of science, as we know it, had to bide its time. As Seyyed Hossein Nasr has pointed out, "The scientific revolution itself came not in the Renaissance but during the seventeenth century when the cosmos had already become secularized, religion weakened through long, inner conflicts, metaphysics and gnosis in the real sense nearly forgotten, and the meaning of symbols neglected. . ."[3] Only in a world in which the higher possibilities of the human intellect were no longer viable could such a gargantuan expenditure of effort on the plane of physical research have taken place.

As Nasr notes, science in the contemporary sense began when men had quite forgotten that the things of Nature bear reference to a higher plane—to the spiritual order, no less, from whence they derive their essential content. And as a type the modern scientist no doubt perpetuates this anti-metaphysical tendency. It is plain that the possibility of a metaphysical symbolism—the idea that "The whole of the spiritual world appears mystically represented in symbolic forms in every part of the sensible world for those who are able to see"[4]—holds little fascination for him. Nor is he apt to be moved when St. Paul declares that "The invisible things of him from the creation of the world are clearly seen, being understood by the things that are made, even his eternal power and Godhead." (*Rom.* 1:20). To the eye of post-medieval man the natural world had become a closed and more or less self-sufficient realm which no longer pointed beyond itself to transcendent causes. Perhaps Sherwood Taylor was stretching a point when he wrote that "Before the separation of science and the acceptance of it as the sole valid way of apprehending Nature, the vision of God in Nature seems to have been the normal way of viewing the world, nor could it have been marked as an exceptional experience"[5]; but in any case (exceptional or not), the experience was far from unknown in medieval times. It was an age, as we know, in which St. Hildegard could still perceive Nature as the living garment of the Holy Ghost, and could transmit words addressed to her by the Spirit. For a moment, at least, let us listen to these words, which cast such an unaccustomed light upon our world:

> I am that supreme and fiery force that sends forth all the sparks of life. Death has no part in me, yet do I allot it, wherefore I am girt about with wisdom as with wings. I am that living and fiery essence of the divine substance that flows in the beauty of the fields. I shine in the water, I burn in the sun and the moon and the stars. Mine is that mysterious force of the invisible wind; I sustain the breath of all living. I breathe in the verdure, and in the flowers, and when the waters flow like living things, it is I. I found those columns that support the whole earth...I am the force that lies hid in the winds, from me they take their source, and as a man may move because he breathes, so doth a fire burn but by my blast. All these live because I am in them and am of their life. I am wisdom. Mine is the blast of the thundered word by which all things were made. I permeate all things that they may not die. I am life.[6]

To the scientific mentality of a later age, of course, such testimony smacks of superstition; or at best it is seen as "poetry" in the exclusively horizontal sense we have come to attach to this term. With the advent of the Renaissance the Spirit was banished, as it were, from this visible world; and at the hands of Galileo and Descartes even the so-called qualities have been relegated to a subjective limbo that has haunted philosophers ever since. In place of "that living and fiery essence" of which St. Hildegard had sung, the Newtonians perceived only a self-moving machine, governed by mechanical laws.

Today one knows that the Newtonian picture was but an empty dream. Yet even to the incomparably more sophisticated eye of modern science, the universe appears no less disenchanted and de-spiritualized than before: there has been no change of direction in that regard. One knows today from considerations of a philosophical kind that this disenchantment is implied by the very methodology of the scientific enterprise: one can say with certainty that if there were "spirits"—or entities of a non-material kind—in the universe, they would not be picked up by our scientific instruments or show on our mathematical maps. But this epistemological insight actually carries little weight: after all, the entire thrust of our official education is to convince layman and specialist alike that science constitutes indeed "the sole valid way of apprehending Nature," and that whatsoever does not appear on its prestigious charts belongs *ipso facto* to the subjective realms of fantasy.

Over a period of several centuries, and by successive stages, our civilization has fallen into its present horizontal and reductionist Weltanschauung. The rise of an arid rationalism and a concomitant diminution of the symbolist spirit were no doubt among the primary causes which initiated this development, and have led (as noted before) to the birth of modern science: but no sooner had this new science come to birth, than it began to react upon the intellectual scene, with the result that the secularizing and desacralizing tendencies which had initiated the scientific advance have in turn become amplified and greatly exacerbated. Our civilization thus finds itself caught in a circle which is vicious indeed; for it threatens to deprive us of such spiritual wisdom as we may yet possess.

★   ★   ★

There is a conflict, a certain antagonism, then, between science and religion. Let there be no mistake about it: science is not quite as innocuous or "neutral" as many would have us believe; much less is it a spiritualizing influence. The much-disputed conflict between science and religion does exist; only it lies much deeper than is generally thought.

The conflict—let it be said at once—is not between "scientific fact" and traditional Christian belief. We must understand, in the first place, that scientific fact, pure and simple, is virtually an unknown quantity. It is hard for the epistemologically innocent to realize how much of human subjectivity has of necessity been incorporated into our scientific knowledge. We must not forget that *the world is for us:* it is after all something that confronts us, something that we perceive and imagine, or conceive of and speculate upon. This is not to say that our knowledge is purely subjective; we are not suggesting that the world as we know it is no more than a mental construct or an apparition. What we are saying is that subjectivity and objectivity do not exclude each other: on the contrary, they go hand in hand. We may know the world by way of mental representations, yet what we know is nonetheless the world. The point, however, is that we know it not simply as it is. Inasmuch as our knowledge comes to us through an instrument (beginning with the mind), it is necessarily conditioned—and diminished, as one might say—through the intrusion of subjective elements. What St. Paul has intimated with reference to our knowledge of spiritual realities applies evidently to mundane knowledge as well: "For now we see through a glass, darkly." (*1 Cor.* 13:12).

Science, then, is a particular kind of "glass." It is a glass, firstly, which filters out a major portion of the spectrum: all the higher octaves of being, in fact. And this is why *homo scientificus* cannot perceive "that living and fiery essence," and why even the familiar qualities which we do perceive with our senses are missing from what science is pleased to call "the physical universe."[7]

But the glass also functions as a lens: it magnifies and frames what it transmits. It "magnifies" in the sense that it brings us in touch—like a microscope—with domains of reality which we do not ordinarily perceive; and it "frames" in that it imposes a perspective in terms of which the given content can be received. And that is of course where the elements of subjectivity come into play.

Now this in itself does not impair the objectivity of our knowledge (as we have already said), nor is it *per se* illegitimate or harmful. If this relativized knowledge could be received for what it is and integrated into an adequate world-view, it would then indeed be not only innocuous and "neutral," but presumably enlightening and spiritually useful as well. Under existing conditions, however, this is hardly possible. In the absence of any effective metaphysical knowledge it is virtually inevitable that the world-pictures arising out of the scientific enterprise should be absolutized and thus misunderstood. Unlike the biologist who looks through his microscope and realizes that the ameba is *not* in fact enclosed in a narrow circle, we lack the intelligence to compensate effectively for the phantasms which the complex *modus operandi* of science have imposed upon the universe. To sort these things out is more, surely, than most of us can handle. And we must remember, too, that the scientific development has come about as an expression of anti-metaphysical tendencies: under such auspices, how can one expect prodigies of metaphysical acumen? It is by no means surprising, therefore, that the artful and fragmentary "models" which enshrine our scientific knowledge—or better said, their popularizations—should have come to be regarded by most as a faithful picture of the way things are in reality. And so we find ourselves in effect enclosed within a drab and meaningless universe, a world consisting of empty space and blurred particles whirling perpetually to no discernible end, in which the great truths of religion cannot but appear strange and suspect in the extreme.

"Science is our religion," Theodore Roszak has wisely said, "because we cannot, most of us, with any living conviction *see around it*."[8]

Science itself, moreover, does all it can to prevent us from ever doing so. Through an education which predisposes against all traditional beliefs, through the relentless popularization and vulgarization of its own theories, through the cumulative impact of technology and the artificial environment, and finally through the systematic and well-subsidized channeling of our collective intellectual resources, it has established itself within our civilization as the prime authority in high matters and the sole purveyor of authentic knowledge. But that is not all; for as Roszak points out, "Soon enough the style that began with the natural scientist is taken up by imitators throughout the culture."[9] Before long that prestigious "style" imposes itself upon virtually every sphere of human endeavor—from biblical exegesis to marketing or making love. And so, by stages and degrees, the scope of the scientific enterprise expands so as to span the full gamut from science in the authentic sense all the way to the banal and the absurd. It is no doubt also one of the "undernoted facts of history" that science inevitably begets pseudoscience and its own brand of sorcery.

★   ★   ★

Worst of all, perhaps, as a result of its humanist and scientistic propensities, our age has evolved a thoroughly skewed perception of history. Science and humanism—the twin pillars of modern civilization—have joined forces to discredit and cast aspersions upon our pre-modern past. In essence we have been told that whatsoever cannot be caught in our contemporary scientific nets does not exist, and what does not conform to our humanist criteria of worth is *ipso facto* bereft of value. It does not seem to occur to these savants of modernity that this argument is plainly circular and self-serving. To be sure, an exception is frequently made in our evaluation of the past when it comes to the artistic and literary spheres, or what we take to be high insights of an ethical kind. But in matters of objective truth and "social values," it is generally taken for granted that our ancestors were "unadvanced" and rather wide of the mark. They were children and dreamers, one thinks, because they believed in realities which do not show on our scientific charts, and "unliberated" because they chose to honor the mandates of a supra-human God. "One need only ponder," writes Roszak, "what people mean in our time when they counsel us to 'be realistic'. They mean, at every point, to forgo the claims of transcendence, to spurn the magic of imaginative wonder, to regard the world as *nothing but* what the hard facts and quantitative abstractions of scientific objectivity make it out to be."[10]

It is hardly surprising, therefore, that looking back into the more distant past, the sophisticated individual of our day should behold mainly ineptitude and superstition. As Maximilian Hasak has put it, "The greater the ignorance of modern times, the deeper grows the darkness of the Middle Ages."[11]

From a less provincial point of view, on the other hand, one perceives that is is *we* who live in considerable darkness. Our collective intellectual horizon has in reality become greatly constricted, and the contemporary plethora of "hard facts and quantitative abstractions" cannot by any means compensate us for this loss. On the contrary; as Schuon has observed, a meaningless knowledge "is not a knowledge that enriches, but one that impoverishes."[12] Nor is this all; for if one looks more closely at the modern phenomenon, one can see that it is ominous, and indeed, frightening. Seyyed Hossein Nasr is certainly not exaggerating when he writes:

> There seems to be in this movement from the contemplative to the passionate, from the symbolist to the factual mentality, a fall in the spiritual sense corresponding to the original fall of man... He has lost a paradise of a symbolic world of meaning to discover an earth of facts which he is able to observe and manipulate at will. But in this new role of a "deity upon earth" who no longer reflects his transcendent archetype he is in dire danger of being devoured by this very earth over which he seems to wield complete dominion, unless he is able to regain a vision of that paradise he has lost.[13]

Meanwhile our humanist and scientistic gurus continue to proclaim the gospel of Progress. Only by now the idea of future progress has become solidly allied with a systematic devaluation of our pre-modern past. And so, too, the contemporary apostles of progress busy themselves, not only with the building up of a new order, but equally with the destruction of whatever yet remains of the old. The idea of progress has thus become distinctly subversive: it has become revolutionary, in fact.

We will not speculate at this point as to what might be the ultimate source of that boundless fascination—this veritable mania, one is tempted to say—which has apparently taken hold of the activists, the dedicated leaders in this worldwide movement. Suffice it to say that the rank and file is still somewhat passive and lukewarm, and thus needs constantly to be prodded by progressivist propaganda of one sort or another.[14] Most importantly, however, there are two main factors or "arguments" which in the eyes of the public lend credence to the dogma of progress: the first are the miracles of technology; and the second is the Darwinist theory of evolution, perceived as a scientific fact.

The technological argument is hard to refute, and most men, one fears, have little chance of doing so. In recent times, as we know, it has disarmed and carried off even eminent theologians, men of the cloth well versed in Holy Writ. The idea suggests itself that the feats of our contemporary technological prowess may indeed be "signs and wonders, to seduce, if it were possible, even the elect." (*Mark* 13:22). But be that as it may, it cannot be denied that technology has become the number-one producer of signs and wonders in our contemporary world, and that "The technological repertory of the artificial environment takes the place of the miraculous,"[15] as Roszak has pointed out. These are the only miracles in which we still believe with any real confidence, and it is the modern super-state that pulls them off.

Another prime argument, as we have said, is Darwinism, decked out as a scientific discovery based upon "incontrovertible evidence." Who, after all, can argue with facts, especially when no one has any idea what they are! Such a notion, once it has been drilled into our collective psyche—from grade school to post-graduate encounters—is hard to beat. And if it be true that we have evolved from primate stock, then it is clear on even the most pessimistic evaluation of our present status that there has indeed been progress. It is now only a small step to the conclusion that our more distant forebears—especially those with whose views we do not agree—had not yet altogether cast off their simian vestiges; and so we arrive at last, by seemingly scientific and sober considerations, at the credo of Progress in its full-blown format.

★   ★   ★

The foregoing observations—which admittedly are all too brief—may nonetheless suffice to convey at least a rough idea of Teilhard's intellectual ancestry. Teilhard takes over—lock, stock and barrel—all the humanist and scientistic conceptions of our day, and adds a few touches of his own. His great gift is to synthesize and epitomize these notions, these contemporary tendencies, and bring what is most typical to a sharp point. Moreover, he not only draws together, but magnifies and exalts; in fact, he deifies.

There is first of all his unbounded enthusiasm for science. Most men admire science; but Teilhard goes into ecstasy. Most think that science is a good thing, or perhaps even an incomparable boon to humanity; but for Teilhard it is "the source of Life."[16] Scientists refer on occasion to the joy of scientific discovery; but Teilhard exults in "the divine taste of its fruit"[17] (a phrase, incidentally, which from a biblical point of view is rather interesting).

To anyone who has read his way through the Teilhardian corpus it must be clear that this pervasive predilection for unrestrained eulogy when it comes to science is not just a literary mannerism—it is not simply an instance of what Medawar has called "that tipsy, euphoric prose-poetry."[18] We need rather to take Teilhard at his word when he tells us that "Research has for long been considered by man an accessory, an eccentricity or a danger. The moment is approaching when we shall perceive that it is the highest of human functions."[19] He is absolutely serious: scientific research is not just sublime, or useful, or wonderful—it is precisely "the highest of human functions." And let us not fail to observe what this implies: if scientific research is the highest of human functions, then it is *ipso facto* the religious function par excellence. Science, then, in its full-blown form, is the true and ultimate religion, the quest which by right fulfills and replaces all that men have previously designated by that term. Teilhard himself, moreover, confirms this conclusion: "It will absorb the spirit of war and shine with the light of religions."[20] Here we have it: Science is to be the world religion, the final religion of mankind which incorporates into itself all that was true in the great religions of the past while presumably discarding their errors and limitations. Teilhard even goes so far as to add a distinctly Christian note to this account of the future scientific enterprise: "But let there be no mistake," he declares. "He who wishes to share in this spirit must die and be reborn. . ."[21]

But these are matters which we shall need to take up later, when we come at last to consider the question whether "this is still, of course, Christianity." Meanwhile a simple observation might not be out of place: there is nothing in the teachings of Christ to suggest (however remotely) that the way of salvation might have something to do with natural philosophy or "scientific research." On the contrary, the Gospel conveys very much the opposite impression: "Verily I say unto you,

Whosoever shall not receive the kingdom of God as a little child, he shall not enter therein." (*Mark* 10:15). Think of it! To receive the kingdom of God "as a little child"—the expression, one feels, would hardly fit a modern research team. To put it as impartially as possible: the biblical and the Teilhardian teachings do not agree on this point. What, then, is to be done? Do we cast our lot with Teilhard, when he preaches the religion of scientific discovery? or with St. Paul, when he declares: "Where *is* the wise? where *is* the scribe? where *is* the disputer of this world? hath not God made foolish the wisdom of this world?"

★   ★   ★

Teilhard's view of science dovetails with his view of history—and, of course, Evolution. In his eyes science existed from the start (in a kind of embryonic form) and constitutes the prime vocation of man; it is the tangent vector, one could say, of the evolutive trajectory beyond the simian stage. "As soon as man was man," we are told, "the tree of science began to grow green in the garden of the earth. But only slowly and much later did it flower."[22] In point of fact, of course, the tree of science (at least as Teilhard understands the term) did not begin to flower until Sir Isaac Newton appeared upon the scene—which could account for Teilhard's distinctly low estimate of pre-modern civilization. Where mathematical physics (or perhaps paleontology) has become the gauge of enlightenment, our more distant ancestors do not fare too well. And Teilhard leaves little doubt on that score:

> Yes this must be said, to our own honour and that of those who have toiled to make us what we are: that between the behaviour of men in the first century A.D. and our own, the difference is as great, or greater, than that between the behaviour of a fifteen-year-old boy and a man of forty. Why is this so? Because, owing to the progress of science and of thought, our actions today, whether for good or ill, proceed from an incomparably higher point of departure than those of the men who paved the way for us towards enlightenment.[23]

It is noteworthy that Teilhard has singled out the first century A.D. in this comparison—the age when Christ walked upon the earth and the New Testament was recorded by His disciples. If the Apostles (and one fears, Christ, too!) may be legitimately compared with a fifteen-year-old boy, it is small wonder that, in Teilhard's view, "the Old Church" stands in need of being gradually moved to "new foundations."[24]

But not only was ancient man inferior to us: there is a mechanism of "social inheritance," Teilhard believes, which ensures that the highest achievements of one generation are faithfully transmitted to the next. "Plato and Augustine are still expressing, through me, the whole extent of their personalities,"[25] he tells us (quite seriously!).

Now the one thing that can be said in defense of this (obviously far-fetched) view is that such a mechanism of transmission does in fact exist within the modern scientific enterprise. It belongs in fact to the very concept of science as originally formulated by Francis Bacon. Scientific knowledge, in the Baconian sense which we have made our own, is thus by definition something that is shared and transmitted. It is a cumulative and public kind of knowledge, an information that can be gleaned through the labors of innumerable individuals and stored in libraries and computer banks. There is something distinctly quantitative about this knowledge—its content as well as the manner in which it is obtained. "And too, as Bacon predicted," writes Roszak, "we arrive at a vast and proliferating research—a 'knowledge explosion'—under the auspices, for the most part, of just such small and ordinary minds as he foretold us would be capable of utilizing his method."[26]

Incidentally, it may be worth pointing out that Bacon ranks high among the intellectual forebears of Teilhard de Chardin, and that there is more than a passing resemblance between the two. Thus, according to Charles Gillespie, Bacon was the prophet, not so much of science as such, but of "an image of scientific progress which has been vastly more popular than science itself can ever think to be."[27] And let us not forget that in the *New Atlantis,* Bacon's third and last *magnum opus,* his vision of the scientific utopia begins to assume apocalyptic dimensions. As Roszak observes, "Bacon was among the first Europeans to identify the secular future as the New Jerusalem."[28]

But let us get back to Teilhard's "social inheritance": the idea is applicable, then, to the modern scientific enterprise. And if it be supposed that this is all that matters, then in a sense it is true that the highest attainments of mankind are constantly being passed on and added to. But even if that were the case, this would still not mitigate the plain silliness of Teilhard's remark regarding "Plato and Augustine"; for it should be obvious that the accomplishments of these men—let alone "the whole extent of their personalities"—have little to do with the Baconian quest, to say the least.

What Teilhard has evidently failed to grasp is that the modern scientific enterprise is not simply the culmination of a development that began "as soon as man was man," but actually represents in many respects a new start and a radical departure from the perennial mainstream. To be sure, there is a certain continuity: Paracelsus no doubt contributed to the progress of medicine, Kepler (who was quite a Pythagorean) discovered laws of planetary motion still to be found in our calculus textbooks, and as is often pointed out, our chemistry has evolved out of alchemy. Yet something very essential has been lost; and in a way everyone acknowledges this: one knows very well that the modern sciences are nothing like the old. But of course, in keeping with our progressivist and scientistic mentality, we generally take it for granted that what has been discarded or forgotten was fundamentally worthless. What has been lost, supposedly, was nothing but a superstition. And this is almost correct: a superstition, after all, is "any belief or attitude that is inconsistent with the known laws of science *or with what is generally considered in the particular society as true and rational.*" (Webster). Only when it comes to what might legitimately be termed the traditional sciences, there is in reality no actual conflict with the "known laws" of *our* science: even Ptolemy has never been disproved! The real point of difference (as we have already suggested a number of times) is that the ancient sciences were in large measure concerned with the *symbolic significance* of natural phenomena, as opposed to their "operationally definable" attributes and positivistic laws.

But there is more to be said. The traditional sciences formed an integral part of a culture that could well be described as religious, spiritual and metaphysical in its primary orientation. We are generally astonished to learn, for instance, that there was an intimate connection between traditional science and sacred art (all art, in fact), and that as late as the fourteenth century Jean Mignot (the builder of the Milan cathedral) could say that "Art without science is nothing." Few things, perhaps, are more strange and incomprehensible to the modern mind than the idea that beauty should have anything whatsoever to do with truth—with scientific truth, no less. It appears that the very conception of culture, in the traditional sense, has disappeared from the intellectual horizon of our age; what to speak, then, of its reality.[29]

The fact is that much—very much—has been lost; the mechanisms of "social heredity" do not function quite as well as Teilhard would have us believe. What may hold true of our sciences does not apply to all culture and all human wisdom without exception. Baconian science has its own limitations and its stringent though perhaps invisible boundaries. Moreover, even within the scientific sphere (using the term in its traditional or premodern sense) it represents no more than one particular avenue of approach. And however sublime, marvelous or practically useful it may be, Teilhard's contention that this Baconian enterprise sums up and incorporates within itself all that is highest in the cultural and intellectual history of mankind is patently absurd.

★   ★   ★

What impedes Teilhard's perception of history is not just the typical mind-set of our age: Teilhard has outstripped his contemporaries in that respect. He has fashioned a theoretical instrument, one might say, which systematically constricts our view. Now, as one can readily surmise, that instrument is none other than his central "Law of Complexity." It is by means of this imagined Law that Teilhard has in effect cut down our field of vision to dimensions of smallness never before attained: to a single one-dimensional continuum, so to speak, coordinatized by a postulated "parameter of complexity."

The question arises, of course, how this all-important parameter—this universal gauge—has been defined: how does one set about to measure the "complexity" of a civilization, or compare the respective complexities of different cultures?

And as we have noted earlier (in Chapter 3), no one has really the slightest idea; even in the comparatively simple realm of inorganic chemistry, such a marvelous index has not yet been found. There can be no question, then, whether the Teilhardian concept of complexity is adequate or reliable as a gauge of human culture: for in point of fact the parameter does not exist.

There does exist, of course, an intuitive notion of complexity, which is not without significance. But the difficulty is that "complexity," in this general and distinctly pre-scientific sense, does not constitute a quantitative or quasi-numerical notion; in mathematical parlance, it is not a variable taking values in an ordered set. One needs to recognize that there exist different *kinds* of complexity, and that these are in general not comparable. What is more "complex," for instance: a Byzantine icon, or the blueprint of some complicated machine? Does the question even make sense?

Corresponding difficulties, moreover, arise on the opposite side of the Teilhardian divide: "consciousness" too, no less than complexity, is not to be conceived in such one-dimensional and inherently quantitative terms. But obvious as this may be, Teilhard seems to believe that both can somehow be measured, that both constitute a "variable" in much the same sense in which this can be said of such things as temperature or barometric pressure. What else is the so-called Law of Complexity, after all, than a stipulated equation or proportionality between "complexity" and "consciousness," each conceived as a quasi-numerical parameter? Thus, tricked (as it would seem) by his famous Law, Teilhard fails to recognize the obvious: that there are, namely, many kinds of complexity and many different modes of consciousness, and that not everything can be neatly parcelled out on a numerical scale.

There is the complexity of the icon, for example, as well as the complexity of the blueprint; and no doubt these go hand in hand with corresponding modes of consciousness. There is an undeniable connection: a certain "language of forms," one can say, which translates an outer structure into an object of consciousness, a Gestalt of some sort, replete with its own significance and unique value: all art, clearly, depends upon this fact. Getting back to our example, there is evidently a profound *qualitative* difference between the icon and the blueprint:

whether we consider the two objectively (in terms of "complexity," let us say) or subjectively (in terms of "consciousness"), we find in either case that they are indeed "worlds apart." We know this, we sense it clearly; but we are quite unable to *measure* this difference; the concept of number, or of quantity in the widest conceivable sense, does not apply to the realities in question, or shed light on what is actually at stake.

If we must speak of "complexity" at all, then let us realize that in the case of the icon, at least, that concept cannot be taken in a purely "mathematical" sense. We know, for example, that icons involve color, and that colors are used not simply to differentiate one region from another (as might be the case with blueprints), but on account of a certain symbolic significance. It would never do, for instance, to interchange blue with red, and so forth. Each color has its own characteristic "value," and there is a special significance, too, in the combination of colors. In the chromatic sphere no less than in the tonal, one can speak of harmonies and of chords. To be sure, this implies that the "complexities" in question have also a quantitative aspect: there is a mathematical side to art (which brings us back to Jean Mignot). But the point is that quantitative considerations —such notions as wavelength, frequency, ratio, distance or area—pertain only to one aspect, one "dimension" of the phenomenon. The icon (and indeed, every work of art) has also a qualitative aspect, which is perhaps tantamount to saying that it has a symbolic value. There is a vertical dimension to art (so long, at least, as it is authentic), a reference to spiritual realities; and that is of course the essential thing.

In modern times, on the other hand, art has to a considerable degree lost that quality of vertical reference: as Ananda Coomaraswamy has pointed out, our Western art has become transformed from a "rhetoric" into an "aesthetic"—which is to say that it is no longer meant to enlighten, but only to please. The transition was inevitable; as our Weltanschauung flattens, so does our art. It is no accident: art mirrors culture. In fact, it is not Teilhardian complexity but art that actually constitutes a faithful and universal gauge of human culture. To see what has happened—to comprehend that momentous transition from the medieval to the modern world—we need but to open our eyes: all the forms, not only of what we are nowadays pleased to call "fine art," but of art in the much wider and original sense—in a word, all man-made forms speak (most eloquently!) of that cultural metamorphosis. And the message is clear: our civilization has moved from "the age of the icon," let us say, into the "age of the blueprint"—into the age of sheer quantity, the age of the machine.

But needless to say, Teilhard de Chardin does not look at the matter quite that way. As an intellectual heir, however distant, of the great French rationalists (notably Descartes), it never occurs to him that art could have anything whatsoever to do with intellection. Facts and concepts (or thought) are all that counts. Art, in fact, is hardly ever mentioned, and when Teilhard does occasionally refer to it, he leaves little doubt that in his eyes this sphere of human endeavor has to do mainly with the Freudian libido.[30]

What is more, Teilhard is bound and determined (as we have already pointed out) to perceive the entire pageant of history within the preconceived framework of his so-called Law. A single, quasi-numerical parameter of "complexity" is supposed to measure the height and depth of human culture—inclusive, even, of the religious phenomenon. The fundamental idea is simple enough: the universe begins with scattered particles. Then gradually, and mostly by chance, these particles come together to form aggregates. First come atoms, then simple molecules, then bigger and more complex molecules; then come cells and simple multi-cellular organisms. Moreover, in parallel with this progressive complexification, there is a concomitant rise of consciousness. Somehow complexity begets consciousness: that is the general idea. And finally we come to man (presumably the most complex and most highly conscious of creatures), where the entire evolutive process has apparently reached its term. At least most Darwinists have thought so, and even Teilhard admits that there is not the slightest reason to believe that *homo sapiens* have become biologically upgraded since the species first appeared. At this point, however, Teilhard proceeds to add a decisive touch of his own: that is where the Law of Complexity comes into play. Having first of all persuaded himself that this imagined Law has been somehow verified (by means of the same "mountains of evidence," presumably, which are supposed to have established organic evolution as a "scientific fact"), he now claims (by extrapolation, so to speak) that this same Law guarantees a further evolution—not, to be sure, of *homo sapiens* as such, but of the human collectivity. Henceforth it is presumably the process of socialization that is building up ever more complicated aggregates, and will in course of time give birth—if all goes well—to a collective super-organism endowed somehow with a supra-human consciousness. For the moment a few observations will suffice. What mainly complexifies the world, according to Teilhard de Chardin, is the progress of science and technology. He is thinking in terms of such things as burgeoning libraries and research institutes, giant industries, and radio-waves beaming tons of information around the globe. But if we recall what has been said above— that there are in fact many different *kinds* of complexity—then it becomes immediately clear that Teilhard is looking at only one particular aspect of human culture: the most external and ontologically inessential, no less. By adhering to his celebrated Law, he has systematically restricted his outlook so as to exclude from its purview all qualities, all art, all symbolism, all vertical reference of any kind. Now this in itself is not necessarily illegitimate—what makes it so is the contention that the resultant picture is adequate, that in fact it brings to view what is most essential in the human phenomenon, and exhibits the true mechanism behind the dynamics of world history.

Let us not fail to observe, however, that unfounded though it be, this Teilhardian contention has obviously been persuasive. And the reason, moreover, for this success—this phenomenal prestige and influence—is not really far to seek: by seizing upon the notion of complexity as if it were the single all-important factor, and pretending that this concept is capable of being quantified, Teilhard has laid the foundations of a pseudo-doctrine which purports to provide a solid scientific basis for our humanist dreams. And not just our humanist dreams, but also our Christian ideals—our highest spiritual aspirations—have been supposedly justified and re-established on this new footing: after millenia of groping, at last we *know!*

This is the great promise; and it is reputedly secured by the Law of Complexity. This presumed Law is supposed to hold the key to the problem of life. On the strength of this ostensibly scientific principle Teilhard would have us believe that our

civilization can complexify itself, not just into a humanist utopia, but right into the New Jerusalem.

We need not detain ourselves too long with the observation
that the actual facts point very much in the opposite direction.
Teilhard himself, moreover, admits as much when he writes
(in one of his letters) that "I feel resolved to declare myself
a 'believer' in the future of the world, *despite appearances*"[31]; or
when he observes that "at close quarters and on the individual
level we see the ugliness, vulgarity and servitude with which
the growth of industrialism has undeniably sullied the poetry
of primeval pastures."[32] Yet elsewhere (when the Muse of Progress beckons) he seems literally to gloat over the fact that
"mechanized masses of men have invaded the southern seas,
and up-to-date airfields have been permanently installed on what
were until yesterday the poetically lost islands of Polynesia."[33]

Teilhard seems to forget, moreover, that what is being systematically obliterated is not just "the poetry of primeval pastures,"
but every last vestige of pre-modern culture. The sad fact is
that "mechanized masses of men" do not simply build airfields
—they bulldoze entire civilizations. And whatever might be the
gain, it cannot be denied that the presumed advantages are com-
pensated by a certain cultural impoverishment and an irrepara-
ble loss. It is after all not just idle curiosity which causes modern
city-dwellers to jet across the seas in order to spend a few days
on whatever yet remains of "the poetically lost islands of Polynesia," or in some other still "unspoiled" region of the globe.
Teilhard conveniently forgets that man does not live by such
things as airfields alone. And needless to say, he also forgets
that industrial civilization is coming more and more to resem-
ble an avalanche in process of breaking loose, and that from
a great many points of view the entire development threatens
not just the well-being of mankind, but its very survival.

It cannot be said, moreover, in any absolute sense, that the
"social organism" is becoming complexified. In the scientific
and technological spheres, of course, an ongoing and progressive complexification is very much in evidence; but in other
domains of culture the very opposite is taking place. Thus, in
conformity with our egalitarian leanings, all forms of hierarchic order are in process of being dismantled, and it appears
that the notion of a "classless society" has established itself

just about everywhere as the ultimate desideratum. In recent decades, moreover, even the division of the sexes (which, as we have noted before, mirrors the primordial duality itself) has become a prime target of egalitarian zeal, and the charming prospect of "unisex" is now before us. Despite an increasing vocational specialization, therefore, associated with the technological advance, it is plain to see that human society has in modern times become levelled-out and homogenized in other respects. And here again one may conjecture that this transition is inevitable: as our Weltanschauung flattens, so does our culture. More precisely, civilization flattens by losing its verticality—its hierarchic order and qualitative differentiations—as opposed to distinctions which pertain more or less to the quantitative domain. And as it flattens, it expands. This is the point we have made before: when being loses its "upper stories," human culture has nowhere to go but "forwards." Under such auspices, science and technological conquest remain basically as the only viable frontier.

But this entire state of affairs is exceedingly unnatural, and dangerous in the extreme. One can see (in the light of what has been said earlier about the ongoing Fall) that the erosion of the traditional social order and all religious ties threatens to cut us off, more completely than ever before, from the primordial Center and the Source of life. Having all but severed our spiritual moorings, we stand helpless in the face of that ominous "attraction of the periphery" against which there is no "secular" defense. And we can clearly see the effect of that Force: all indicators point to the fact that society is now set upon an accelerating centrifugal course. Who can deny that the image of the avalanche is far from inapt?

Just about everyone, moreover, is beginning to sense this. A pronounced disenchantment with the idea of scientific progress has begun to set in. Having but recently experienced the horrors of two world wars, and finding ourselves condemned to live henceforth under the shadow of ecological doom and nuclear holocaust, we are anxious as never before. The euphoria of the nineteenth century has clearly departed from our generation, presumably never to return. Uncertainty and frustration bordering upon despair have begun to take hold of our post-Christian civilization, and underneath such progressivist hoopla as yet remains one senses a growing *Angst.* Our literature is full of this mounting unease, and its signs are etched on the faces of even the young.

But let us get back to Teilhard de Chardin: against this darkening backdrop of gathering clouds, the priestly scientist declares himself a "believer" in the future of the world *"malgré les apparences":* despite all appearances to the contrary. What is more, he claims to have validated our modernist hopes and even our spiritual aspirations by the one thing in which our disillusioned civilization still believes with unabated vigor—and that is scientific law. Now what could be more attractive to a post-Christian generation, or to a society which finds itself sinking gradually into the quicksands of despair, than a gospel of Hope and Progress, based, not upon Revelation or faith, but upon the incontrovertible evidence of science? Rendered invincible, as it were, through the possession of his magic Law, Teilhard presents himself as the appointed prophet and champion of mankind.

Never mind that this Law operates with a fictitious parameter, that it abstracts from reality and ignores what is most essential; these are technical points, which seem never to have bothered the multitude of Teilhardian enthusiasts. Never mind that, scientifically speaking, all this is empty talk. Medawar was right: it *is* the style—aided, no doubt, by "hope's élan"—that creates "the illusion of content."

NOTES

1. *Man and Nature* (London: Allen & Unwin, 1968), p. 64.
2. *Forgotten Truth* (New York: Harper & Row, 1977), p. 120.
3. Op. cit., p. 68.
4. St. Maximus the Confessor, *Mystagogy,* P.G. 91:669C; quoted by Archimandrite Vasileios in *Hymn of Entry* (Crestwood, N.Y.: St. Vladimir's Seminary Press, 1984), p. 67.
5. *The Fourfold Vision* (London, 1945), p. 91; quoted by S.H. Nasr, op. cit., p. 41.
6. Quoted by S.H. Nasr, op. cit., p. 102.
7. We have discussed this question at considerable length in *Cosmos and Transcendence* (La Salle: Sugden, 1984), pp. 13-42.
8. *Where the Wasteland Ends* (Garden City, N.Y.: Doubleday, 1973), p. 124.
9. Op. cit., p. 31.
10. Op. cit., p. 124.

11. Quoted by Ananda Coomaraswamy in *Christian and Oriental Philosophy of Art* (New York: Dover, 1956), p. 29.
12. *Light on the Ancient Worlds* (London: Perennial, 1965), p. 44.
13. Op. cit., pp. 37-38.
14. See, for instance, Jacques Ellul, *The Technological Society* (New York: Knopf, 1964).
15. Op. cit., p. 125.
16. FM, p. 20.
17. HE, p. 165.
18. *Mind,* Vol. 70 (1961), p. 99.
19. HE, p. 38.
20. HE, p. 38.
21. HE, p. 38.
22. HE, p. 165.
23. HE, p. 18.
24. FM, p. 23.
25. FM, p. 18.
26. Op. cit., p. 157.
27. Quoted by Roszak in op. cit., p. 137.
28. Op. cit., p. 137.
29. On the subject of traditional culture we would refer the interested reader especially to the pertinent works of Ananda Coomaraswamy, Frithjof Schuon, Titus Burckhardt, Seyyed Hossein Nasr, Martin Lings, Gai Eaton and Lord Northbourne.
30. See, for example, HE, p. 129, where Teilhard tells us that love, "which I understand here in the strict sense of 'passion';. . . is nevertheless well known to be the inspirer of genius, the arts and all poetry."
31. *Lettres de Voyage, 1923-1955,* Edition Grasset, p. 107 (the italics are our own).
32. FM, p. 261.
33. FM, p. 131.

Chapter IX
Socialization and Super-Organism

One of Teilhard's most original ideas is that the formation of social aggregates constitutes a strictly biological phenomenon. Socialization supposedly continues and extends the process of organic evolution which is said to have produced the living organisms inhabiting our globe. "We see Nature combining molecules and cells in the living body to construct separate individuals," Teilhard tells us, "and the same Nature, stubbornly pursuing the same course but on a higher level, combining individuals in social organisms to obtain a higher order of psychic results. The processes of chemistry and biology are continued without a break in the social sphere."[1]

That is the theory; but where is the proof? On what grounds has Teilhard put forth this remarkable claim? And as one might have come to expect by now, it turns out once again that Teilhard's bold contention is buttressed by nothing more substantial than an assortment of metaphors. He speaks, for example, of "the development, through the increasingly rapid transmission of thought, of what is in effect a nervous system, emanating from certain defined centers and covering the entire surface of the globe"[2] —as if such things as telephone wires and radio transmitters could constitute an actual nervous system by the mere fact of contributing to "an increasingly rapid transmission of thought." To be sure, there is a functional analogy here: both telephone wires and neurons have something to do with the transmission of thought or information of some sort. Yet it is clear that one must not press such correspondences too far; an airplane, after all, is in certain respects analogous to a bird; but does this mean that it also lays eggs? If there are analogies between the technical and the biological realms, there are also differences of the most fundamental kind; how, then, could anyone be so naive as to take such metaphors as that of the nervous system (or the bird) at face value? Yet this is precisely what Teilhard does when he announces that "the processes of chemistry and biology are continued without a break in the social sphere." What he means, quite plainly, is that a radio transmitter is not just analogous (in certain respects) to a nervous system, but that it *is* a nervous system (or more precisely, a part of one). There is not only a partial analogy between the two, but a complete continuity of process.

No wonder that Henri de Lubac (faithful defender that he is) has tried hard to play down this contention—even though it happens to be central to the Teilhardian theory. For indeed, so far from being a secondary or negotiable issue, the biological interpretation of socialization and technology is nothing less than the key idea upon which Teilhard's entire vision of the future has been staked. It is the great extrapolation, validated supposedly by the Law of Complexity, on which Teilhard would found his ethics, his social, political and religious doctrines, and his highest mystical speculations. As Teilhard himself informs us in his major work, "All the rest of this essay will be nothing but the story of the struggle in the universe between the unified *multiple* and the unorganized *multitude:* the application throughout of the great *Law of complexity and consciousness.*"[3]

Enough has already been said with reference to this "great law" in other parts of this book (especially in Chapters 3 and 4). To put it bluntly, there *is* no such law: the notion is in reality a myth. And the same holds true, of course, of the Teilhardian extrapolation from this professed Law; this, too, is a myth—a modern version, perhaps, of the Prometheus motif. Or as the French biologist Louis Bounoure has said (from a slightly more prosaic point of view): "The presumed Super-evolution is nothing but the result of a puerile confusion between biological evolution and human progress."[4]

★   ★   ★

Let us nonetheless examine Teilhard's theory in somewhat greater detail. To begin with, there is another central contention which it behooves us to reflect upon. Not only does the aggregation of "human particles" give rise to a biological super-organism, but what is even more surprising, the process is supposed to "personalize" these so-called human particles to an unprecedented degree. "The tightening network of economic and psychic bonds in which we live and from which we suffer," Teilhard tells us, "the growing compulsion to act, to produce, to think collectively, which so disquiets us—what do they become. . .except the first portents of the super-organism which, woven of the threads of individual men, is preparing (theory and fact are at one on this point) not to mechanize and submerge us, but to raise us, by way of increasing complexity, to a higher awareness of our own personality?"[5] In a word, "socialization personalizes"; so goes the formula.

Now in the first place, what does this mean? It should be clear from the start that in the framework of Teilhard's theory the person can be nothing other than the center (real or imagined) of reflective consciousness: it is the ego, the subjective pole of our thought. Teilhard is moving (as one can see) within the magic circle of the *cogito ergo sum.* To be sure, he has no more use for the Cartesian *res cogitans* or "thinking entities"—a "static" notion which has no place in a thoroughly evolutive universe. In Teilhard's eyes, the ego is not so much a being as it is a process; it is essentially an act. As he tells us in *The Phenomenon of Man,* "The ego only persists by becoming ever more itself, in the measure in which it makes everything else itself. *So man becomes a person in and through personalization.*"[6] But we must remember that the ego "makes everything else itself" precisely by way of thought. And so we find that the *cogito ergo sum* is still in force, and holds, in fact, in a more radical sense—for whereas in the philosophy of Descartes the formula "I think therefore I am" is to be understood in the sense that thought implies the existence of a thinker, in Teilhard's philosophy it means, essentially, that the thinker is nothing but the center of the thought.

We still need to ask ourselves, however, what "personalization" is supposed to mean when the term is applied to "human particles," to "particles," therefore, which are already personalized. In other words, what does it mean to personalize a person?

After the miracle of reflective consciousness has already taken place, what more can we ask? Nothing, it seems, other than to demand that the mental outreach should widen, that the human ego-in-progress should to an ever higher degree "make everything else itself." And this, presumably, is what is taking place through the advance of science and technology in a society dedicated to the Baconian enterprise. This is what is happening, for instance, when we watch the evening news and see distant events unfold before our eyes. And let us not forget that these things are brought into our consciousness, to be "made ourself" in thought, by way of that "collective nervous system" of which we have spoken before.

There is a certain logic, then, in the idea that socialization personalizes. Within the framework of the Teilhardian theory such a phenomenon (or such an "effect") can indeed be envisaged up to a point. Not, to be sure, to the full extent that Teilhard would have us believe. For example, under Teilhardian auspices there can be no question at all of any personal immortality (a *bona fide* survival of Peter and Paul); and as we have seen before, even the survival of the human race beyond the habitable lifespan of our planet is also *de facto* unthinkable, despite all of Teilhard's efforts to establish the contrary.

But even with these restrictions clearly in view, there is yet something deceptive and illusory in the Teilhardian notion of a progressive personalization of mankind. The concept of personalization, thus defined or interpreted, is after all exceedingly artificial and somewhat trivial at that. It can hardly be denied that the cultural value of such things as global news coverage is limited, and perhaps even the staunchest advocate of progress might flinch before the contention that TV heightens the "terrestrial consciousness." We suspect, therefore, that the Teilhardian concept of "personalization" could actually arouse little enthusiasm if it were not for the fact that the term is generally misunderstood and overestimated. Consciously or unconsciously, Teilhard is utilizing to his own advantage certain overtones which have no more place in his system. We must remember that for centuries our civilization had entertained a vastly more profound conception of personhood, an idea rich in associations which still, presumably, resonate to some degree in our soul. And so, whether one speaks of "person" or of "personalization," the very word has yet a certain ring that inspires and exalts. It has spiritual overtones, one might say, which refer to another domain entirely.

It is worth recalling, in this connection, that a person, in the authentically Christian sense of that term, is said to be an *imago Dei*. The person is thus incomparably more than the ego (in the modern sense), the phenomenological "I" which is inextricably tied to our thought. One could put the matter this way: whereas thought depends upon the person, the true person does not in turn depend upon thought. And that is of course the reason why the person as such can survive the catastrophe of death, by which, after all, the brain—the instrument of thought—is unquestionably annihilated.

We need to understand, in the first place, that the person in us did not (and could not) come into existence as a result of an evolutionary process, an "aggregation" of some sort. Our bodies—perhaps; but not our personhood. "And the Lord God formed man of the dust of the ground, and breathed into his nostrils the breath of life; and man became a living soul." (*Gen.* 2:7). To say that our bodies were formed "of the dust of the ground" does in fact suggest quite strongly that they were formed through a process of aggregation; but it is all the more noteworthy that this alone is not enough to make a man, and that Adam did not become "a living soul" until God had infused into him a certain higher principle. The reference to "breath," moreover, points to a spiritual principle, and even suggests a certain continuity or kinship with the divine: what God has infused into Adam appears to be a "spark," as it were, kindled by the Fire of God.

But then, if it is not the case that our personhood came into being through an evolutive process of aggregation, it becomes unreasonable to suppose that we shall be further "personalized" through a process of socialization conceived along evolutive lines; to think thus is simply to compound the initial Darwinist error. One can still, presumably, speak of "personalization" in the sense of a spiritual self-realization, or spiritual growth. But if it be true that our personhood derives "from above," then it must also be true that our "personalization" depends upon a spiritual influence. Under favorable circumstances, moreover, such an influence may be transmitted through the medium of a human collectivity; and this was indeed the rationale, one could say, of the traditional civilizations, and pre-eminently of the institutional Church. But it cannot be said that every collectivity (regardless of the principles upon which it is based) is able to fulfill that function. When it comes to specifically modern societies, moreover, societies based upon the ideals of secular humanism, one finds that the dominant thrust points exactly in the opposite direction: such societies (be they capitalist or communist) are inherently anti-traditional. There is a crucial difference here, which we must not overlook: despite all their shortcomings, pre-modern societies were yet to some degree "traditional" in the true sense of transmitting a beneficent spiritual influence to the population at large; that is what "tradition" (from *tradere,* to "deliver" or "transmit") actually signifies. There was human failing, of course, a pervasive falling off from the values and standards upon which these traditional societies were based. And yet a spiritual and spiritualizing influence continued to flow, as it were, through multiple channels of transmission. In modern times, however, the picture has changed: what impedes us today is not simply a falling short on the part of individuals, but an inbuilt godlessness, a Promethean spirit of disobedience which has been officially inscribed, as it were, upon our tablets of law. A certain collective neo-humanist *hybris* has effectively insulated us, *en masse,* from the higher spiritual world. It is not a question of having outgrown the past (as we like to believe), but of spiritual incomprehension and a concomitant rebellion; in our gradually emerging Brave New World the breaking of sacred vessels has come to be regarded as a meritorious act and a mark of enlightenment.

Now in such a society, "personalization" in the authentic sense is indeed an untypical occurrence. Yet the phenomenon continues to exist. There will always, presumably, be souls able to swim against the stream; and let us not forget that numerous traditional channels, both religious and cultural, are still operative—in other words, the great Revolution is still incomplete.

It follows from these admittedly cursory observations that "personalization," in the truly Christian sense, can mean nothing more nor less than spiritual growth—which is not to say, of course, that our contemporary gurus are incapable of using the term to designate very much the opposite. After all, the devaluation and debasing of linguistic coinage has ever been a favorite enterprise of the anti-traditionalists, and constitutes moreover an especially effective mode of what we have termed "the breaking of sacred vessels." But be that as it may, the fact remains that within the modern technological society personalization has become untypical, as we have said. In a sense, and to some degree, we all participate in the ongoing collective Fall. There is an analogy here with the theological concept of Original Sin: in certain respects every member of an aberrant society suffers from the misdeeds and infidelities of those who have contributed to the formation of the given *status quo*. Not that we are morally responsible for the sins of another; what has been placed upon us is not the onus of sin, but of a certain incapacity. Yet it is not by any means an absolute incapacity, one that cannot be overcome—that is the crucial point. As Eric Voegelin has well put it, "No one is obliged to take part in the spiritual crisis of a society; on the contrary, everyone is obliged to avoid this folly and live his life in order."[7]

Which leads us to a final observation: the fact is that the highest degree of personalization is to be found precisely in those heroic men and women rightfully referred to as "saints." One needs but to read an account of their lives, and a few of their utterances, perhaps, to realize how unique and powerful a personality shines through these outer forms. It might not be too much to say that just as every flower has its own inimitable fragrance, so every saint has a "spiritual perfume" all of his own, by which he (or she) can be recognized. And let us not forget to observe also that for the most part this spiritual growth, this true personalization, has been achieved without any of the collective means which Teilhard prizes so much: no research institutes, no scientific congresses, no stupendous technology. As a rule these spiritual giants live as simple children of the Church. Their circle of physical contact has often been limited in the extreme; and not a few of their number have lived out their years in the isolation of deserts and caves.

The conclusion that emerges from these various considerations is clear: it is *not* true that "socialization personalizes." This, too, is a humanist illusion, and another Promethean myth.

★   ★   ★

Having touched upon the subject of "spiritual influences," it behooves us to recall that these can be of very different kinds. We know from Christian tradition that there are (within the created order) many categories or grades of spiritual beings, and we know too that not every spirit is beneficent. This is a fundamental truth which has been much overlooked in modern times: there *are* malefic spirits in the world—it is not fable. We know this, not only on the authority of Scripture and tradition, but also from hard empirical facts; one does not exorcise a fable!

Now from this point of view as well we see that traditional societies hold the edge over the modern world inasmuch as they recognized the existence of such malign influences and tried (not always successfully) to protect against calamity. Presumably a great deal of what in our eyes is superstition was instituted to ward off or neutralize malefic forces of one sort or another. On a perhaps loftier plane, moreover, there were wise men about to warn against these perils and preach spiritual prudence (as there are still to some extent today), but most importantly, the populace at large was yet sufficiently "superstitious" to pay heed. This, too, has changed. Under the influence of humanist notions the idea of evil has become discredited, and meanwhile a popularized science has convinced most of us that "spirits" do not exist. Nothing, therefore, could be more suspect, nowadays, than the idea of evil spirits (even though, in the wake of increasingly frequent outbursts of satanism, some folks are beginning to reconsider the issue). But be that as it may, "our modern soul" (to use Teilhard's phrase) does not much resonate to the idea, so much so that even believing Christians tend to become curiously inattentive when they hear (if indeed they still do) that "We wrestle not against flesh and blood, but against principalities, against powers, against the rulers of the darkness of this world, against spiritual wickedness in high places." (*Eph.* 6:12).

Getting back to Teilhard de Chardin, we need now to observe that on this fateful issue, too, the French Jesuit is solidly aligned with the neo-humanist camp. Apart from any other considerations, this follows already from his evolutionist premises, or if you will, from that Law of Complexity which is supposed to be the key to just about everything—for if spirit is the specific effect of an aggregation which can be gauged in terms of a postulated parameter of complexity, then spiritual nature does indeed submit to the notions of "more" or "less," but not to *bona fide* qualitative distinctions. In particular, the distinction between beneficent and malefic spirits becomes inconceivable under these auspices. If spirit is the product of evolution, and if evolution is desirable or beneficent (as Teilhard ardently believes), then spirit is invariably good. That is what it comes down to. Never mind that this theory makes no sense even from a purely materialistic point of view; Teilhard speaks as if every sufficiently complex molecule were *ipso facto* a nutrient or a vitamin, and as if there were no such things as cyanide. The more "complex," the better and the more spiritual: that is the gist.

Let us not fail to observe that in the social and political spheres this means of course that every form of totalitarianism or collectivization—no matter how brutal—can on principle be accorded high rank, provided only that it complexifies "the human mass" to a sufficient degree. It also means that every "center of centers" can be assimilated to Omega, provided only that it attracts "human particles" and causes them to aggregate. Within the framework of Teilhard's theory it becomes impossible to conceive of an intrinsically bad society—of a mode of social aggregation, namely, which is inherently harmful or productive of evil. Where evil is conceived as nothing but disorder, order of whatever kind becomes beneficent. In the sphere of human collectivities no less than in the domain of molecules, Teilhard is committed to the risky notion that every complex is a vitamin, and that cyanide does not exist.

What Christianity calls "discernment of spirits" has thus been ruled out. There is no more difference between angels of light and angels of darkness; and one doubts, in fact, that there are any angels left at all. In a Teilhardian universe there can be no such thing as "spiritual wickedness in high places." The idea that demons not only exist, but can also congregate, has become inconceivable; in Teilhard's world there is no room for a "synagogue of Satan." (*Rev.* 2:9). What is more, Teilhard has deftly done away with Satan himself: the concept of a nether pole of attraction, an anti-Omega, has also been ruled out. As we are told repeatedly in *The Divine Milieu,* all human labors—all human acts without exception—are done under the aegis of the Risen Christ. At one point Teilhard goes so far as to say (with an inconsistency that is not untypical) that even "evil spiritual powers" [sic.] are His "living instruments."[8] Think of it! All those monsters of iniquity—from Jack the Ripper to Adolf Hitler—the "living instruments" of Christ!

*   *   *

In Teilhard's eyes the one great desideratum—literally "the one thing needful"—is the building up of the technological super-state. And from a thoroughgoing evolutionist point of view, there is indeed a certain logic in this position. As Teilhard points out, "To all appearance the ultimate perfection of the human *element* was achieved many thousands of years ago, which is to say that the individual instrument of thought and action may be considered to have been finalized." In other words, on the plane of the human individual, evolution has reached the end of the line. "But there is fortunately another dimension," he goes on to explain, "in which variation is still possible, and in which we continue to evolve."[9] Now that other dimension, of course, refers to the social domain, the sphere of the human collectivity. From an evolutionist angle of vision there is only one viable path, one viable option before us, and that is collectivization: to act collectively, to produce collectively, and even to think collectively—that is "the growing compulsion" from which there is supposedly no escape.

Teilhard realizes, of course, that to most of us the prospect of compulsory collectivization is distinctly unpalatable. As we have noted earlier, as yet it is chiefly the activists—the professional collectivizers, one could say—who seem to be sold without reservation on the idea of a joyous serfdom to the emerging super-state. The rest remain disquieted and apprehensive in varying degrees. And for good reason: if facts mean anything, there is little ground indeed for optimism. Even Teilhard admits that "The modern world, with its prodigious growth of complexity, weighs incomparably more heavily upon the shoulders of our generation than did the ancient world upon the shoulders of our forebears."[10] And he admits, furthermore, that so far as "recent totalitarian experiments" are concerned, the results have been none too good, to say the least.

But we must not give up so easily. "In so far as these first attempts may seem to be tending dangerously towards the sub-human state of the ant-hill or the termitary, it is not the principle of totalization that is at fault, but the clumsy and incomplete way in which it has been applied."[11] The "recent totalitarian experiments" (Teilhard is speaking before the French Embassy in Peking in the year 1945) refer of course mainly to the exploits of Hitler and Stalin (Mao Tse Tung's "experiments" had not yet run their course); it is interesting, therefore, that Teilhard seems not to be unhappy with "the principle of totalization" exemplified by these developments, but only with the manner in which that principle has been put into operation. We are not told in which respects this praxis was "clumsy" (admittedly in both instances the methods were not particularly refined!) and "incomplete"; perhaps the experimenters neglected to liquidate a sufficient number of people (five or six million apiece might not have been enough). In any case, Teilhard leaves us in the dark on these issues. The only thing we are told in no uncertain terms is that sooner or later the experiment will succeed.

It must, because there is no other way—that is the bottom line. Repeatedly, in fact, Teilhard works his way through an elaborate dialectic to prove that all other roads are barred. He does so, for instance, in an essay entitled "The Grand Option," in which he confronts us successively with three alternatives. In each case the desired option is exhibited as the second of two possibilities, the first of which is always patently objectionable. Each "fork in the road," moreover, leads on to the next, until one arrives at the final conclusion. As Teilhard informs us at the end of this complicated tour:

> Our analysis of the different courses open to Man on the threshold of the socialization of his species comes to an end at this last fork in the road. We have encountered three successive pairs of alternatives offering four possibilities: to cease to act, by some form of suicide; to withdraw through the mystique of separation; to fulfill ourselves individually by egoistically segregating ourselves from the mass; or to plunge resolutely into the stream of the whole, in order to become a part of it.[12]

Now the only difficulty with this argument is that in each instance the stipulated alternative turns out to be spurious: the whole exercise is consequently a classic example of what we have previously referred to as the method of false alternatives. It is true enough that the first three options listed above are unacceptable—but this in itself does nothing to establish the fourth.

Let us consider, for example, the second presumed alternative: "On the one hand there are those who see our true progress only in terms of a break, as speedy as possible, with the world...And there are those on the other side, the believers in some ultimate value in the tangible evolution of things...withdrawal, or evolution proceeding ever further? This is the second choice that human thought encounters in its search for a solution to the problem of action."[13] The crucial implication, of course, is that if we reject the first of the two proposed options (the straw man), then we have *ipso facto* committed ourselves to the second. But this is not actually the case; there happens to be a middle ground between the two. We are not in reality standing before a Y in the road.

An ancient inscription (to be seen at Fatehpur Sikri) comes to mind in this connection: "Jesus says"—so reads the inscription—"the world is a bridge: pass over it, but build no house thereon." Here we have the answer, the Christian response, no less: the world is not an evil to be shunned, or an illusion from which to liberate oneself; but neither is it destined to be our permanent home. It is a bridge. There are those, perhaps, who would jump off, and those who would build houses thereon; but "Jesus says: pass over." The world does have a purpose—but it is there, not simply to torment or to please, but to teach wisdom and kindle charity. And this it does as much by its insufficiencies as by its plenitude, as much, perhaps, by its sharp cruelties as by its tender mercies. The Christian—yes, the Christian optimist—has no reason to suppose that the world is destined to become better and better; it fulfills its function just as it is. It is *we*—and not the world—who need to become better.

The Christian is thus concerned, not so much with the world at large, or with the human collectivity, but with himself and his neighbors; his love extends, not to some super-state, but above all, to God, and in second place, to his brothers and sisters in Christ. And it is men and women, let us remember, who are to be saved—not the state! That convergence of mankind which Teilhard postulates, and the attendant notion of a collective salvation—these ideas are utterly foreign to Christianity. Christ never promised that the world at large is destined to evolve into a utopia. It is only a bridge: pass over it, but build no house thereon.

There *is* a third option, then, a way of living and acting in the world which entails neither withdrawal ("as speedy as possible"), nor yet a belief in progress and a commitment to the formation of a collective super-organism. And this observation —simple as it is—suffices to invalidate Teilhard's argument: his entire long-winded exhortation has failed to establish the desired conclusion. It thus remains to be seen whether "We can do no other than plunge resolutely forward, even though something in us perish, into the melting-pot of socialization." Nor does it help his case when Teilhard adds (in ostensibly Christian accents): "Though something in us perish? But where is it written that he who loses his soul shall save it?"[14] For indeed the possibility remains that there may be more than one way of "losing one's soul."

★   ★   ★

To plunge resolutely forward "into the melting-pot of socialization": that is the great imperative. In Teilhard's eyes this option is nothing less than the true Way of Salvation which leads straight into the New Jerusalem.

Now basically this means that the Marxist and the Christian are fellow-travelers: they may not know it yet, but despite certain inessential differences of outlook they are proceeding more or less along the same path and towards one and the same goal. As Teilhard has put it:

> Take the two extremes confronting us at this moment, the Marxist and the Christian, each a convinced believer in his own particular doctrine, but each, we must suppose, fundamentally inspired with an equal faith in Man. Is it not incontestable. . .that despite all ideological differences they will eventually, in some manner, come together on the same

summit?...Followed to their conclusion the two paths must certainly end by coming together: for in the nature of things everything that is faith must rise, and everything that rises must converge.[15]

Let us carefully consider these words (which in the light of recent developments have evidently been swallowed by millions). To begin with, we must object to the idea that what the Christian believes is "his own particular doctrine." Actually, nothing could be further from the truth; even Christ declared: "My doctrine is not my own, but his that sent me." (*John* 7:16). To speak of the Christian as "a convinced believer in his own particular doctrine": what a travesty! Either Teilhard does not understand what Christianity is, or he does not accept its claim. To set the record straight: the doctrine of Christianity is *not* a man-made ideology, on a par with Marxism, but a revealed truth. It is a truth taught by God, speaking to us, first through the prophets, and at last through His incarnate Son. It is a teaching, moreover, which "flesh and blood" cannot receive; for as St. Paul declares, "No man can say that Jesus is the Lord, but by the Holy Ghost." (*1 Cor.* 12:3).

Nor can it be maintained that the Christian and the Marxist are "fundamentally inspired by an equal faith in Man." For in the first place, what fundamentally inspires the Christian is not in fact a faith in Man: he is not a humanist. The Christian believes, first and foremost, in God: in the God of Revelation, "the living God of Abraham," as distinguished from "the God of the philosophers." The Christian does, of course, uphold a certain faith in man—he believes in the dignity of man, in certain inalienable rights, and above all, in his high calling as a potential son of God. But he does not believe in man as an autonomous being; not for a moment can he accept the notion that the human individual, or the human collectivity, is at liberty to deny God or reject His mandates. He thus abhors secular humanism, whether it be conceived along individualist or collectivist lines. His faith in man, therefore, is qualified. The Christian knows that God alone is absolutely good, and that in the last analysis, all strength and all glory belong to God alone. He knows full well that our own strength is weakness, and our human wisdom mere folly before God. The true Christian, therefore, does not put too much stock in such human factors as the strength of numbers, the power of wealth, or the efficacy of Five Year Plans. He sees everything from a higher point of vantage. He knows, for example, that God can accomplish the mightiest works through the most frail and humble instruments. And he knows, too, that whatever man does simply on his own cognizance and in his own name will eventually fail. Cities and empires will crumble into dust, and even our boast of scientific knowledge will prove hollow in the end; like Isaac Newton, he realizes that we can do no more than gather a few pebbles by the seashore, while the ocean of God's truth lies undiscovered before us.

What utter foolishness, then, to maintain that the Marxist and the Christian are "fundamentally inspired with an equal faith in Man"!

But there is more to be said: the Christian knows that he belongs to a Kingdom that is not of this world. It is a Kingdom, moreover, which does not lie simply at the end of the collective road: nothing could be further from the truth. "Neither shall they say, Lo here! or, Lo there! for, behold, the kingdom of God is within you." (*Luke* 17:21). And so, unlike the Marxist utopia, the Kingdom of God exists at this very moment, and is close at hand—only the world sees it not and knows it not. And the reason has also been told: we do not see that Kingdom, because we are looking in the wrong direction. We need a change of heart, a true *metanoia* or "repentance"—not just in the sense of feeling sorry for our misdeeds, but in the incomparably more profound sense of a veritable "turning around." The call of St. John the Baptist is still "relevant" today: "Repent ye: for the kingdom of heaven is at hand." (*Matt.* 3:2).

Meanwhile it appears that the neo-humanist gurus of the future paradise are paying little heed to this call, and that the world at large is heading precisely in the wrong direction. Let us be clear about it: the Bible speaks not only of "brotherly love," but of a few other things besides—the phrase "*vanitas vanitatum*" ("Oh vanity of vanities!"), for instance, is also to be found in the Good Book. And harsh as it may sound, the true concern of the Christian is not so much to assist in the accomplishment of collective projects as it is to convert souls. His is an unwelcome voice: for it is his vocation as a Christian to convict the world of its folly, and to call all men (and first of all himself!) to a *metanoia*, a radical change of mind and heart.

Christian charity, therefore, is something quite different from humanist philanthropy, not to speak of Marxist fanaticism: for we must never forget that the prime object of this charity is to bring souls to Christ.

Teilhard, of course, does not perceive any intrinsic opposition between the following of Christ and the way of the world. He thinks that such opposition as there appears to be is due in large part to an antiquated understanding of what Christianity is about, based upon a pre-evolutionary conception of the universe. From an evolutionary point of view, to be sure, it is apparent that Christianity can be nothing more than one particular manifestation of the human spirit, one particular expression of a single universal human drive. "Look well," Teilhard declares, "and we shall find that our Faith in God, detached as it may be, sublimates in us a rising tide of human aspiration." And he adds: "It is to this original sap that we must return if we wish to communicate with the brothers with whom we seek to be united."[16]

To this the Christian—the "pre-evolutionist" Christian, to be precise—is bound to reply: Look well, and you shall find that our Faith in God derives from an incomparably higher source. As with Peter, so with us: "Flesh and blood has not revealed it unto you, but my father which is in heaven." (*Matt.* 16:17). And so, too, that Faith impels us in a new direction, and towards a very different end: it wars, in fact, against the "human aspirations" of the carnal man, the man who lives on the level of "flesh and blood." St. Paul speaks in principle for all Christians when he declares: "I delight in the law of God after the inward man; but I see another law in my members, warring against the law of my mind, and bringing me into captivity to the law of sin which is in my members." (*Rom.* 7:22, 23). Now what else is that "law of sin which is in my members"— what else could it possibly be—than that "original sap" on which Teilhard has his eye? Let him say what he will: the fact remains that the Christian and the neo-humanist are *not* fellow-travelers. There is indeed a parting of the way, a clearly marked fork in the road—and it is up to each and every one of us to make his choice.

★   ★   ★

At one point Teilhard himself broaches the natural question whether the neo-humanist "religion of conquest" which he extols might not in fact be Promethean. In an essay commemorating the first explosion of an atom bomb—after having informed us that "Thus the greatest of Man's scientific triumphs happens also to be the one in which the largest number of brains were enabled to join together in a single organism"[17] —he proceeds to contrast what he takes to be the Promethean and the Christian spirit. Teilhard perceives the former as "the spirit of autonomy and solitude; Man with his own strength and for his own sake opposing a blind and hostile Universe; the rise of consciousness concluding in an act of possession."[18] And opposed to this, on the Christian side, he envisages "the spirit of service and of giving; Man struggling like Jacob to conquer and attain a supreme center of consciousness which calls to him; the evolution of the earth ending in an act of union."[19]

Now these definitions call for comment. Let us begin (on the side of Prometheus) with "the spirit of autonomy and solitude." What, precisely, does Teilhard have in mind? He is thinking no doubt of the self-centered human individual, the egoist who lives for himself and fends for himself. The universe appears hostile and blind to such a man simply because, quite obviously, it is not specifically designed to serve his own selfish ends. And what are these ends? Wealth and power, mainly; or, as Teilhard puts it, "an act of possession."

The Christian spirit, on the other hand, is said to be "the spirit of service and of giving," and also, of course, "the spirit of love."[20] But what kind of love? That is the crucial question. Everyone, to be sure, speaks of love; and the heretics, it would seem, do so the most. What, then, is Teilhard alluding to? Is it the true Christian *agape*? Is it the love which Christ enjoins upon us in "the first and great commandment" (*Matt.* 22:38)? Or in the second, perhaps: "Thou shalt love thy neighbor as thyself"? And what about the idea of union—union with what? Here, too, there is a certain ambiguity which needs to be resolved. What, then, is actually the object of adoration which Teilhard has placed before us: is it God or is it Man?

By now the answer to this basic question should be plain: Teilhard's gaze is obviously fixed upon Mankind, upon the emerging super-state, upon that super-organism which is supposedly being formed by way of "planetization": "the evolution of the earth ending in an act of union," as he tells us—that is evidently what his teaching is about.

But is this Christianity? Is this the teaching of Christ? Once again Teilhard has muddied the waters with his dialectic of false alternatives. To begin with, he has misconstrued the Promethean ethos. If it be admitted that Teilhard's egoist is indeed a Promethean type (a question which is debatable), he represents in any case a comparatively harmless variety: there is another kind, far more dangerous, which Teilhard has left out of account. Who would deny, for instance, that the fanatical Nazi, the individual who is ready at the drop of a hat to suffer martyrdom for *Reich* and *Führer*, is any less Promethean than the more familiar (and far more innocuous) egoist? Teilhard is very much mistaken when he identifies the Promethean characteristic with the egoistic bent—as if Prometheanism were simply a question of being selfish or antisocial. He forgets that devils, too, can collaborate. No; that is not the point at all. What characterizes the Promethean spirit—let it be clearly understood—is not the pitting of an individual human "I" against the human collectivity, but the pitting, rather, of man (whether individual or collective) against God.

To glorify oneself, or to glorify some human conglomerate: is there really quite so sharp a distinction between the two cases as Teilhard leads us to believe? Is there no such thing as a family egoism, a national egoism, or an ethnic egoism? The "I" and the group, the human collectivity with which I identify: are these not simply the two complementary poles (like the two foci of a single ellipse) around which the carnal man inevitably circulates? Is this not already implied by the fact that man is inherently a "social creature," a being who cannot actually be conceived in isolation from his group? And is it not clear, too, that even robbers act in union with one another, and that even murderers take care of their own?

What Teilhard has done is to misconstrue the Promethean ethic by restricting its scope to what in reality can be no more than a limiting case: the extreme of individualistic egoism. And having done so, he then proceeds immediately to misconstrue the Christian ethos by confusing it with the complementary extreme of the Promethean: it becomes basically Marxism, the worship of Collective Man.

Now it is true, certainly, that both Christianity and Marxism are opposed to the ideals of the crass egoist, the individual who has not yet learned to identify with anything larger than the local self. But this in itself does not validate Teilhard's contention to the effect that Christianity and Marxism are somehow equivalent. It obviously takes more than a common opposition to the egoistic ideal to establish the remarkable conclusion that Christians and Marxists are fellow-travelers.

Teilhard conveniently forgets, moreover, that Prometheus stole the fire from Heaven, not just for himself, but precisely for the benefit of mankind. And what indeed could have been more in accord with Teilhard's own program? If there be yet any doubts on that score, the following elucidations should certainly suffice to settle the matter:

> Thus considered, the act of the release of nuclear energy, overwhelming and intoxicating though it was, began to seem less tremendous. Was it not simply the first act, even a mere prelude, in a series of fantastic events which, having afforded us access to the heart of the atom, would lead us on to overthrow, one by one, the many other strongholds which science is already besieging? The vitalization of matter by the creation of super-molecules. The remodelling of the human organism by means of hormones. Control of heredity and sex by manipulation of genes and chromosomes. The readjustment and internal liberation of our souls by direct action upon springs gradually brought to light by psychoanalysis. The arousing and harnessing of the unfathomable intellectual and effective powers still latent in the human mass.. .[21]

It is interesting, moreover, that this Faustian fantasy culminates in the following proclamation: "In laying hands on the very core of matter we have disclosed to human existence a supreme purpose: the purpose of pursuing ever further, to the very end, the forces of Life. In exploding the atom we took our first bite at the fruit of the great discovery, and this was enough for a taste to enter our mouths that can never be washed away.. ."[22]

Now apart from the fact that this is of course Promethean-ism, pure and simple, we should not neglect to point out yet another "mythical concordance" which is no less worthy of note. A "fruit of great discovery," a fateful "bite," a taste "that can never be washed away"—where have we heard this before? And what about "the very core of matter," wherein reside "the forces of Life": is this not indeed reminiscent of the Tree of Life which is said to stand at the exact center of this earthly realm? Teilhard reminds us, moreover, that by its very nature this fateful drama of discovery relates to the conflict of good and evil; he perceives "the light of a growing unanimity" set against "the nightmare of bloody combat."[23] And what, let us ask, is the nature of that light-bearing concord? Is it not the very "unanimity" through which man has been enabled to split the atom and thus discover, as Teilhard tells us, "another secret pointing the way to his own omnipotence"[24]? What a revealing phrase: "another secret pointing the way to his own omnipotence"! Is this not precisely the ancient temptation, the promise that has tantalized our race: "Ye shall be like gods"? Even the biblical plural fits: this is no solitary venture!

★   ★   ★

No one need be surprised that Teilhard exhibits a special interest in the Pauline teaching concerning the Mystical Body of Christ. Teilhard's approach to Christian dogma, as we have seen, is selective: what it amounts to, basically, is that he accepts those articles of Faith which can (with suitable modifications) be somehow fitted into his evolutionist scheme, and does away in effect with the rest. Now the Mystical Body, so Teilhard believes, can be made to fit. He points out, first of all, that "To this mystical super-organism, joined in Grace and charity, we have now added a mysterious equivalent organism from the domain of biology: the 'Noospheric' human unity gradually achieved by the totalizing and centering effect of Reflection."[25] What Teilhard is driving at, of course, is that these two "super-organisms" are actually the same, and that it behooves us to recognize this fact: "How can these two super-entities," he tells us, "the one 'supernatural', the other natural, fail to come together and harmonize in Christian thought?"

It is a diplomatic way of announcing the presumed identity. We must remember that in 1947, when this "prophecy" was made, that identification would have been patently unacceptable in official theological circles (a question which is no longer

196 Teilhardism and the New Religion

quite so clear today). Meanwhile it appears that the anticipated fusion had already taken place in Teilhard's own thought; in a footnote (on the same page), in fact, he alludes to "the collective human organism ('the mystical body')," as if the issue had already been decided. It is interesting, moreover, that what has been put under quotes is "the mystical body"—as if the so-called collective human organism ("from the domain of biology") were indeed the concrete reality to which the theological phrase ultimately refers. And is this not also the reason, presumably, why the adjective "supernatural" has been put in quotes when Teilhard refers to "these two super-entities, the one 'supernatural', the other natural"? It seems to be Teilhard's way of informing us that the Mystical Body is supernatural only from the standpoint of a pre-evolutionist Christian thought in which the two conceptions have not yet merged.

Meanwhile it will be of interest—at least from a "pre-evolutionist standpoint"—to see what Scripture and Christian tradition have to say on the subject. There are biblical references, of course, to the Mystical Body; but are there not also allusions to that other "super-organism"—the one which is to be built up through the collective enterprise of men?

There are such references, certainly; and the most striking, no doubt—the example which immediately comes to mind and has become proverbial—is to be found in the story of Babel or Babylon. "And they said, Go to, let us build a city and a tower whose top may reach unto heaven" (Gen. 11:4): what could be more unequivocal than that? "A tower whose top may reach unto heaven": is this not indeed reminiscent of the Omega hypothesis? There is even a reference (in the same pericope) suggesting the key notions of "planetization" and "unanimity" which figure so prominently in the Teilhardian venture: "The whole earth was of one language and one speech." (Gen. 11:1). "One language": could this not be interpreted (in the present context) as "the universal language of science"? And "one speech": might this not refer to a single global system of communication, the very thing which Teilhard conceives as the actual nervous system of a gargantuan super-organism in the process of formation?

These are exegetical speculations, of course; but they are by no means incongruous. Let us note in this connection that St.

John speaks of Babylon at considerable length in an apocalyptic context, a setting to which the indicated line of interpretation might certainly apply. Here the reference is evidently to future events which the Prophet of Patmos was able to foresee. But whether it be the Babylon of Genesis or of the Apocalypse, the basic idea remains the same: in either case it is a city or a "social organism" constructed through the concerted efforts of men for their own (individual or collective) self-aggrandizement. And it is worth noting how accurately this symbol fits the description of Teilhard's "collective human organism": for indeed, that super-organism, like a city, is composed of both "human elements" and man-made artifacts, the products of technology.

It is also interesting to observe that both Genesis and Revelation stress the Promethean character of this collective venture, which consists not so much in a denial of God (Prometheus himself was no atheist!) as in the fateful notion that man, by his own collective endeavor, is able to accomplish what by right appertains to God. Now this putting of man in the place of God—is this not precisely the hallmark of the Promethean? And what, let us ask, is the object of this presumption: what is it that Promethean man sets out to accomplish? Is it not indeed "to build us a tower whose top may reach unto heaven"? In other words, is not the Promethean aspiration tantamount to the idea that through collective enterprise, guided by reason, mankind can "reach up to heaven": can establish itself in "the world to come," in the Heavenly Jerusalem? The great presumption, then, the Promethean sin, is not simply the hope that Heaven can be attained, but the notion—the "evolutionist faith"—that it can be attained through concerted human effort.

And this is what (figuratively speaking) brings down "the wrath of God": Babylon always falls, it is always shattered in the end. It is indeed a city built upon sand, a vain thing; and as the Good Book likewise teaches, it is not Babylon, but that other City—the one that is built upon a Rock—which will prevail and be victorious, and will endure *in saeculum saeculi* ("for ever and ever").

There are two Cities, then: one built by man, the other by God, or by "the sons of God," as we are also told. "The Lord came down to see the city and the tower which the children of men built." (*Gen.* 11:5)—this is how the Old Testament describes Babylon: it is the city "built by the children of men," the "earthly city," as St. Augustine observes, built not by "the sons of God," but by "that society which lived in a merely human way."[26]

There are two Cities, then: the earthly and the heavenly, the natural and the supernatural. And not only are the two different, but they are actually opposed; this, too, we learn from the Bible. God Himself takes up arms, as it were, against Babylon: "So the Lord scattered them abroad from thence upon the face of all the earth: and they left off to build that city." (*Gen.* 11:8). The "unanimity" of which Teilhard speaks will eventually give way to conflict—that is what the Bible predicts. And the Tower will crumble into dust long, long before Heaven (or Omega) is reached.

★   ★   ★

To speak of the Two Cities is to refer to the inherent opposition between the way of the world and the following of Christ. And despite its current unpopularity, this recognition is of vital importance: the Two Cities—or the Two Ways—are always before us, and they are mutually antagonistic.

Physics teaches that bodies move invariably along the path of "least action"—the path of least resistance, if you will; but the Christian does just the reverse: he moves perpetually "against the stream."

The way of the world, one could say, is like that of a river which descends (as all rivers do) and broadens as it runs its course; but the way of Christianity may be likened to a mountain path which ascends and narrows as it approaches the summit.

A striking description of the Two Ways is to be found in the Gospel according to St. Matthew: "Enter ye in at the straight gate: for wide is the gate, and broad is the way, that leadeth to destruction, and many there be which go in thereat: Because straight is the gate, and narrow is the way, which leadeth unto life, and few there be that find it." (*Matt.* 7:13, 14). And it is certainly not without interest to observe that the Gospel immediately goes on to say: "Beware of false prophets, which come to you in sheep's clothing, but inwardly they are ravening wolves." (*Matt.* 7:15).

No wonder, then, that the Christian life commences with an act of repentance, with a *metanoia* or "conversion," as we have noted before. The fact is that on account of Original Sin we are by nature or by instinct, as it were, headed in the wrong direction. And so, too, the humanist mainstream leads, not to the Promised Land—as the apostles of Progress would have us believe—but to a deadly precipice: as Christ has many times forewarned us, great will be the destruction of those who shall be swept over its fearful brink. Repent, therefore; change your course before it is too late! That is the Christian message.

But needless to say, such is not the teaching of Teilhard de Chardin. The closest he ever comes to admitting that there is after all a difference between the Christian and the humanist ideals is when he likens the two to vectors pointing in orthogonal directions, which need henceforth to be combined. "OY and ox, the Upward and the Forward," he tells us: "two religious forces, let me repeat, now met together in the heart of every man; forces which, as we have seen, weaken and wither in separation. . ."[27] But this, too, is untenable. In the first place, inasmuch as true religion is indeed concerned with the supernatural and derives "from above" (unless, of course, we assume from the outset that its claims are invalid), it is something altogether different from neo-humanism in any of its forms, which is clearly a man-made ideology. Thus, to place these two things on the same plane and speak indiscriminately of "two religious forces" is already to confuse the issue, to say the least. And it is questionable, too, that Christianity is supposedly destined to weaken and wither away unless it joins forces with the neo-humanist camp: has it not waxed strong and thrived for at least a millenium and a half simply on its own? And if we look carefully at the subsequent decline (which began precisely with the advent of modernist ideas), do we not find that the very opposite has actually occurred: that Christianity has become weak and lifeless in proportion as it has become mixed with humanist ideals?

It is no wonder, moreover, that this should be the case—if only we recall that according to the explicit teachings of Christ there can be no such mixing, no such compromise. "No man can serve two masters" (*Luke* 16:13), we are told. As Christians we are called upon to love and serve God, not just halfway, but "with all thy heart, and with all thy soul, and with all thy mind" (*Matt.* 22:37)—what could be more unequivocal than that?

There can be no mixing of the Christian and neo-humanist ideals, no merging of the two vectors, as Teilhard suggests. We must choose, therefore. We are free to take either path; no one compels us. Meanwhile two voices impinge always upon our ears: there is the loud, external voice of the world calling us to that broad mainstream on which "the many" seem always to be embarked; it speaks to us of Progress, of the conquest of Nature, and the setting up of a kindgom upon this earth; it speaks of Evolution, of a Promethean venture: "Ye shall be as gods"; and there is also a second voice, soft and gentle, a voice that is heard in stillness and in poverty of spirit: "Come unto me, ye who labor and are heavy laden." It is a voice that calls us, not to the Promethean enterprise of those who would be like gods, but to that spiritual heroism so abundantly exemplified by the saints and martyrs of the Church.

These are the two options, the two paths. And so far from being destined eventually to converge, it appears that the inherent opposition between the two will become only more sharply manifest as we approach that limit-point of history which Christianity knows as the Parousia, the Second Coming of Christ. "And ye shall be hated of all men for my name's sake," Christ declares (with reference to those latter days): "but he that endureth to the end shall be saved." (*Matt.* 10:22). We are given to understand, in fact, both in the apocalyptic discourses of Christ and in the Book of Revelation, that there is to be a vast counter-movement to Christianity which will gain enormous power as mankind passes into the final phase of its earthly existence. What confronts us here is not simply an "axis ox" set at right angles to "the Christian axis oy," but a hostile force of supra-human proportions and a final battle to the death. It appears that this counter-movement will be realized by a collective human organism replete with its own Antichristic "center of attraction": it will in all respects be a caricature, a kind of satanic imitation, of the true Mystical Body. And this super-organism will grow and wax great by deceiving vast multitudes with its clever lies and marvelous feats. And in the end it will hoist religious colors and proclaim itself divine.

It is hardly surprising, however, that Teilhard has little to say on that subject, and seems to avoid it like the plague.

*   *   *

Dietrich von Hildebrand relates how in the course of a conversation with Teilhard de Chardin he happened to say something about St. Augustine. "Don't mention that unfortunate man," Teilhard is said to have exclaimed violently; "he spoiled everything by introducing the supernatural."[28]

To which one might add that long before the Bishop of Hippo, Christ had obviously committed the same offense when He declared: "My kingdom is not of this world."

It is not often, however, that Teilhard exhibits his "crass naturalism" (as von Hildebrand calls it) quite so openly. There are times, moreover, when Teilhard himself seems to admit the existence of the supernatural; for example, when he says (with reference to the Mystical Body) that "This kingdom, in its essence, goes beyond the domain of life that is, in a strict sense, called supernatural."[29] If there exists a domain that can, "in a strict sense," be termed supernatural, then perhaps St. Augustine was not really quite as "unfortunate" as Teilhard suggests. But on closer examination we see that the actual thrust of the preceding observation is not so much to affirm the supernatural as it is to blur the distinction between the two domains. And since no one, presumably, entertains any serious doubts regarding the existence of the natural order, it is the supernatural that suffers by being swallowed up and in effect eliminated.

What Teilhard is telling us, basically, is that all forms of "progress"—and most especially our scientific and technological advances—are actually taking place under the aegis and inspiration of Christ (unacknowledged though this fact may be), and that all these activities are contributing to the formation of the Mystical Body, which is therefore coextensive with the emergent social organism.

Now this surmise constitutes one of Teilhard's crudest mistakes. Ostensibly he bases his conclusions upon the presumed universality of Christ: if Christ is universal—so the implicit argument goes—then His Kingdom can have no bounds. But

what he fails to grasp is that while Christianity maintains that
the whole of humanity has indeed been redeemed by the Risen
Saviour, everyone is free to participate in that Redemption or
to exclude himself therefrom. In a word, we are saved
potentially—"for the asking," if you will—but we are not as
yet actually saved: there is a crucial choice to be made, as we
have noted before. We begin to participate in the supernatural
life (we "receive the Holy Ghost") as soon as we have done
our part, but not a moment before. What is needed is a conversion, a catharsis, and an initiation—and we may leave it to the
theologians to spell out more precisely what this entails. In
any case, there is a decisive step that needs to be taken consciously and with deliberation; and it is by this step that we
become *bona fide* members of the Mystical Body, also known
as the Church.

The universality of Christ, therefore, and of the Redemption
which He has won for mankind upon the Cross, must not be
interpreted to mean that the Mystical Body is coextensive with
humanity at large, or that it will be such in the future. Christ
Himself has made this perfectly plain; for instance, when He
speaks of the good grain and the tares growing together in
the same field.

Let us also remember that for those who are prepared to receive the gift, the supernatural life begins here and now: we
need not wait for death and Judgment to occur. Through Bap-
tism (and all that by right pertains to this Sacrament) we are
born into a new life: we "put on Christ," as St. Paul declares.
Now it may well be true that a Christian is able to live his
Christianity not only in the performance of what are commonly
regarded as religious acts, but in virtually all worthy occupa-
tions. St. Paul himself continued to make tents, and he no doubt
transformed this métier into a profoundly Christian act. And
this is just the point: an action which ordinarily is profane can
be Christianized, so to speak, and thus taken up into the supernatural life, which is the life in Christ. It is then profane no
longer, nor is it any more a merely natural act. An infusion
of grace has occurred, a descent of the supernatural—a trans-
figuration, one could almost say. But this does not mean that
the line of demarcation between the Kingdom of Christ and
the profane world has been blurred or obliterated; it does not

mean that near its outer fringes, so to speak, the former ceases to be strictly supernatural. To say such a thing is to misunderstand completely the meaning of the Christian life.

According to Teilhard's theory, salvation is in effect the ultimate product of socialization; it will come about through scientific research and the development of a fantastic technology. But this is a colossal mistake: mankind is to be transformed into a super-humanity, not by some linkage with itself through technical means, but by union with God through spiritual means. *Deo volente,* we shall all be one in the Spirit of God; but that Spirit is not something that has evolved, or that shall evolve, as Teilhard maintains. It is eternal; and the problem of life, therefore, is not to create that Spirit, but simply to receive the divine gift, to become receptive. And this is a matter, not so much of the brain, but of the heart: it is "the pure in heart" that shall see God. Teilhard is hopelessly mistaken when he thinks that the truly spiritual life will be achieved through a kind of super-cephalization; he is looking in the wrong direction. The brain, after all, is only an instrument; it is a computer, if you will—and most assuredly no one becomes spiritual through calculation. There is something else in us—call it soul, intellect or spirit—and this is what needs to be purified and awakened. If the sanctified man can "see God," it is certainly not by way of cerebral activity! And let us not forget that it is ultimately through spiritual sight that we enter into the Kingdom of God: for "this is life eternal, that they might know thee the only true God, and Jesus Christ, whom thou hast sent." *(John* 17:3).

But needless to say, the brain has nothing to do with this supreme knowledge. It has to do, rather, with the outer life: our life in this world. It is an instrument, one could say, adapted to this particular sphere of existence—something that is needed precisely so long as we are *not* in the Spirit.

Now, one might perhaps object to this statement on the grounds that Christianity speaks, after all, of a resurrection of the body. But does the dogma in question imply that in life eternal we shall possess a brain made up of neurons? Certainly not! What it does indicate is that this earthly brain made up of neurons manifests a spiritual reality—an archetype, if you will—and that by virtue of this fact it can be realized or exemplified on a higher plane. The body can be spiritualized, it can be transfigured, precisely because it is *not* just an aggregate of particles. It has another dimension, one is tempted to say; there is about it something that survives the dissolution of particles. And this means also that even here and now the particulate brain is not really the essential thing.

But let us get back to the Mystical Body of Christ. Scripture teaches that this Body came into being through a supernatural influx of the Holy Ghost: "I came to cast fire upon the earth..." (*Luke* 12:49). Thus it sprang into existence "from above," and not "from below," as Teilhard's theory implies. And what is more, it was created suddenly—in a single instant—as befits the action of the Holy Ghost: "And suddenly there came a sound from heaven as of a rushing mighty wind, and it filled all the house where they were sitting." (*Acts* 2:2). Nothing could be further from the Christian truth than the notion that the Mystical Body has gradually evolved.

Now the Body that came to birth at Pentecost is indeed a supernatural organism, or a spiritual organism, if you will. It belongs to a different plane; or better said, it constitutes a new creation, a new world. Strictly speaking, the Mystical Body is none other than "the World to Come": it is the New Jerusalem, the Kingdom of Heaven. And yet it has entered into this world, entered into history. It is not a thing of the future any more (as it was in the days of the Old Testament), but of the present. That is the great mystery: "The time is fulfilled and the Kingdom of God is at hand." (*Mark* 1:15). Whether we realize it or not, the New Jerusalem is already standing before us; it has penetrated into our world. We are living, therefore, in "the latter days." The old order, the purely "natural" world, is still there, to be sure; but that world is on its last legs, so to speak—its days are numbered. For even now, rising up in its midst, the Christian seer beholds the Mystical Body, the new creation which is destined to supplant and supersede the old.

This is the veritable "super-organism" of which Christianity speaks; and let us be careful to add that it is indeed supernatural. Though *in* the world, it is yet separated therefrom: like soul and body, the two do not mix. For all its proximity, the Mystical Body is by no means continuous with the natural order, but is situated, as one might say, on a higher ontological plane. It is therefore invisible to our natural organs of perception, and to the profane intelligence which is geared, as we know, to the realities of the sense-perceived world: "Flesh and blood has not revealed it unto you..." (*Matt.* 16:17).

*   *   *

The Mystical Body, we have said, does not evolve out of human society by a natural process or through human means, but came into existence suddenly, through the descent of the Spirit. It is God's free gift to mankind. This "super-organism," moreover, is an accomplished fact: it stands before us here and now. It is not at all our task, therefore, to set about with Promethean might to construct the New Jerusalem; the one thing needful, rather, is to make ourselves receptive through humility and love. All that Christ asks of those who would enter the Kingdom of Heaven is that they be "poor in spirit." (*Matt.* 5:3).

That is the supreme goal which Christianity has set before us; and let us understand clearly that it has nothing to do with any collective enterprise. It is Peter and Paul—and not some human collectivity—that is to be incorporated into the Mystical Body. And this happens (when it does) in a single instant— because the miracle is wrought, not through human effort, but through the operation of the Holy Ghost.

There are, of course, degrees of adhesion to the Mystical Body of Christ. Yet it remains true that a certain knowledge imparted by the Holy Spirit is indeed "the hallmark and seal of the believer," as Archimandrite Vasileios has put it. Every true Christian has known (however faintly) the "flavor" of the life in Christ, and the "taste" of holiness. Whether he fully realizes it or not, he lives already on two planes and knows two lives; but the worldly-minded know only one. It is always thus: the higher includes and transcends the lower. When we grow up we do not cease to understand the pastimes of childhood; we only lose our relish for these former things. We have no more desire to engage in these once-fascinating activities, because we have found something better. There is an inherent asymmetry here, which betokens a change of level, a change of plane.

The Christian can very well live in a technological society, and can even participate to some extent in its projects. Yet his heart is not set upon these goals. And when it comes to the satisfaction of his deepest aspirations, he has no need for any secular institutions; at that point such things as research institutes, industries or universities are of no use to him at all. To put it very simply: the authentic Christian experiences a need to withdraw periodically into the contemplative solitude of his heart, into that inner "closet" which Christ bids us enter. (*Matt.* 6:6). There he communes with God, and there he drinks to his heart's content of the spiritual nectar. And having done so—having become filled and fortified with the gifts of the Spirit—he descends, as it were, into the humdrum world, to share his riches with his brethren, and serve his neighbor who is in need. That is the fully Christian life. It is a life lived on two planes; or better said, it is a heavenly life lived here and now upon this earth.

In truth it is the men of this world, those sophisticated builders of the Teilhardian "super-organism," who are childish and misguided. They seek Heaven in the building of some gigantic Babylon, not knowing that Heaven is already at hand, that it lies within easy reach. What a pity! What a tragic farce.

Meanwhile the Mystical Body is extending its sway. It is forming in the quiet of deserts and mountain caves, and it is forming amidst the tumult of great cities. It exists wherever a human heart loves Christ. We have argued earlier that on the whole our modern preoccupation with science and technology has not been congenial to spiritual growth; and that is another point. Yet the fact remains that spiritual life is possible everywhere; the Spirit, like the wind, "bloweth where it listeth" (*John* 3:8)—even in factories.

Yes, spirituality can blossom wherever there is to be found a human heart that has not yet been killed. And this heart needs to be ignited by being brought into living contact with the Mystical Body of Christ (which is the Church): these are the two requisite factors. Apart from this nothing is needed—nothing at all.

NOTES

1. FM, p. 136.
2. FM, p. 137.
3. PM, p. 61.

4. *Recherche d'Une Doctrine de la Vie* (Paris: Laffont, 1964), p. 155.
5. FM, p. 120.
6. PM, p. 172.
7. *Science, Politics & Gnosticism* (South Bend, Ind.: Gateway, 1968), pp. 22-23.
8. DM, p. 127.
9. FM, p. 16.
10. FM, p. 122.
11. FM, p. 123.
12. FM, p. 49.
13. FM, p. 36.
14. FM, p. 54.
15. FM, pp. 198-199.
16. FM, p. 200.
17. FM, p. 149.
18. FM, p. 153.
19. FM, p. 153.
20. FM, p. 153.
21. FM, p. 149.
22. FM, p. 151.
23. FM, pp. 151-152.
24. FM, p. 148.
25. FM, p. 232.
26. *City of God,* XVI.5.
27. FM, p. 278.
28. *Trojan Horse in the City of God* (Chicago: Franciscan Herald, 1967), p. 227.
29. SC, pp. 16-17.

Chapter X
The New Religion

Before the advent of Teilhard de Chardin it was generally assumed in evolutionist circles that religion *per se* had become an outmoded superstition, and the expectation was rife that in time these "primitive vestiges" would give way before the advancing front of scientific enlightenment. There were still believers, of course, and there was yet the Old Church rising up like a medieval fortress within the modern world. But the stronghold was obviously under siege, and by human reckoning, at least, it seemed that its days were numbered.

This is where Teilhard enters upon the scene. He proceeds forthwith to develop a position of his own through a number of successive steps, beginning with the simple recognition that science and the various forms of neo-humanism constitute basically a single integrated movement of worldwide scope. From thence he goes on to observe that there is something distinctly religious about this contemporary movement: "a religion of the earth is being mobilized against the religion of heaven,"[1] he declares. And this recognition leads to a third step: having diagnosed that a single neo-humanist "religion" of global proportions is being marshalled against "the religion of heaven" (by which Teilhard obviously understands Christianity), he goes on to conclude that this new faith can be nothing more nor less than the expression of the evolutive thrust on the collective human plane. Evolutionist that he is, he naturally concludes from this premise that the movement in question constitutes indeed the one and only true religion. And this leads finally to the last turn in this Teilhardian dialectic (it represents the only option Teilhard has left at this point, short of openly repudiating his Christian faith): he insists that Christianity and neo-humanism must henceforth join forces, that in reality the two are pointing in the same direction.

It now appears that Teilhard has deftly turned the tables on the evolutionists of the old school: religion (and Christianity, no less), so far from being a thing of the past, has become *the thing* of the future. It is no wonder that loud cheers and bursts of applause could be heard rising up from behind the ramparts of the Old Church. Nor is it too surprising that before long some of the gates of the Fortress should have been opened from within.

But the question remains whether the proposed merger between Christianity and the neo-humanist mainstream is legitimate. It may be comforting to think that the Church is no longer under siege, and that her erstwhile opponents have now become at one stroke ardent champions of her cause. And for many, no doubt, who had been teetering in their faith, the idea that science itself can guarantee the essentials of Christian truth must have come as a blessed relief. But of course, such feelings, exhilarating though they may be, prove nothing. Profound theological questions stand at issue—and Huston Smith may yet be right when he observes that "only an exhausted theology, one about to sink into the sands of science like a spent wave, could fail to sense the enormous tension between its claims and those of a scientific world view."[2]

One needs to ask oneself whether the Teilhardian scientization of Christian belief may not indeed be destroying the very thing which it is supposed to save. Now it appears that Teilhard himself has experienced at least momentary qualms on that score. In one of his earlier letters, for example, he admits that "Sometimes I am a bit frightened to think of the transposition to which I have to subject the vulgar[3] notions of creation, inspiration, miracle, original sin, resurrection, and so forth, in order to be able to accept them."[4] But it seems that before long Teilhard was able to overcome these trepidations. In fact, he became reconciled to the idea that what he was actually doing is not so much a matter of interpreting Christianity as it is of founding a new religion. He has made it plain on a number of occasions that such was indeed his intention; he does so, for instance, in a letter to Leontine Zanta, where he writes:

> As you already know, what dominates my interest and my preoccupations is the effort to establish in myself and to spread around a new religion (you may call it a better Christianity) in which the personal God ceases to be the great neolithic proprietor of former times, in order to become the soul of the world; our religious and cultural stage calls for this.[5]

It thus turns out, finally, that Teilhard is not after all the champion of a besieged Christianity, but the founder of a new religion destined to supplant the old. Despite Teilhard's contention, moreover, that "you may call it a better Christianity," it happens that the new cult is not anything like the Christianity of bygone days. It is so radically different, in fact, that Teilhard refers to it at one point as "a hitherto unknown form of religion—one that no one could as yet have imagined or described, for lack of a universe large enough or organic enough to contain it."[6] Not only, then, did this religion not exist in ancient times, but it would not have been possible, even, to conceive of it in a pre-scientific and pre-Darwinist age. And as if this were not enough, Teilhard adds by way of further clarification that the new religion "is burgeoning in the heart of modern man, from a seed sown by the idea of evolution."[7] But then, if it has sprung, not out of Christianity, but out of a scientific hypothesis which began to be entertained during the nineteenth century, it follows that this religion is new not only in the sense of having been hitherto unimaginable, but also in the sense of having entirely different roots. It appears in fact that the true founder of the new cult is not Yahweh or Christ, but Charles Darwin. One cannot but wonder whether the French Jesuit was playing square with us when he declared that "This is still, of course, Christianity."[8]

★   ★   ★

Perhaps those shouts of jubilation from behind the ramparts were premature; and perhaps some of those who unbolted gates

are having second thoughts. In any case, it does not fall within
the planned contours of this monograph to consider the impact
of Teilhard's doctrine upon Christianity at large, or upon the
Roman Catholic Church. A few words on this subject, however, may not be inappropriate.

So far as the Catholic Church in most parts of Europe and
America is concerned, it might not be too much of an over-
statement to contend that Teilhardism has indeed become the
dominant trend. One can see this, for instance, in such recent
phenomena as the radical involvement on the the part of the
American bishops in political and economic issues (generally
left of center), the waning of faith in the supernatural, and the
ongoing deconversion of clergy and laity alike from all "staticist" beliefs—not to speak of "liberation theology"! The trend
is unmistakable: Christianity (as personified, firstly, by major
contingents of the Roman Catholic hierarchy, and secondly, by
a number of Protestant and inter-denominational institutions,
such as the World Council of Churches) has begun to turn
in the direction mapped out by Teilhard de Chardin. Whether
or not these segments of official Christendom have as yet fully
"embraced in love" what Teilhard terms "that tremendous movement of the world which bears us along,"[9] it is clear in any
case that a concerted effort to merge the "two religions" is
well under way.

The Teilhardian connection, of course, has often enough been
observed. As Albert Drexel, a Catholic ecclesiastic, explains:

> The modernism or neo-modernism within Christianity, and
> especially within the Roman Catholic Church after the Second
> Vatican Council, is above all characterized by a turning away
> from the supernatural and an exclusive predilection for this
> world, the Aggiornamento of Pope John XXIII interpreted one-
> sidedly and hence misapplied. Teilhard's ideology was a defini-
> tive precondition for this. Inasmuch as he turned his back to
> the past, fused God and the supernatural with the process of
> a universal evolutionism, and proclaimed religion to be an ac-
> tive participation in a progressive development ending in Point
> Omega, the basis was given for a humanist cult of the secular
> ("ein humanistischer Diesseitskult").[10]

It remains to ask what has been the result. And the answer
to this delicate question (for the Catholic domain) that has

recently been given by the top theologian at the Vatican is this: "The results were totally opposite to the hopes of all," admits Cardinal Ratzinger in an interview.[11] "We had hoped in renewed Catholic unity and the results have been a pattern of autocriticism leading to self-destruction. We had hoped for a new enthusiasm, but the results have been discouragement and boredom." He concludes that the post-Conciliar period has been "decidedly negative for the Catholic Church." In place of the "renewal" we have heard so much about, the Cardinal now speaks of a pressing need to "restore the Church." It is clear that Cardinal Ratzinger does not believe in a marriage of Teilhard's "two religions"; indeed, the Cardinal is quite emphatic on the point: "He is totally ignorant of the nature of the Church and of the nature of the world who believes that these two can meet without conflict or that they may be somehow mixed," he declares. And he urges the bishops to change their course and oppose "the many worldly cultural tendencies adopted by post-Conciliar euphoria."

Whether or not Cardinal Ratzinger's voice will prevail, it is in any case significant that twenty years after Vatican II such a voice should have been raised at all.

*   *   *

Getting back to Teilhard's program, it is to be noted that the idea of a new religion has not been much publicized. There is no hiding the fact that major changes have been proposed, but it is claimed that the sole objective of these radical transformations is a more highly evolved Christianity. In an evolutive universe (so the argument goes), how can the Church stand still? What is actually at stake, we are told at one point, is "the laying of new foundations to which the old Church is gradually being moved."[12] Yet the crucial question remains whether the newly-founded structure will still be the Church.

To begin with, it is a strange idea that the foundations of the Church could be shifted at will, considering that it had always been understood that these foundations have been established, once and for all, by God Himself: "Thus saith the Lord God, Behold, I lay in Zion for a foundation a stone, a tried stone, a precious corner stone, a sure foundation." (*Isaias* 28:16).

And St. Paul (whom Teilhard delights to quote at other times) has this to say on the subject: "For other foundation can no man lay than is laid, which is Jesus Christ." (*1 Cor.* 3:11). Nor must it be supposed that this everlasting Foundation is simply Jesus Christ conceived *in abstracto,* so to speak, as if prophetic and apostolic tradition had nothing to do with that stipulated Foundation. Paul himself makes this quite clear when he speaks elsewhere of the living Church as having been "built upon the foundations of the apostles and prophets, Jesus Christ himself being the chief corner stone." (*Eph.* 2:20).

So long, therefore, as we take seriously the word of Scripture, the question of moving the Church to new foundations has been definitely set at rest. But what if we do not? As we have noted before, Teilhard is always willing to take biblical teachings *cum grano salis* and jettison in effect those parts which do not harmonize with his preconceived ideas. Now that in itself, of course, makes him a heretic according to the classical definition of that term. But perhaps this concept, too, needs nowadays to be revised or discarded. Perhaps, in the light of evolutionist discoveries, we need to give up the old "staticist" way of looking at things and adapt our religious outlook to the newly-discovered facts. And so we come back once more to the notion of moving the old Church to new foundations.

To be sure, from a humanist point of view, the Church, like any other institution, can be revamped at will whenever it may seem expedient to do so. And as to the question whether "This is still, of course, Christianity," it could be argued that this too presents no major problem: are we not free to call the revised institution or cult whatever we please? Here too expediency is apt to be the ultimate criterion: words are cheap in this nominalistic age.

Now the first thing that needs to be observed in the face of such arguments is that Teilhard's position can indeed be attacked, but *not* on the basis of theological premises or metaphysical principles, the validity of which he radically denies. In order to be cogent and effective, the refutation of Teilhardism must be carried out first of all on Teilhard's own turf, that is to say, on scientific ground. We must remember that time and again Teilhard has made it a point to disavow both theology and metaphysics—which permits him, in effect, to offend against either discipline with impunity, provided only that he is able to convey the impression of speaking as a scientist. Now his central claim, in effect, is that the Church must be "moved" because its erstwhile teachings do not harmonize with the newly-discovered truths of science: but it happens that this claim is *demonstrably* false (as we have had ample opportunity to see). Thus it can be said with certainty from a strictly scientific and indeed profane point of view that *science as such neither demands nor can authorize the revisions for which Teilhard pleads in its name.*

But there is something else that needs also to be said: when it comes to the Church and its doctrines, the profane point of view does not reach very far. The real Christianity is not to be known from the outside; "flesh and blood" do not suffice for the discovery of its truth. Contrary to profane opinion, its doctrines cannot actually be examined and weighed by unbelievers. What Philip said to Nathaniel applies to all of us: "Come and see." (*John* 1:46). We must bestir ourselves and take a few steps away from the "fig tree" of this world; and like Nathaniel, too, we need to be "without guile." Then alone will we gain firsthand experience of what Christianity is about. And then shall we realize (strange as it may sound) that the Church lives, not so much in time, as in eternity; for it lives in truth by the Holy Spirit. In a real sense, therefore, the Church does not change at all: it changes, of course, in some of its outer manifestations, but not in its essential truth and innermost life. As Georges Florovsky has put it, "In the life and existence of the Church time is mysteriously overcome and mastered; time, so to speak, *stands still.*"[13] Our task as Christians, then, is not to recreate the Church (by tampering with its foundations) but to drink ever more deeply from its sacred vessels and savor the timeless draught. And when we shall have received the Holy Spirit as we should, we will no longer perceive the Church in temporal or evolutive terms, but truly *sub specie aeternitatis.*

*   *   *

Teilhard does not always speak of shifting the old Church to new foundations; more often than not, he speaks as one who would bring the Church back to its essential truth. For example, in an essay entitled "Introduction to Christianity," he takes it upon himself to exhibit the essentials of Christian dogma in the form of three successive articles of faith. They are as follows:

1. Faith in the (personalizing) personality of God, the focus of the world.
2. Faith in the divinity of the historic Christ (not only prophet and perfect man, but also object of love and worship).
3. Faith in the reality of the Church *phylum,* in which and around which Christ continues to develop, in the world, his total personality.[14]

"Apart from these three fundamental articles," Teilhard informs us, "everything else in Christian teaching is basically no more than subsidiary development or explanation (historical, theological, ritual)."[15]

Now it is true, certainly, that each of the three articles (despite linguistic quirks) admits of an orthodox interpretation. But what about Teilhard's contention to the effect that this meager catechism comprehends all that is essential to Christian doctrine? Gone, first of all, is "God, the Father Almighty, creator of heaven and earth"; gone, too, is the Holy Spirit; and in the realm which theologians are wont to designate *"ad extra,"* gone is the Resurrection of Christ, the communion of saints, the forgiveness of sins, and many other things besides. Are these matters, then, indeed inessential to the Christian faith? Is the Resurrection of Christ, in particular, to be counted as a "subsidiary development or explanation"? Just a moment ago Teilhard had quoted *1 Corinthians* 15:28 (one of his favorite verses); but he does not seem to stand with the Apostle when the latter declares: "If Christ be not raised, your faith is vain." (*1 Cor.* 15:17).

It is unrealistic, furthermore, to suppose that a list of statements (of whatever length) could enshrine the essentials of Christian doctrine; nor is this what a catechism is meant to do. For it is only within the living tradition of the Church that such "dogmatic definitions" can be rightly understood. Those, therefore, who have cut themselves off from that tradition (or who have never, perhaps, participated therein) are not apt to be enlightened by such formal means. What is more, even the most orthodox formulations of Christian dogma can be misinterpreted. When it comes to the Teilhardian "articles," moreover, the possibility of heterodox interpretation has become virtually assured due to the fact that Teilhard has deftly installed a few "signposts" of his own. Taken within the context of his own doctrine (as they are meant to be), one sees in fact that these artful statements amount to no more than a reaffirmation of Teilhardian themes. Thus interpreted, the first article, for instance, reduces evidently to the affirmation of Point Omega: no more, and no less.

But what about the second article ("Faith in the divinity of the historic Christ"): what could be more orthodox than that? Yes, but what exactly does Teilhard have in mind when he speaks of "divinity"? Faith in "the divinity of the historic Christ": what can this possibly mean under the auspices of Teilhard's theory? The question is not entirely simple, and that is perhaps the reason why Teilhard comes to our aid. He has provided us with a hint (placed in parentheses): "not only prophet and perfect man, but also object of love and worship." This is a bit vague, of course; and yet the suggestion is unmistakable: the divinity of Christ is actualized through the love and worship accorded to Him by mankind. He is divine, in other words, insofar as He is actively fulfilling His role as "the focus of the world." We need not be surprised: has not Teilhard told us often enough that henceforth mankind can believe in no other God save Point Omega?

So far as the third article of the Teilhardian catechism is concerned, suffice it to observe that in speaking of "the Church *phylum*" (a funny phrase), Teilhard is dropping a broad hint to the effect that the Church (like everything else) has evolved and represents at bottom a biological phenomenon. It is only that our Christian forebears were too primitive to recognize this fact; they still believed in the supernatural, and in an "extrinsicist" God "whom no one in these days any longer wants."[16] This is indeed one of Teilhard's favorite themes, to which he returns repeatedly: "For hundreds of centuries (up to yesterday, one might say)," we are told, "men have lived as children, without understanding the mystery of their birth or the secret of the obscure urges which sometimes reach them in great waves from the deep places of the world."[17]

It could hardly have been put in plainer terms. "Up to yesterday"—until Darwin came along—men were unable to comprehend the source and true meaning of their deepest aspirations. The sages and prophets of old were mistaken when they interpreted the mystic urge as the beckoning of God, the response of the human heart to His call. They did not realize that these urges are in reality biological, that they spring "from the deep places of the world."

But let us get back to the new catechism. Having singled out his "three fundamental articles" (replete with evolutionist guideposts) and turned his back upon Christian tradition (which by his own reckoning is to be classified among "the whims and childishness of the earth"[18]), Teilhard is free at last to unfold the new theology. And it is hardly surprising that at his magic touch, everything acquires a new meaning. It may be of interest to give a few examples.

Speaking of "grace," Teilhard tells us: "From the Christian, Catholic and realist point of view, grace represents a physical super-creation. It raises us a further rung on the ladder of cosmic evolution. In other words, the stuff of which grace is made is strictly biological."[19] Let us try to enter into this remarkable train of thought. The first statement is more or less orthodox, except for the adjective "physical," whose meaning in this context is not initially clear. Presumably it is there to guide us into the universe of discourse within which the second statement is to be comprehended: we are now in the domain of evolutionist thought, where the "super-creation" of Christianity has become simply "a further rung on the ladder of cosmic evolution." And indeed, Teilhard loses no time to draw the desired conclusion: "In other words," he tells us, "the stuff of which grace is made is strictly biological." With seeming logic Teilhard has taken us from an isolated proposition, which might sound Christian enough, to a statement about the nature of grace which affirms very much the opposite of what Christians had always believed: for it belongs to the very essence of grace to be, not a natural attainment, but a supernatural gift. What Teilhard has actually done under the pretext of interpreting the term is to deny that such a thing as grace exists. His "grace" is actually a non-grace, if one may put it thus.

Another example of what can happen to Christian terms pertains to the notion of infallibility: "In reality," Teilhard tells us, "to say that the Church is infallible is simply to say that, in virtue of being a living organism, the Christian group contains in itself, and to an eminent degree, a certain sense of direction and certain potentialities: ill-defined though these are, they enable it to grope its way, constantly probing in this direction or that, to maturity or self-fulfillment."[20] Now it is admittedly difficult to formulate the concept of ecclesiastic infallibility in precise terms, and there is no doubt room for certain differences of interpretation. But one need hardly be a theologian or a canonist to realize that the stipulated infallibility derives from the fact that the Church is not just a "living organism," but indeed a theandric organism (which is tantamount to saying that this infallibility derives ultimately from the mystery of the Hypostatic Union). In a word, the Church is infallible in a certain sense because in a distinctly supernatural way it stands under the inspiration and guidance of the Holy Spirit. But of course this traditional concept is no longer tenable within the confines of Teilhard's evolutionist system. And so once again Teilhard's pretended definition of the term turns out to be in effect a denial that the thing in question exists. For indeed, if the Church is infallible "in virtue of being a living organism," then we arrive at the strange conclusion that this infallibility is shared by amebae and buffalo! And since (as everyone knows) amebae and buffalo are not in fact infallible, one must conclude that neither is the Church.

Getting back to the authentically Christian concept of infallibility, let us also observe that this notion does *not* apply to the sphere of action—it has nothing whatever to do with "groping one's way towards maturity and self-fulfillment." Instead, it applies to the doctrinal sphere, to the fundamental formulations of the Christian faith. Thus, by misrepresenting the idea of infallibility as a kind of pragmatic wisdom, Teilhard has also by implication denied the universal validity of doctrinal pronouncements. It is obvious that so long as the idea refers to a self-corrective groping (such as is to be found in the behavior of animals or even of servo-mechanisms), it cannot apply to such things as the Christological affirmations of the Councils.

It will hardly be necessary to follow Teilhard any further on his victorious sweep, as he proceeds to explain in succession the Trinity, the divinity of Christ, Revelation, Miracles, Original Sin and Redemption, Hell, and finally, the Eucharist. Everywhere it is the same story: all that exists in the end is the evolutive process—"That, when all is said and done, is the first, the last, and the only thing in which I believe."[21]

★   ★   ★

It is literally true that Teilhard has deified evolution. One might add that from the start the concept of evolution has been—not simply a scientific hypothesis to be tested or verified—but an idea charged with a kind of religious significance, to be preached and circulated. Yet Teilhard de Chardin was presumably the first to be totally possessed by the concept, the first to be fully intoxicated, as it were, with the new wine. Darwin himself was still to some extent rooted in the past; he was not yet completely "liberated," it would seem. In any case, not until Teilhard stepped upon the stage did Evolution find its full-blown prophet. It was through his mouth that the religious pretensions which had been latent in the evolutionist movement all along have finally burst forth—with a fury, as one can say. At Teilhard's hands the Darwinist theory has been transformed into a full-fledged religion: it has actually been turned into a cult.

This explains (among other things) what Medawar calls "that tipsy, euphoric prose poetry," and those "alarming apocalyptic seizures": that is nothing unusual in a man fired with a sense of religious mission. Teilhard thinks he sees, not just for himself, but for all mankind—nay, for the cosmos at large. At his best, he does not write: he cries out with a loud voice. But unlike the prophets of old, his is not the voice of Tradition. Quite to the contrary, it is manifestly the voice of anti-Tradition: "A new victorious passion is beginning (we seriously believe) to take shape, which will sweep away or transform what have so far been the whims and childishness of the earth,"[22] he cries.

What is especially ominous, moreover, is that the new cult masquerades under Christian colors. One cannot say "in Christian garb," because it is only too evident that the new religion is diametrically opposed to the old on just about every count. What has happened (as we have just seen) to the ideas of grace and infallibility is by no means untypical: it turns out to be the rule. And what else could one expect once it has been admitted that "We no longer want a religion of regulation: but we dream of a *religion of conquest*"[23]? One sees that even the *Pater Noster* has become reversed: henceforth it is no longer "Thy will," but ours, that is to be done. The fact is that Teilhard stands clearly on the side of that "religion of the earth" which according to his own testimony "is being mobilized against the religion of heaven." Yet at the same time he persists in the blatant claim that "This is still, of course, Christianity." And with telling effect: for as the exiled Jesuit had shrewdly foreseen, the newly-hatched anti-creed has come to be accepted by millions as the true Christianity. In the eyes of the "liberated" it is indeed perceived as the ultra-Christianity which Teilhard declared it to be.

★   ★   ★

It is true that Teilhard preaches Jesus Christ. But we must also ask ourselves on what basis it is possible for an evolutionist to do so. Millions are impressed when a man of science proclaims Christ to be the focus of the world. They do not know, first of all, that the so-called "Omega Point of science" is a fake. Neither is it clear how someone who has rejected tradition—someone who thinks that until yesterday "men lived as children'—could know that Jesus of Nazareth became Point Omega. We know Jesus almost entirely through Christian tradition; and if we reject that tradition and its claims, we know next to nothing about Him. How, then, can Teilhard speak of Jesus Christ as the universal center of attraction? As von Hildebrand has very aptly pointed out, "An unprejudiced mind cannot but ask: Why should this 'cosmic force' be called Christ?"[24] Why indeed? Is it because Jesus Christ enjoys a certain "popularity" in our world? But then, so does Buddha, and so does Mohammed; and so, too, do many secular figures upon the world stage.

We need not belabor the point: from a scientific perspective the connection between Jesus of Nazareth and Point Omega is flimsy in the extreme. It is not enough to say that there is no evidence for such a claim; for even if it were admitted that Omega exists, the Christological connection would still be, not only unverified, but scientifically inconceivable. The fact is that Christ can be known *only* by way of the Christian tradition, and only on that basis could He be recognized as the true Center of the world. But once that tradition has been undercut, what then? If it be true that our Christian forebears were infantile and their religious beliefs mere "whims and childishness of the earth," on what basis can Teilhard preach Christ? Clearly, *there is no such basis.* This, too, is a fake.

★   ★   ★

Despite his clerical garb, Teilhard's attitude towards traditional Christianity is distinctly negative and critical. It is not clear whether there is anything at all in the old religion of which he approves. At times he does of course extol certain Christian conceptions (the idea of personalization, for instance); but on closer scrutiny one invariably finds that the praises he sings apply, not to the old, but to the new "Christianity."

Teilhard never loses an opportunity to criticize and discredit whatever is not to his liking or stands in his way. Nor does he hesitate to cast aspersions even upon the words of Christ. Even the Beatitudes do not escape the ire of his reformist zeal: "There can be no place for the poor in spirit," and no place for "the sad of heart,"[25] he exclaims.

His central complaint, to be sure, is that (traditional) Christianity is not "scientific," by which he means, first and foremost, that it does not harmonize with the evolutionist outlook. It is therefore "staticist" and needs to be revised.

A second objection, moreover, closely related to the first, is that the old beliefs are not compatible with our so-called "discovery of Space and Time." Now on this score Teilhard may have a point. It can hardly be denied that when it comes to the physical dimensions of the universe—and more generally, to the material sphere in the specifically modern sense of that term—our forebears may indeed have been somewhat naive. But Teilhard forgets that numerical or physical magnitude—the immensity of Avogadro's number, or of the Hubble constant—is not everything. There is also a spiritual immensity (a *qualitative* plenitude, if you will); and that is, after all, the true immensity: it is the plenitude of life itself, which is infinitely greater than the enormity of its outer shells.

If the Weltanschauung of Christianity seems narrow to Teilhard de Chardin, this may be due in part to the fact that he has never approached the subject without preconceived notions of a scientistic kind and the arrogance of one who thinks that he has outstripped all who came before.

It is evident that Teilhard does not resonate to the biblical world-view. Not only does he find it staticist and narrow, but he thinks that it is based upon "the Alexandrine" cosmology (whatever that might be). What Teilhard fails to grasp, however, is that the biblical Weltanschauung is actually based, not upon any theory or abstract model of the universe, but quite simply upon sense perception. The Bible speaks of the world as it is revealed to us—not through Geiger counters or telescopes—but through the God-given instruments. Christianity has never claimed, moreover, that this perceived world is absolutely real (we now see "through a glass, darkly"). But even so, as St. Paul declared, it has a truth-value—an immense and unlimited truth-value, in fact—inasmuch as it points beyond itself to "the invisible things of God." The heavens above and this solid earth beneath our feet—everything without exception is charged with a higher significance; even what Teilhard refers to disdainfully as "the illusion of terrestrial flatness" may not be without meaning to the wise. In a word, the world is a symbol, an icon; and that is what both explains and justifies the biblical world-view.

Actually the shoe is on the other foot: it is Teilhard who is duped. It is he who has mistaken a mere abstraction, a mere "model," for the reality itself. As Alfred North Whitehead would say, he has succumbed to "the fallacy of misplaced concreteness." Let those who disavow philosophy stay clear of the despised discipline!

Another frequent Teilhardian complaint pertains to the so-called "juridical" notions of traditional Christianity. Now it may well be true that there has been a tendency in certain quarters to overemphasize this aspect of Christian doctrine. But Teilhard should have been cautioned by the fact that juridical ideas do obviously constitute an integral part of the Judeo-Christian heritage and play a major role in the discourses of Christ. At the same time he ought to have realized that these juridical conceptions do not cover the entire ground, and that it was never intended that they should. And that is of course why so many metaphors, so many symbols, so many parables have been put before us. Each of these has something unique and precious to say: Christ did not speak vain words. And yet Teilhard takes it upon himself to dismiss the entire gamut of juridical images as a mere vestige of a so-called "neolithic symbolism" which has nowadays become outmoded.[26]

In point of fact, authentic symbolism never becomes outmoded: for it is rooted in the nature of things. All that can happen is that in a superficial age—an era in which spiritual vision has become almost extinct—such symbolism may no longer be comprehensible, especially in the more "educated" strata of society. And when this comes to pass our religious outlook (if it survives at all) does indeed become rather minuscule and exceedingly anthropocentric. As Vladimir Lossky has pointed out, "A theology impoverished by that rationalism which recoils before these, the images of the Fathers, necessarily loses the cosmological perspective of Christ's work."[27] Now it may well be that this is in the main the kind of theology to which Teilhard had been exposed during his seminary years—as we have noted before, the malady of which we speak goes back to the Renaissance, and constitutes a characteristic of the modern age. To be sure, Teilhard does not stand alone in having all but lost the capacity to read symbols of a metaphysical kind. But this does not alter the fact that when he objects (quite rightly!) to a Christianity whose views have become somewhat narrow and bereft of cosmic grandeur, the beam is actually in his own eye.

Another source of displeasure are the so-called miracles, beginning with the miracles of Christ. Teilhard is careful for the most part not to deny outright that such things have taken place. Yet he is obviously at pains to minimize their importance. Repeatedly he informs us that miracles, though they may have played a certain role in the early development of Christianity (on account of their "propaganda value," as one could say), have all but lost their significance in the present scientific age. But here again Teilhard is overlooking something of the utmost importance: miracles are profoundly significant insofar as they render visible, so to speak, the reality of the spiritual world. Diseases which Nature could only heal slowly or not at all are cured in a trice; future happenings which seem to hinge upon a host of imponderables are perceived in advance (like the crowing of the cock in the Gospel); and much else that is no less an affront to our scientific wisdom. The crucial question, of course, is whether such things have actually taken place. But assuming that they have, it would indeed be foolish to perceive in these preternatural happenings nothing but a psychological device to prod people into accepting the Christian religion. What is of far greater moment, surely, is that these eruptions of the miraculous reveal to us—more eloquently than any metaphysical argument—the stupendous inadequacy of our ordinary naturalistic notions, the very conceptions which Teilhard tends to absolutize.

Finally, Teilhard is not particularly pleased with our Christian saints. Even their charity offends him: "It is the fire of a love which is almost exclusively 'ascensional' in type, its most operative and most significant act being always represented in the form of a painful purification and a joyless detachment." And he adds: "For the neo-humanists we all are now, this soon produces an atmosphere which we find unbreathable, and *it must be changed*."[28] What apparently bothers Teilhard the most is that these fervent men and women of "ascensional" type are not especially concerned with what he deems to be human progress. We do not find them congregating around universities and research institutes. Worst of all, there is ample reason to believe that they are wont to commune with God in ways that are distinctly beyond our ken. Let us admit it outright: the saints are a living reproach, not just to Teilhard de Chardin, but to all of us: to all who are not as heroic, not as self-sacrificing, not as pure, and not as intoxicated with the love of God. And if we happen *not* to be neo-humanists, we find in them—not an "unbreathable" atmosphere of gloom—but a shining example, a living inspiration, and a perennial source of strength and joy.

There is also something else that needs to be pointed out in this connection: the saints exemplify at times a spiritual knowledge which is literally beyond imagining, a knowledge which our Nobel laureates know nothing of. We must not think of this as something "mystical" in the popular sense: it is not a cognition of vague things in the sky. And while that knowledge does no doubt penetrate into the invisible reaches of the subtle and spiritual realms, it does not on that account lose touch with the corporeal sphere. The *bona fide* contemplative is able, no less than we, to perceive the realities of this world; but he can do so by different means, and in a different manner. As we learn from one of the Byzantine masters, "He beholds this multitude of things and all this perceptible world, not by perception, nor by thought, but by the power and grace proper to the God-like intellect, which makes distant things [appear] as if before their eyes, and in a manner beyond Nature presents things to come as if they were already there."[29] No use trying to picture to oneself what such knowledge might be like. As one Oriental sage has said: "You cannot pour four seers of milk into a one-seer pot."

*   *   *

The Christian life is the following of Christ; it is the Way of the Cross. And Teilhard agrees. But what does he have in mind? Here is how he explains the essential idea:

> If you ask the masters of the ascetical life what is the first, the most certain, the most sublime of mortifications, they will all give you the same answer: it is the work of interior development by which we tear ourselves away from ourselves, leave ourselves behind, emerge from ourselves. Every individual life, if lived loyally, is strewn with the outer shells discarded by our successive metamorphoses—and the entire universe leaves behind it a long series of states in which it might well have been pleased to linger with delight, but from which it has continually been torn away by the inexorable necessity to grow greater. This ascent in a continual sloughing off of the old is indeed the Way of the Cross.[30]

It is interesting, in the first place, that this account makes no reference (open or implied) to the Crucifixion. Teilhard speaks of the Way of the Cross as if Jesus of Nazareth had never lived. Unlike the authentic Christian "masters of the ascetical life," he seems to have totally forgotten that Christ "suffered under Pontius Pilate" and was crucified. His "Faith in the divinity of the historic Christ" apparently does not entail the slightest belief in the saving efficacy of the Sacrifice for the sake of which

Christ was born.

But let us go on. Teilhard is also forgetting something else: there is more than one way of "sloughing off" shells. To be sure, the Christian ascetic is busy casting off something of himself; but this alone does not suffice to characterize the Christian trajectory. If it were true, as Teilhard implies, that a single law of metamorphosis is the universal rule of life, then basically every creature in the universe—every caterpillar—would be doing just what the Christian ascetic does—which is of course precisely what Teilhard is driving at. As he tells us himself, "All that rather involved way of putting it is simply a way of expressing the most commonplace and frequently met experience of our lives—the painfulness of hard work."[31]

Amazing! The Mystery of the Cross reduces at bottom to "the painfulness of hard work." As always, we arrive in the end at a complete banality.

This remarkable interpretation of the Cross is of course entirely consonant with Teilhard's doctrine of "creative union" and the misbegotten notion that "Every process of material growth in the universe is ultimately directed towards spirit, and every process of spiritual growth towards Christ."[32] Does he not know that the world is full of enterprises in which material growth is coupled with a blighting of the spirit? And does he not know, too, that there are evil spirits, and individuals who out of foolishness or ill-intent work destruction? And this man calls himself an empiricist!

On *a priori* grounds Teilhard has locked himself into a position which forces him to believe that all vectors point in one and the same direction. In Teilhard's one-dimensional universe there is only one way to go, one destination, one Point Omega down the universal road. In such a constricted universe there is no room in which to turn around, no room for "conversion." And where there is no Fall and no *metanoia*, there can be no Redemption and no Cross. The Cross does not fit into a one-dimensional continuum; it consists, after all, of two perpendicular lines. And this iconographic fact has a profound metaphysical significance: it teaches us that the Christian life— which is the Way of the Cross—is indeed set at right angles to the plane of the world. And so, too, it leads out of the world, not simply at the end, but right from the start: to become a

Christian is already to have departed from the horizontal plane of this world.

There is, then, after all, a difference between the Way of the Cross and the way of a caterpillar, even as there is a difference, too, between the Mystical Body of Christ and the profane world. Not all change is for the better, not all material growth is directed towards the Spirit, not all complexities are destined to be immortalized in the World to Come, and not all voices that beckon us on are the Voice of Christ.

★   ★   ★

Here and there, in some of his more intimate writings, Teilhard reveals himself in the posture of a mystic; and who can tell whether this extraordinary person may not have been gifted with a certain preternatural sight? We have no reason, surely, to doubt his word when he intimates that experiences of a mystical kind have played a decisive role in the formation of his doctrine, and that he saw in these revelations a direct confirmation of his most essential beliefs.

There is an interesting parallel in this regard between Teilhard de Chardin and Carl Jung, which it may be worthwhile to point out. Jung, too, as we know, presented himself as a man of science, and propounded his far-flung theories on purportedly scientific grounds—only to let it be known in the end that he was in truth a prophet. He too, moreover, billed his doctrine as a kind of grand synthesis between science and religion, and as Philip Rieff observed, "has supplied a parody of Christianity."[33] In Jung's case the definitive statement on the subject was issued in his famous memoirs (*Memories, Dreams, Reflections*), dictated in the last days of his life. And Rieff might well be right when he notes with irreverent candor that this revelation had been carefully planned. "To avoid martyrdom," he conjectures, "Jung delayed announcing his full membership in the confraternity of prophets until after his death, by arranging a posthumous publication of his autobiography, which is at once his religious testament and his science, stated in terms of a personal confession."[34]

The parallels are obvious enough. In the case of Teilhard de Chardin, of course, there are those who think that martyrdom has in fact been inflicted and suffered. But even so, it is obvious that things could have been far worse, and that Teilhard lived out his days rather comfortably as a Jesuit in comparatively good standing.

There is an analogy, too, between the Jungian *Memories* and Teilhard's most intimate essay, "The Heart of Matter," belonging to the last period of his literary career. Here too one can speak of a posthumous publication "which is at once his religious testament and his science, stated in terms of a personal confession."

To be sure, we must not press these parallels too far. The element of "personal confession" and the detailed glimpses into his mystical workshop, for instance, to be found in Jung's autobiography exceed by far what Teilhard has to offer along these lines. And despite the indicated similarities it must not be forgotten that the two men represent quite different intellectual and spiritual types. Nothing, for example, could have been further from Jung's mind than to eulogize such things as Baconian science, the unbridled proliferation of technology, and the formation of totalitarian states; we can be certain, moreover, that the Swiss psychiatrist would have had some less-than-complimentary observations to make concerning his French counterpart if only Teilhard's theories had been more widely known at the time. Teilhard, on the other hand, would have been profoundly offended by Jung's alchemical speculations, by his generally high regard for "primitive" societies and all manner of ancient lore, by his scathing critique of modernism in at least some of its manifestations, and by a number of other Jungian traits, which are obviously opposed to his own.[35]

Teilhard's mysticism, too, is of a different stamp. It is evidently much less "pictorial," and much less intricate from a symbolist point of view, than the visionary experiences recorded by Jung. Teilhard seems to be concerned more with concepts than with symbols of a predominantly iconographic kind. We are told, for example, how *Cosmic Convergence* and *Christic Emergence* "made themselves felt in the very core of my being," and how "They reacted endlessly upon one another in a flash of extraordinary brilliance, releasing by their implosion a light so intense that it transfigured (or even 'transubstantiated') for me the very depths of the World."[36] Despite their seemingly

amorphous character, moreover, experiences of this kind were
no doubt immensely significant in Teilhard's eyes. "How is it,
then," he exclaims, "that as I look around me, still dazzled by
what I have seen, I find that I am almost the only person of
my kind, the only one to have *seen*?"[37] To be "the only one
to have *seen*"—in this expressive phrase Teilhard has undeniably
staked out his prophetic claims. "I cannot, when asked, quote
a single writer," he goes on to say, "a single work, that gives
a clearly expressed description of the wonderful 'Diaphany' that
has transfigured everything for me."[38] In himself alone, we are
told two pages later, have "love of God and faith in the world"
come together in just the right proportion so as to fuse spon-
taneously. And Teilhard predicts that what has thus far happened only in himself will eventually take place on a grand
scale: *"Sooner or later there will be a chain reaction,"*[39] he declares
(in italics). "This is one more proof"—so reads the concluding
line of "The Christic," completed one month before his death—
"This is one more proof that Truth has to appear only once,
in one single mind, for it to be impossible for anything ever
to prevent it from spreading universally and setting everything
ablaze."[40]

When it comes to impassioned utterances such as this, one
can hardly doubt the sincerity and indomitable force of Teilhard's prophetic convictions. Here we come face to face—not
with a scientistic pretender, one who "cheats with words"—but
with a mystic of sorts, a soul afire. What then—the question
can scarcely be avoided any longer—what could be the source
of these compelling visions? Whence come these astonishing
revelations? This is ever the crucial issue where mysticism is
at stake.

Now it is certainly not our intention to propose a definitive
answer to this delicate and somewhat uncomfortable question.
We will, however, point out certain signs which strike us as
being significant. In particular, we would draw attention to one
of Teilhard's early compositions, a piece entitled "The Spiritual
Power of Matter" (dated August 8, 1919), which seems to be
a dramatized account of a mystical experience through which
Teilhard had recently passed. And significantly enough, Teilhard himself has appended this piece (along with another) to
"The Heart of Matter" (his "Confessions"), to "express more

230 Teilhardism and the New Religion

successfully than I could today the heady emotion I experienced at that time from my contact with Matter."[41] Let us see what Teilhard has to say in this illuminating "fantasy."

"The man was walking in the desert, followed by his companion, when the Thing swooped down on him": so it begins. We need not concern ourselves with all the dramatic particulars—what interests us is the impact of this strange encounter upon "the man." It has been impressively described:

> Then, suddenly, a breath of scorching air passed across his forehead, broke through the barrier of his closed eyelids, and penetrated his soul. The man felt he was ceasing to be merely himself; an irresistible rapture took possession of him as though all the sap of all living things, flowing at one and the same moment into the too narrow confines of his heart, was mightily refashioning the enfeebled fibres of his being.[42]

A striking passage, to be sure, which one feels could easily have come from the pen of a *bona fide* Christian mystic. But let us continue: "And at the same time the anguish of some superhuman peril oppressed him, a confused feeling that the force which had swept down upon him was equivocal, turbid, the combined essence of all evil and all goodness."[43] Could this, too, have come from the pen of a Christian mystic? We believe not; the sentence smacks in fact of Gnosticism.[44] A presence that gives rise to oppression and confusion, a force that is "equivocal, turbid, the combined essence of all evil and all goodness"—could this be an Angel of Light? "You called me: here I am," says "the Thing"; "grown weary of abstractions, of attenuations, of the wordiness of social life, you wanted to pit yourself against Reality entire and untamed," the young seer is told in this distinctly Faustian scene. The spirit himself, moreover, disclaims his own holiness: "I was waiting for you in order to be made holy," he declares. "And now I am established on you for life, or for death...He who has once seen me can never forget me: he must either damn himself with me or save me with himself." To which the seer replies: "O you who are divine and mighty, what is your name? Speak." It is strange indeed that Teilhard should address as "divine" a spirit that is not holy, and susceptible of being damned.

Such are the "signs" Teilhard de Chardin the mystic has left behind—meager perhaps, but not insignificant. For in fact they suggest, quite strongly, that once again the laconic words of Hermes to Prometheus may hold the key: "It appears you are stricken with no small madness..."[45]

NOTES

1. SC, p. 120.
2. *Beyond the Post-Modern Mind* (New York: Crossroad, 1982), p. 108.
3. Dietrich von Hildebrand may be right when he observes that this use of the term "vulgar"—though perhaps not meant in the pejorative sense—is indicative of a "Gnostic" attitude. See *Trojan Horse in the City of God* (Chicago: Franciscan Herald Press, 1967), p. 239.
4. A letter dated December 17, 1922; quoted by Philippe de la Trinité in *Rome et Teilhard de Chardin* (Paris: Fayaard, 1964), p. 47.
5. *Lettres à Léontine Zanta* (Paris: Desclée de Brouwer, 1965), p. 127; quoted by von Hildebrand, op. cit., p. 240.
6. AE, p. 383.
7. AE, p. 383.
8. HM, p. 96.
9. PM, p. 298.
10. *Ein Neuer Prophet?* (Stein am Rhein: Christiana, 1971), p. 115.
11. *El Paris,* Zaragoza, Nov. 7, 1984. This material has since been published in full as *The Ratzinger Report* (San Francisco: Ignatius Press, 1985).
12. FM, p. 23.
13. *Collected Works* (Belmont, Mass.: Nordland, 1972), Vol. I, p. 45.
14. CE, p. 152.
15. CE, p. 152.
16. FM, p. 279.
17. HE, p. 32.
18. HE, p. 32.
19. CE, p. 152-153.
20. CE, p. 153.
21. CE, p. 99.
22. HE, p. 32.
23. SC, p. 103.
24. Op. cit., p. 238.
25. FM, p. 75.
26. The point has been made, for instance, in CE, p. 202.
27. *Orthodox Theology* (Crestwood, N.Y.: St. Vladimir's Seminary, 1978), p. 114.
28. CE, p. 217.
29. Gregory Palamas, quoted in Archimandrite Vasileos, *Hymn of Entry* (Crestwood, N.Y.: St. Vladimir's Seminary, 1984), p. 37.

30. SC, p. 69.
31. SC, p. 69.
32. SC, p. 68.
33. *The Triumph of the Therapeutic* (New York: Harper & Row, 1968), p. 139.
34. *Ibid.*
35. An analysis of Jung's doctrine and *modus operandi* has been given in *Cosmos and Transcendence* (La Salle: Sugden, 1984), pp. 110-133.
36. HM, p. 83.
37. HM, p. 100.
38. HM, p. 100.
39. HM, p. 102.
40. HM, p. 102.
41. HM, p. 61.
42. HM, p. 68.
43. HM, p. 68.
44. Only a Gnostic could speak of "a combined essence of all good and all evil." According to Christian teaching, evil is a *privatio boni*, a mere absence or privation of the good; and as such it has no essence at all. We believe that Teilhard's affinity with Gnosticism can be rigorously demonstrated (as it can also in the case of Hegel, Marx, Nietzsche and Jung); but this would require a separate study.
45. Aeschylus, *Prometheus Bound*, 977.

Appendix
Gnosticism Today

This appendix by Dr. Wolfgang Smith was written as an article for Homiletic and Pastoral Review *and is reprinted here with the kind permission of the publisher.*

To speak of Gnosticism as a contemporary movement, it is first of all necessary to disengage the essential features of this type of philosophy from the welter of notions (often exceedingly strange) to be met in the ancient Gnostic schools. To be sure, the curious doctrines of Simon Magus, of Marcion or Valentinus are dead and gone—unless, perchance, they have been recently resurrected by some outlandish sect. But that, in any case, is not our present concern. What interests us here, rather, is the little-known and indeed astonishing fact that Gnosticism, in its quintessential sense, has reasserted itself in post-medieval times, not in the form of some marginal mysticism, but precisely in and through the mainstream of modern culture.

Classical Gnosticism, as one knows, did not present itself in the form of a homogeneous teaching or unified doctrine; the very opposite, in fact, has ever been one of its salient characteristics. In the first place, it was syncretistic in the extreme. As Hans Jonas points out, "The Gnostic systems compounded everything—oriental mythologies, astrological doctrines, Iranian theology, elements of Jewish tradition (whether biblical, rabbinical or occult), Christian salvation-eschatology, Platonic terms and concepts..."[1] And as if that were not enough, individual

233

Gnostic gurus were hardly reticent in contributing novelties of their own. As St. Irenaeus informs us, "Every day every one of them invents something new."[2] It is small wonder, therefore, that within the domain of Judeo-Christian Gnosticism alone scholars have counted as many as thirty different speculative systems.[3]

Nonetheless, there exist of course common doctrinal elements (failing which one could hardly speak of "Gnosticism" at all); and the most distinctive of these, it appears, is what may be termed *the Gnostic devaluation of the cosmos.* Now this tenet, which always plays a crucial role in the economy of Gnostic thought, can most readily be defined as the negation of a corresponding Christian belief—the thesis, namely, that the world was created by Almighty God and is inherently good. According to this perception, which incidentally was fully shared by the Greeks, the cosmos is a masterpiece, no less, fashioned by the divine Artificer, and therefore perfect in its foundations—as perfect, at any rate, as anything outside of God could be. It is in fact a theophany, a kind of image or reflection of God Himself; for indeed, "The invisible things of him from the creation of the world are clearly seen, being understood by the things that are made, even his eternal power and Godhead." (*Rom.* 1:20). And if, moreover, such be not the case in our own experience, the fault for this incomprehension rests ultimately with us; we are "without excuse," as St. Paul goes on to say. If it happens (as it generally does) that we live in ignorance and misery, it is not the Creator of Heaven and earth, but we ourselves—our "vain imaginations" and "foolish heart" (*Rom.* 1:21)—that are at fault.

Now this is just what the Gnostic can never admit. According to the Gnostic gurus, we are not fallen creatures in an inherently good and indeed theophanic world, but divine beings, no less, who through no fault of their own have been cast into an alien, cruel, and perfectly senseless universe. And if we engage (as we frequently do) in base and vicious acts, it is always the world—or the fact of our immersion therein—that is to blame; what has happened is simply that the terrestrial environment has cramped our godly style. One is reminded in this connection of Rousseau's "noble savage," and of Freud's view of neurosis as the resultant of externally imposed inhibitions.

In any case, this is one of the points on which Gnostics of every stripe always agree: in the final analysis it is the world, the cosmos, with its inexorable law—its *heimarmene,* however conceived—and not our "foolish heart," that holds us in chains. But let us observe what this implies. If all our misery stems from the external environment, or from the conditions of the terrestrial abode into which we have been undeservedly cast, then it behooves us above all to revolt against an unjust and arbitrary fate, and seek by appropriate means to escape from the dungeon of this world. Under such auspices it would seem that nothing further is required for the attainment of ultimate bliss than to divest ourselves once and for all of an unbearable status quo. And this brings us to the second major tenet of classical Gnosticism: the idea, namely, that the *summum bonum* is to be attained through a radical separation from the conditions of our terrestrial habitat. One should add that in ancient times this liberating act was typically conceived as a mystic journey, a mysterious flight into higher worlds.

A word of warning, however, is called for at this juncture: we must not be too quick to perceive a Gnostic journey in every form of ancient or Eastern mysticism we may chance upon. If Plotinus, for example, speaks of a "flight of the alone to the Alone," it does not instantly follow that he is a Gnostic. Our point here is that there are numerous modes of "mystic flight"—ranging from the authentic to the counterfeit—and that in this domain (more, perhaps, than in any other) one needs to exercise caution and restraint.

Once the Gnostic's "mystic flight" has come to be perceived as the decisive liberating act, there remains but one crucial question: what are the means or *modus operandi,* namely, by which the desired exodus—the Gnostic Passover, one might say—can actually be achieved? Now the generic answer to this question—from which the Gnostic sects derive their collective appellation—is that "the one thing needful" is indeed *gnosis*: a sovereign knowledge of some kind. And this belief in liberation through gnosis constitutes another doctrinal element of Gnosticism—the third and last in our succinct enumeration. To summarize, the Gnostic scheme entails, firstly, a devaluation of the cosmos; secondly, the notion of a mystic journey as the liberating act; and finally, a claim to the possession of the "gnostic secret" by means of which this act is to be consummated.

It has sometimes been said that the belief in a liberating gnosis constitutes, all by itself, the definitive characteristic of Gnosticism. But if that were the case, it could well be argued that religion per se is Gnosticism, for where indeed does one encounter a major religious tradition which does not, in one way or another, allude to a gnosis of this sovereign kind? Certainly Christianity, despite its emphasis on love, is no exception in that regard: "Ye shall know the truth, and the truth shall make you free." Think of it: "The truth shall make you free." What could be more "Gnostic" than that? If these words had been discovered on some ancient papyrus, some experts, one fears would straightway conclude that it must be a Gnostic text. And this brings us to our immediate point: neither the notion of a mystic flight, nor the concept of liberation through gnosis, taken *in abstracto,* constitutes an infallible hallmark of Gnosticism. What actually makes the Gnostic, let it be said at once, is not simply a belief in gnosis, but a claim to possess what in fact he does not.

Gnosticism, as we have seen, involves not one, but three fundamental doctrinal ingredients, which are inseparably connected, and of which the first is overtly at odds with a fundamental Christian belief. And this initial heresy, to put it plainly, suffices to spoil and invalidate all the rest; for as St. Thomas has said, "A false idea about the nature of creation always reflects itself in a false idea about God."

Meanwhile, one should not fail to observe that the Gnostic depreciation of the cosmos invariably goes hand-in-hand with a rejection of perennial norms and spiritual traditions. In the first place, the Gnostic is always a nonconformist. He finds it hard to agree even with fellow-Gnostics ("Every day every one of them invents something new."). It would appear, moreover, that when it comes to the beliefs and aspirations of the non-Gnostic portion of mankind, his sympathies run thin. The Gnostic's native attitude towards the hallowed views and practices of his forefathers is typically one of rejection and contempt. By natural disposition he is a breaker of norms, be they ethical, social or political. His antipathy towards the cosmic order extends as a matter of course into the cultural sphere; it applies to every order which presents itself as a given, a status quo of some kind. In a word, the Gnostic is a born revolutionary. And so, too, he is invariably a man of *ressentiment.* Understandably so! For indeed the postulate of senseless and unmerited misery, which, as we have seen, forms an essential part of the Gnostic creed, is apt to arouse frustration and bitterness in even the gentlest soul. Hence, if Christianity be the religion of love, Gnosticism could well be termed "the religion of animosity."

Now this in itself, one might add, suffices to invalidate the Gnostic claim to world transcendence. Where there is anger or frustration, there can be no peace; and where there is no peace, there can be no gnosis. Authentic world transcendence comes calmly, in the fullness of time—like the falling of a dry leaf. Or, it is like breaking the shell of a ripened fruit. Its Gnostic imitation, on the other hand, is always hasty and premature; it is forced and "inorganic," one could say, an aggressive act which only spoils what it pretends to liberate. One does not ripen fruit by tearing off the skin.

If Christ had only said, "The truth shall make you free," He might indeed have been a Gnostic. But He also said: "Love thine enemies, do good to them that persecute you." And no Gnostic has ever been able to say these words!

One more general point regarding Gnosticism: the Gnostic liberation is to be achieved without the consent or blessing of "God, the Father Almighty, Creator of Heaven and earth." Indeed, as we learn from the texts of Jewish and Christian Gnosticism, it is to be achieved precisely in opposition to this Almighty Father. As a rule, the dethronement and eventual "murder" of God constitutes one of the key "mysteries" of Gnostic religion.

*   *   *

To the casual observer nothing, presumably, seems more dated and indeed outlandish than the speculations of classical Gnosticism. One must remember that with the advent of the Renaissance the dominant interest of Western man began to shift markedly from God and transcendence to the exploration and eventual mastery of this visible world. It was an age when philosophical rationalism and a generally skeptical mood began to replace the medieval penchant for theological speculation, while in the universities of Europe the ground was being prepared for the scientific revolution which was soon to get under way. It would seem that by the fifteenth century or thereabouts men had generally become disenchanted with the mystical quest and were ready to give themselves wholeheartedly to more tangible and mundane pursuits. A new spirit, a new enthusiasm was in the air. Rarely, one feels, had the world seemed so fair to mortals, and quite so worthy of possession; and rarely, too, had eschatological prospects seemed more tenuous. A brave new breed of men had made their appearance and were fast taking over the helm—hard-headed pragmatists, one might say, formidably insulated against even the faintest glimmer of transcendence. And so, by the time of the so-called Enlightenment, something quite unprecedented had taken place; for indeed, as Huston Smith points out, "The modern West is the first society to view the physical world as a closed system."[4] Never before in history had the intellectual elite forgotten so completely the existence and use of what our ancestors were wont to call "higher spheres."

Under such auspices Gnosticism is still of course conceivable as a sub-culture or counter-culture, in opposition to the prevailing *Zeitgeist*. But how could there be Gnosticism *within* the cultural mainstream of a civilization which has abjured transcendence? How indeed could anyone speak of a Gnostic "flight from this world" when this world has in effect become all? To do so, obviously, the ancient symbol must first of all be interpreted in a new key. A modern Gnosticism, to be conceivable, must hinge upon a new hermeneutic, a new way of envisioning the Gnostic "flight." And so in fact it does. As Eric Voegelin points out, the requisite reinterpretation has been achieved through what he terms "the immanentization of the Eschaton." In place of an Eschaton which ontologically transcends the confines of this world, the modern Gnostic envisions an End within history, an Eschaton, therefore, which is to be realized within the ontological plane of this visible universe.

Now it is perhaps surprising that this key notion of Neo-Gnosticism was prepared for by Christianity itself. One of the great novelties of Christianity, let us recall, was that it endowed the flux of history with a teleological direction and a determinate end. Thus, under aegis of the new religion, history was no longer viewed as an endless and periodic succession of cyclic phases, but came to be perceived instead as a directed movement converging relentlessly towards a final encounter with Christ, an encounter by which history as such will be forever terminated. Just one more step, it appears, was needed to pass from this Christian conception to the Neo-Gnostic Eschaton: the Parousia needed to be immanentized, that is to say, the End of history needed to be seen as taking place within history itself, as its final phase.

But for this, too, Christianity had prepared the way; for as one well knows, the logical clarity of the Christian teaching had from the start been compromised by chiliastic speculations which tended, in effect, to immanentize the Parousia by confusing it with the imagined millenary reign of Christ. It is true that St. Augustine had labored to put a stop to these notions, and succeeded so far as the official Church was concerned. But it is equally true that chiliasm did survive, and became in fact a dominant influence during the latter half of the Middle Ages. Since the days of Joachim of Flora, it seems, right up to the Renaissance, Europe was rife with millenary speculations, which at times erupted in frenzied movements of unrest and revolt. And in all these diverse manifestations of what historians term "the pursuit of the millenium" we find one and the same underlying idea: the belief, namely, in an imminent state of collective "salvation" to be realized here on earth through a radical transformation of some kind.

To be sure, medieval chiliasm presented itself in Christian colors and was presumably perceived by its votaries as the true Christianity, no less. But as is always the case, heretical Christianity is not in fact Christianity at all, despite superficial appearances and vehement protestations to the contrary. As has often been said, deny one dogma—one seemingly fine point of fundamental theology—and you have implicitly denied all the rest. And this explains why chiliasm (once it had immanentized the Parousia) could readily shed its Christian garb and evolve into a medley of anti-Christian creeds.

The fact is that the millenarian movement of medieval Europe bequeathed to the modern world the key notion of the Neo-Gnostic Eschaton: the seductive vision of a terrestrial and futuristic salvation (generally conceived in collective terms). This immanentization of the Eschaton is the crucial concept, as we have noted before, that enabled classical Gnosticism to transplant itself into the modern age. It is the master-stroke that enabled the post-medieval Gnostic to "fly into a higher world" when there was no longer a "higher world" to fly into. Let us be clear about this matter. The decisive Gnostic revelation of the new age is that there *is* no "higher world," nor shall there ever be, *unless it be first created by man himself.* The heavens and paradises of the religions are but a dream, or the shadow, if you will, of a reality yet to be born. And God Himself, so the Gnostic declares, is but a shadow or premonition of the coming Superman.

But let us again remember that "One myth does not a Gnosticism make"; there are necessarily *three* key ingredients to Gnosticism, beginning with what we have termed the Gnostic devaluation of the cosmos. Now this, too, may at first glance seem like an antiquated notion, one that scarcely fits into our modern outlook. How could it be said, one might well ask, that we have devalued the cosmos when in fact we have elevated it to the status of the prime reality itself? On closer examination, however, it appears that this step itself constitutes a devaluation, and the most radical one at that, for it negates the transcendent origin of being and thus reduces every existing order to the status of a contingency (a mere accident, one could say). Once being has become thus decapitated (to use Voegelin's excellent term), everything, both in the natural and the human realm, has lost its sanction, its legitimacy, and above all, its higher meaning. There can be no doubt about it: *the eclipse of transcendence constitutes the ultimate devaluation of the world.*

Now this eclipse of transcendence, or "decapitation of being," is nothing else than the Gnostic "murder of God," the "mystery" Nietzsche had his eye on when he announced that "God is dead." But needless to say, this is a "murder" which can be accomplished in no other way than speculatively—in the imagination, if you will. And even that is not a simple matter; in fact, it is a task which has occupied the brightest minds of Europe and America for the past several centuries. When the Middle Ages drew to a close, mankind had not yet "progressed" that far. It is true that incipient Neo-Gnosticism was already in possession of its new Eschaton; it had inherited the idea, as we have seen, from heretical Christian sects. But the devaluation of the cosmos along Neo-Gnostic lines had as yet scarcely begun. Nor had anyone yet revealed to mankind "the gnostic keys," the secret knowledge, that is, by virtue of which man will be enabled (individually or collectively, as the case may be) to effect the realization of the proffered Paradise. However, what was still missing was to be supplied in due course. It arrived, if not in linear progression, yet in stages and degrees. The Gnostic gurus did appear. There came Jean Jacques Rousseau, for instance, and Voltaire, and the whole tribe of Encyclopedists; there came Hegel, Nietzsche and Marx; and a host of lesser lights, too numerous to record. The remarkable (and generally unrecognized) fact is that the history of Neo-Gnosticism coincides almost exactly with the intellectual history of the modern West—for as Voegelin has observed, the growth of Gnosticism is indeed the essence of modernity.[5]

★   ★   ★

Carl Jung was presumably right when he remarked that Gnosticism represents the counter-position to Christianity—which means, in effect, that when men despair of the Christian God, they shift their allegiance inevitably to the Teilhardian Omega: *earthly futurity replaces transcendence.* As Voegelin explains,

> Gnostic speculation overcame the uncertainty of faith by receding from transcendence and endowing man and his intramundane range of action with the meaning of eschatological fulfillment. In the measure in which this immanentization progressed experientially, civilizational activity became a mystical work of self-salvation.[6]

And this brings us to a most important point: Gnosticism is not an ivory tower pastime. It is a religion of sorts, a counter-position to Christianity no less; and as such it cannot but express itself in the life, first, of an elite, and eventually of entire civilizations—which is precisely what has happened. Major segments of humanity have become dedicated to a civilizational task which is not simply a question of survival, nor of material self-aggrandizement (as skeptics are apt to think), but represents in the final analysis "a mystical work of self-salvation." Therein, unquestionably, lies the deepest significance of contemporary civilizationism. Beneath the veneer of our sophisticated rationality and pragmatic sobriety there lurks a mysticism. The very words we cherish the most—like "progress," "freedom," or "science"—have acquired a kind of mystic ring; as Martin Lings points out, they have become "words to conjure with," enchanted terms "at the utterance of which multitudes of souls fall prostrate in sub-mental adoration."[7] Behind such words as these one senses the magic of the New Eschaton, the Gnostic Good News of "self-salvation" which happily speeds millions along their mystic way.

But let us not forget that Gnosticism always requires *three* legs to stand upon—which means, in the first place, that the Good News in question would not make the slightest sense to anyone if it were not complemented and supported by what has been termed the speculative decapitation of being. And this means, in more concrete terms, that a second myth (or syndrome of such) is needed to bolster up the first—a cosmological myth, one might say, to complement the eschatological.

Let one example suffice: the theory of evolution. It has been repeatedly demonstrated that the so-called proofs are no proofs at all, and that there is in fact no empirical basis whatever for the Darwinist conjecture. What is more, with the advance of scientific knowledge a host of uncongenial facts have come to light, ranging from mildly hostile to positively damning; and yet the doctrine continues to be proclaimed in the most dogmatic terms. Now, if it were actually a scientific tenet, such a situation would be impossible. As a scientific theory, Darwinism would have been jettisoned long ago. The point, however, is that the doctrine of evolution has swept the world, not on the strength of its scientific merits, but precisely in its capacity as a Gnostic myth. It affirms, in effect, that living beings create themselves, which is in essence a *metaphysical* claim. This in itself implies, however, that the theory is scientifically unverifiable (a fact, incidentally, which has often enough been pointed out by philosophers of science). Thus, in the final analysis, evolutionism is in truth a metaphysical doctrine decked out in scientific garb. In other words, it is a scientistic myth. And the myth is Gnostic, because it implicitly denies the transcendent origin of being; for indeed, only after the living creature has been speculatively reduced to an aggregate of particles does Darwinist transformism become conceivable. Darwinism, therefore, continues the ancient Gnostic practice of depreciating "God, the Father Almighty, Creator of Heaven and earth." It perpetuates, if you will, the venerable Gnostic tradition of "Jehovah bashing." And while this in itself may gladden Gnostic hearts, one should not fail to observe that the doctrine plays a vital role in the economy of Neo-Gnostic thought, for only under the auspices of Darwinist "self-creation" does the Good News of "self-*salvation*" acquire a semblance of sense.

The inherent connection between the two myths, moreover, has nowhere been brought to light more clearly than in the philosophy of Teilhard de Chardin. If atoms have aggregated themselves into molecules, and molecules into living beings of every description, then why should not humanity, Teilhard maintains, aggregate itself right into the New Jerusalem? The Mystical Body of Christ, we are told, is being formed before our very eyes through the exploits of technology and the birth of modern super-states. And this "super-evolution" supposedly continues the Darwinist evolution, the postulated evolution of organic forms. In both instances Teilhard beholds the workings of one and the same sovereign Law—his imagined "law of complexity/consciousness."[8]

Now this so-called Law, let us add in passing, constitutes precisely "the gnostic secret" in the Teilhardian system; as Teilhard himself informs us early in *The Phenomenon of Man,* all the rest of this, his main treatise, is nothing but the application throughout of this one "great Law."[9] It expresses the truth of evolution, we are told, and in a philosophy in which Evolution—as von Balthasar observes—has become "the only category of thought,"[10] this supposed "truth of evolution" becomes indeed the one and universal Truth.

Once this "secret" has been grasped—and it is surprisingly easy to do so—the Teilhardian message becomes readily comprehensible. What the Law tells us, in plain words, is that through the pooling of human resources—the formation of the collective "super-organism," if you will—man is enabled to take control of his own evolution; he can in fact build up the Mystical Body of Christ—which has now become fused with the Neo-Gnostic Superman.

Consider, for instance, the production of the atom bomb:

here, supposedly, we have an effect, or an application, of the "great Law." And this explains why, in Teilhard's eyes, the explosion of the first atomic device in the desert of New Mexico was not simply a miracle of science, but represents, rather, a milestone in the spiritual ascent of man, a milestone "pointing the way to his omnipotence."[11] "In laying hands on the very core of matter," Teilhard declares, "we have disclosed to human existence a supreme purpose: the purpose of pursuing ever further, to the very end, the forces of Life." [12] It appears that the explosion of the atom bomb was but the first step in a gigantic program, "the first bite at the fruit of the great discovery"—the discovery, namely, of how we can at last make good the ancient promise, "Ye shall be as gods"! Let us see how Teilhard envisions this tantalizing prospect. Referring again to the milestone of the New Mexico desert, he goes on to say:

> Was it not simply the first act, even a mere prelude, in a series of fantastic events which, having afforded us access to the heart of the atom, would lead us on to overthrow, one by one, the many other strongholds which science is already besieging? The vitalization of matter by the creation of super-molecules. The remodeling of the human organism by means of hormones. Control of heredity and sex by manipulation of genes and chromosomes. The readjustment and internal liberation of our souls by direct action upon springs gradually brought to light by psychoanalysis. The arousing and harnessing of the unfathomable intellectual and effective powers still latent in the human mass...[13]

Is it necessary to point out that this is the purest Gnosticism? It is strange that even such an odious and overtly Promethean outburst as this did not suffice to forewarn the faithful—when they thronged by the millions to this Prophet of the New Christianity.

And this brings us finally to the moral point: we find ourselves today, both outside and inside the Church, in a predominantly Gnostic environment, and it would seem that no St. Irenaeus has yet appeared to apprise us with spiritual might of this precarious fact. It is now our turn, our own responsibility, to exercise what our Christian forebears used to call "discernment of spirits," and by so doing hold fast to the truth. We must indeed "watch and pray." The hour is late, and the urgency tremendous. "For there shall arise false Christs, and false prophets, and shall show great signs and wonders; insomuch that, if it were possible, they shall deceive the very elect." (*Matt.* 24:24).

NOTES

1. *The Gnostic Religion* (Boston: Beacon Press, 1963), p. 25.
2. *Ad. Haer.* I.18.1.
3. Joseph Lortz, *History of the Church* (Milwaukee: Bruce, 1939), p. 65.
4. *Forgotten Truth* (New York: Harper & Row, 1977), p. 96
5. *The New Science of Politics* (Chicago: University of Chicago Press, 1952), p. 126.
6. *Ibid.*, p. 129.
7. *Ancient Beliefs and Modern Superstitions* (London: Perennial, 1965), p. 45.
8. The "law of complexity/consciousness" has been dealt with at length in Chapter 3.
9. *The Phenomenon of Man* (New York: Harper & Row, 1965), p. 61.
10. "Die Spiritualität Teilhards de Chardin," *Wort und Warheit,* XVII (1963), p. 344.
11. *The Future of Mankind* (New York: Harper & Row, 1964), p. 148.
12. *Ibid.*, p. 151.
13. *Ibid.*, p. 149.

Index of Names

247

By the same author...

COSMOS & TRANSCENDENCE

*Breaking Through
the Barrier
of Scientistic Belief*

$8⁹⁵   168 Pages.
Paperbound

Wolfgang Smith presents an insider's critique of the scientific world-view based upon the sharp but oft-overlooked distinction between scientific truth and scientistic faith. With elegance and compelling clarity he demonstrates that major tenets promulgated in the name of Science are not in fact scientific truths but rather scientistic speculations—for which there is no evidence at all. Step by step the reader is led to the astonishing realization that the specifically "modern world" is based intellectually upon nothing more substantial than a syndrome of Promethean myths.

But this is only half of what the book accomplishes. Its primary contribution is to recover and reaffirm the deep metaphysical and religious insights which have come down to us through the teachings of Christianity. And herein lies the true worth of this remarkable treatise: having broken the grip of scientistic presuppositions the author succeeds admirably in bringing to view great truths which had long been obscured.

This book is powerful and profound. It speaks to the deepest questions of our time—and of all time. It has been hailed by reviewers as an outstanding achievement. A must for everyone who would understand the hidden assumptions which have shaped every facet of the modern world.

Order from—

TAN BOOKS AND PUBLISHERS, INC.
P.O. Box 424
Rockford, Illinois 61105

From the Critics . . .

"*Cosmos and Transcendence* is an excellent book, and would be an asset in any course dealing with science and philosophy, or the history of science. It is also most fascinating reading, and would be a welcome addition to any library."
—Harold Hughesdon, *The Wanderer*

"We are astounded to see the revival of philosophical doctrines long thought dead in a scientific context...Smith has a good grasp of both the scientific and the mystical points of view and thus is able to bring off with occasional brilliance an effort that on its face might seem impossible...This book will repay study, especially its brilliant third chapter, 'Lost Horizons.'" —John C. Caiazza, *Modern Age*

"His chapter on 'The Deification of the Unconscious' is superb and totally destroys the pretensions of Jungian psychology..."
—Rama P. Coomaraswamy, *Studies in Comparative Religion*

"Having traced the degeneration of the mechanistic outlook into subjectivism and pseudoscience, Dr. Smith concludes his book with a profound reflection on the fall of man and its implications for the pursuit of knowledge...This is a serious work which will repay close attention." —Robert P. Rooney, *Homiletic & Pastoral Review*

"Clearly, the arguments for returning to the central premises of Christian thought are compelling, though it is ironic that now only laymen like Smith seem to care. While professional philosophers are busy playing with semiotics and theologians are distributing political manifestos and automatic weapons, it is left to an amateur—a mathematician—to defend the foundations of Western culture..."
—*Chronicles of Culture*

"In an age when specialization is rife, Smith is that rare individual who is singularly well equipped to comprehend and communicate the unitary nature of knowledge...This is an inspiring and rewarding book. Everyone who prizes Truth should read it."
—Urban J. Linehan, *Orthodoxy of the Catholic Doctrine*

"This is a very interesting book for the general reader as for the scientist." —*Fellowship of Catholic Scholars Newsletter*

"The best book in print on science, the philosophy of science and how our Catholic faith is truly a part of what is 'real science' in contrast to passing fashion. This book gets our award for one of the great books of the year." —*Catholic Spiritual Direction*

If you have enjoyed this book, consider making your next selection from among the following . . .

At your bookdealer or direct from the publisher.

Prices guaranteed through December 31, 1992.

ABOUT THE AUTHOR

Born in Vienna in 1930, Wolfgang Smith took a degree in physics, philosophy and mathematics from Cornell University in 1948. After completing an M.S. in physics from Purdue in 1950, he joined the aerodynamics group at Bell Aircraft Corporation, where he distinguished himself through his research on the aerodynamics of diffusion fields; he was the first to investigate the effect of a foreign gas on aerodynamic heating. His analysis and results on the effect of diffusion fields (published in the *Journal of Aeronautical Sciences* in 1954) sparked considerable interest in England and the United States and provided the theoretical key to the solution of the famed re-entry problem for space flight. Following a three-year sojourn in industry Smith resumed his graduate studies at Columbia University, where he received a Ph.D. in mathematics in 1957. Thereafter he held faculty positions at M.I.T. and U.C.L.A. He has been active as a research mathematician and since 1968 has served as Professor of Mathematics at Oregon State University. His extensive scientific publications have spanned a wide spectrum, from his early work in boundary layers to relativistic cosmology and topics in algebraic and differential topology.

From his early years Wolfgang Smith has also been deeply interested in metaphysical and religious questions. As a young man he developed a strong interest in Platonism and Oriental metaphysics, and later took up serious studies in the field of Christian theology. After decades of study spanning many disciplines he has emerged as a profound expositor of traditional Christian doctrine. His first book, *Cosmos and Transcendence* (1984), which could be characterized in part as an insider's critique of the contemporary scientistic Weltanschauung, has been hailed as an outstanding work.